INVASION '44

INVASION '44

'44

The full story of D-Day

JOHN FRAYN TURNER

Airlife
CLASSIC

Printed in England by Livesey Ltd., Shrewsbury (01743) 235651

Distributed in North America by
STACKPOLE BOOKS
5067 Ritter Road, Mechanicsburg, PA 17055
www.stackpolebooks.com

For a complete list of all Airlife titles please contact:
Airlife Publishing Ltd
101 Longden Road, Shrewsbury, SY3 9EB, England
E-mail: sales@airlifebooks.com
Website: www.airlifebooks.com

Preface

SO many component parts were needed to stage the greatest invasion the world has known that the historian would find it virtually impossible to present a picture of D-Day, and those fateful few days that followed, but for the invaluable evidence that has been presented by contemporary writers who have specialized in the parts played by the various units involved.

I gratefully acknowledge the help that I have received from reading a wide selection of the many fine books which present specific aspects of the invasion, and in particular I am extremely grateful for permission to refer to such accounts in the following books:

Above Us the Waves, by C. E. T. Warren and James Benson (Harrap), for the vital piloting task of the two midget submarines; *The Frogmen*, by T. J. Waldron and James Gleason (Evans), for the selfless work of the men who tackled beach obstacles; *The Last Passage*, by J. E. Taylor (Allen and Unwin), for the poignant tale of the old blockships; *The Marines were There*, by Sir Robert Bruce Lockhart (Putnam), for the part played by the Commandos; *The Red Beret*, by Hilary St George Saunders (Michael Joseph), for the airborne assault; *The Second World War*, Volume V, by Winston S. Churchill (Cassell), from which I have quoted the memorandum on piers, with a comment by the author; *The Secret War* (1939–45), by Gerald Pawle (Harrap), for information about certain inventions; *The Struggle for Europe*, by Chester Wilmot (Collins), for facts in the overall pattern; "This was D-Day," by Cliff Bowering (the *Canadian Legionary*), an eye-witness impression by a Canadian soldier; also, for general information, "Air Operations by the Allied Expeditionary Air Forces in North-West Europe" (the *London Gazette*); "The Assault Phase of the Normandy Landings" (the *London Gazette*); *Crusade in Europe*, by Dwight D. Eisenhower (Heinemann); *Invasion*, by John St John Cooper (*Daily Express* Publications); *Normandy to the Baltic*, by Field-Marshal the Viscount Montgomery of Alamein (Hutchinson); *Omaha Beachhead* (United States War Department, Historical Division); *Utah Beach to Cherbourg* (United States War Department, Historical Division).

I am also indebted for their help to the Reference and Photographic Librarians of the Imperial War Museum, and to my friend, Commander John G. D. Ouvry, D.S.O., R.N.

Contents

Illustrations

Maps

I

From Dunkirk to Dieppe

AS the great German juggernaut thundered through the Low Countries in mid-May 1940, within a week the British Expeditionary Force was in drastic danger. An emergency meeting at the War Office on May 19 considered as a temporary measure maintaining it through Dunkirk, Calais, and Boulogne, and as an alarming alternative, partial or total evacuation via the same three places. The need for evacuation was still thought "to be unlikely." Whether we were to stay or leave, however, naval command was to be controlled direct from Dover by Vice-Admiral Bertram Ramsay.[1]

During the next two days conditions on the Continent grew worse each hour, and on May 21 the War Office were considering "emergency evacuation" of very large forces. Throughout the week the now-immortal small ships and smaller-still boats assembled around the Kent coast, while over in Belgium four divisions of the B.E.F. were in imminent danger of encirclement near Lille.

Then, at 10 P.M. on Sunday, May 26, exactly one week after the War Office had thought evacuation unlikely, Ramsay received the order to implement Operation Dynamo. The most expected from this was to save 45,000 men in an estimated two days left before the enemy would reach the coast: one man in eight of the B.E.F.

But for some reason, the German tanks headed away from the retreating British troops, giving them an extra week before the all-out attack.

The result was Dunkirk.

At this moment of memorable defeat one man typified the will to win, which was expressed four years later on the day of deliverance. His name, of course: Bertram Ramsay. How right that Ramsay, the saviour of the B.E.F., should carry the Allies back into France on D-Day.

Although so much must happen before this could come to pass, the very night after France signed a separate armistice with Germany on June 22, 1940, British troops stepped ashore again on French soil. True, this was

---

[1] Afterwards Admiral Sir Bertram Home Ramsay, C.B., M.V.O.

only a reconnaissance raid near Boulogne by 120 Commandos, but it was a beginning, nevertheless. The number was to have been 200, but boats of a suitable kind could not be found—despite the fact that less than a month earlier one-third of a million men had been snatched from the smoke and death of Dunkirk.

The raid provided little intelligence, and one group mistook their port of return in England—to be promptly arrested as deserters by the ever-vigilant British military police!

D-Day was still nearly four years off. But during July Mr Churchill set up a Combined Operations Command to conduct regular small raids on enemy coasts. Then, in October, he instructed the Joint Planning Staff to study the whole question of an offensive in Europe, even mentioning a bridgehead on the Cherbourg peninsula. This was essentially a period of preliminary planning, for, with the Luftwaffe still strong and active over England, the possibility of a German invasion could not yet be completely ignored. We could only look ahead to a time when we should have equal or superior land and air power, and try to keep the Atlantic open for supplies. For, as Admiral Raeder rightly said on December 27, 1940, "Britain's ability to maintain her supply lines is definitely the decisive factor for the outcome of the War."

When Hitler invaded Russia in 1941 the Communists in Britain went suddenly silent, but not for long. Soon they were echoing the pleas of Stalin, who had no hesitation in asking Churchill for a Second Front in France irrespective of our ability to launch one. Only a year had passed since Dunkirk, but it would take two or three more before sufficient forces were built up in Britain to contemplate an attack on the Continent.

The day after the second anniversary of the outbreak of the war between Britain and Germany, Stalin told Churchill, "The Germans consider the danger in the West a bluff and are transferring all their forces to the East with impunity."

Churchill's reply was to point out that all his military advisers insisted that even if an attack were made in the West it could not succeed and would actually result in a withdrawal after a few days. And in a cable to Sir Stafford Cripps, our Ambassador in Moscow, Churchill revealed that far from being able to invade Europe, we still had to contend with the chance of an invasion by Germany in the spring of 1942.

Meanwhile, soon after the Stalin message of September 4, Churchill told the Joint Planning Staff "to complete as a matter of urgency their examination of the plan for operations on the Continent in the final phase, with particular reference to the requirements of all types of special craft and equipment both for the actual operations and for the training of the necessary forces."

On the afternoon of December 7, at Fort Sam Houston, Texas, Colonel Dwight D. Eisenhower was tired out from exhausting staffwork in connexion with prolonged U.S. Army manoeuvres. He went to bed, leaving orders that he was not to be disturbed. But, despite this, he was awoken by an aide with the news that America was at war. Within an hour of Pearl Harbor orders began pouring into the headquarters, and Eisenhower's dream of a fortnight's Christmas leave with his wife was shattered. But his part in the D-Day story does not start until later.

Almost to the day, the Joint Planning Staff produced its first outline for an invasion of France in the summer of 1943, so when Churchill met Roosevelt in Washington on Christmas Eve, for the Arcadia Conference, they had this basis for discussion. There was also much else to talk over, and the conference lasted three weeks altogether. A common command, to be called the Combined Chiefs of Staff, was set up to pool all resources, and secondly, the conference made a momentous decision to exert the efforts of the Allies against Germany before Japan. For the European situation looked as bad as it had ever been, with the Germans near Leningrad, Moscow, and Sevastopol, and no one knowing if the Russians could withstand the Wehrmacht. Simultaneously, the Battle of the Atlantic reached its most serious stage; in one month during this winter eighty-eight ships being lost there and in the Arctic.

It was good to know that President Roosevelt saw the wisdom of the Germany-first strategy and also had the courage to endorse it at a time when his countrymen were more disposed to retaliate against Pearl Harbor than turn to Europe.

By the spring Roosevelt was becoming anxious for some sort of Second Front in Europe during 1942, and on March 9 cabled to Churchill that the losses involved "will be compensated by at least equal German losses and by compelling Germans to divert large forces of all kinds from Russian fronts." So the cry for a Second Front was heard by Churchill from both of his main Allies.

The Americans spent a considerable time deciding where to recommend this Second Front in Europe. They clearly could not get American troops to Russia; attacks through Scandinavia or Spain each presented problems; any decisive invasion via North Africa and Italy was too far from Germany to be effective; in fact, the only possible place to start from was England. Apart from its obvious asset of being directly opposite occupied Europe, England was also the nearest point for the transatlantic trip from the east coast of the U.S.A.

Against this axiomatic truth, however, was levelled by many soldiers and statesmen the argument that the Atlantic Wall being built up by the Germans in France could not be broken by such an assault direct from the Channel shores of England. In fact, only a very few American officers thought it conceivable. Eisenhower was one of the small select group who believed in it, envisaging how air support co-ordinated with ground attack could create an invincible weapon for the ultimate liberation. Yet ground officers, out of prejudice, refused to realize the full scope of air power allied to their forces.

Throughout March the various viewpoints were exchanged, but by April 1 the American Operations Division, under Eisenhower, charged with preparing an offensive strategy, finally submitted an outline to the Chief of Staff, General Marshall. The crux of their scheme was the establishment of overwhelming air power, to be numbered in thousands of planes, so that the enemy air force and land defences could both be neutralized as completely as possible for the eventual invasion.

The Chief of Staff approved the scheme, conferred with Admiral King and General Arnold, and then sought the seal of the President. This Operations in Western Europe plan actually received Roosevelt's approval the same day, and he told Marshall to present the plan to the British Government, taking Harry Hopkins with him.

Just one week later the two men arrived in London to advocate action in Europe at the earliest possible date. The British Government agreed about Marshall's aim for a full-scale invasion in the spring of 1943, but his second suggestion of a landing in France during the present year "as a sacrifice to avert an imminent collapse of Russian resistance" met direct disapproval. While sympathizing with the intention, Britain could not really contemplate an Allied landing in 1942, particularly when Marshall admitted that it would be late autumn before even the minimum level of troops, equipment, and craft could be ready. October was not a good month to launch such an operation, nor the winter a suitable season to maintain it.

On April 14 Marshall was persuaded to abandon the idea of a bridgehead landing in 1942 unless the situation on the Russian front made such a desperate throw necessary. At the same meeting America and Britain made the historic agreement that, whenever the time came, the cross-Channel invasion was to be the main offensive operation in Europe. Neither knew that another twenty-six months must elapse before it could be begun.

Back in Washington, Marshall directed Eisenhower to visit London to bring back recommendations for organizing future American forces in Britain. Eisenhower found that the United States Commander in England had been given no chance to familiarize himself with the war in Europe as it would affect America. He was too far from the Pacific to do anything to help there, and the United States had not yet transferred its attention to the European theatre.

After a ten-day tour Eisenhower returned to Washington on almost the same day as Molotov, who had belatedly accepted an invitation from Roosevelt. The Russian at once told Roosevelt and Marshall that the Red Army might not be able to hold out against Hitler. If Britain and the United States could create a Second Front to draw off forty German divisions, however, things might be better. Roosevelt listened to Molotov politely and then asked Marshall if he could tell Stalin that the Allies were preparing a Second Front. Marshall said yes, and the President authorized Molotov to tell Stalin that they expected a Second Front that year. In later talks Roosevelt reminded Molotov that this must mean a reduction in Lend-Lease ships for Russia in the next twelve months. The Russian refused to accept this, and also managed to persuade the Americans to issue a communique which said:

> In the course of the conversations full understanding was reached with regard to the urgent task of creating a Second Front in Europe in 1942.

Marshall advised Roosevelt to omit "in 1942," but Molotov managed to keep it in the text. On his way home via London, Molotov received an assurance that Britain was preparing for a landing on the Continent in August or September 1942, but could give no promise to do so.

While Molotov negotiated in Washington Eisenhower was busy there too, drafting his Directive for the Commanding General, European Theatre of Operations, in which he envisaged unified command of all American forces in Europe. On June 8 he submitted it to Marshall, remarking that the General should study it in detail in view of its importance.

Marshall replied, "I certainly do want to read it. You may be the man who executes it. If that's the case when can you leave?"

Eisenhower was amazed at these words, which came to him as a complete surprise. Three days later he heard definitely that the appointment had been confirmed. His immediate reaction was alarm at the weight of responsibility involved, but he had little time to worry in the twelve hectic days that followed. In meetings with the Secretary of State, Eisenhower got the impression that the Secretary was anticipating that active operations would be started very soon, so he commented on the long build-up which would have to precede any attack.

Among all the things he had to do before leaving, Eisenhower called on Roosevelt and Churchill, a White House guest at the time. This was his first personal talk with either leader. Despite the defeat at Tobruk, which had just been announced, they both behaved cheerfully, and concentrated on the coming struggle for liberation.

It was at this June meeting between the two that Churchill stressed strongly to the Americans the impossibility of an invasion on the Continent that year. The only major Anglo-American amphibious operation could be in French North Africa. And with the fall of Tobruk Rommel headed towards Alamein and Egypt, an advance which also sent Churchill hurrying back to London.

Eisenhower's son came down from West Point, and spent two days with his parents before his father flew off to Britain with General Clark and some assistants on June 23. Major-General Eisenhower at once assumed command of the European Theatre of Operations, U.S. Army, then comprising two bases—Britain and Iceland.

The commander could hardly have chosen a worse month to arrive, for shipping losses were higher than in any other so far. Merchant ships sank at the devastating rate of one every four hours. And yet the popular cry for a Second Front echoed everywhere. All Eisenhower had in the United Kingdom were two divisions and some small detachments of the U.S. Air Forces, being trained in Northern Ireland. Little of the necessary equipment existed with which to contemplate any form of invasion, and some of the landing-craft, so far from being built had still to be designed. Although this would have been bad propaganda for the public to hear, Eisenhower very soon appreciated that no full-scale operation could be contemplated before mid-1943, and unless almost all Anglo-American production were aimed at this single goal, it would be 1944 before they could begin to liberate Europe.

Independence Day 1942 aptly marked the date of the very first American offensive operation by air against the enemy in Europe. Four German aerodromes in Holland formed the target, and from a force of six Bostons—part of a bigger British group—two were shot down in a furore of flak. So four American crews remained. This was scarcely the time, yet, to talk of invasion. Eisenhower visited these crews on their return, and later made his way thoughtfully back to London, where his headquarters was an apartment building near Grosvenor Square, already the centre of American activity in London. The week of the Holland raid, after talks with British leaders, Eisenhower had to report to Washington that Britain would not consider any cross-Channel attack that year.

The U.S. Chiefs of Staff at once advised Roosevelt to turn his attention to defeating Japan. Eisenhower's message reached General Marshall on July 10, and the U.S. Secretary for War wrote in his diary:

> The British War Cabinet . . . are seeking now to reverse the decision which was so laboriously accomplished when Mr Churchill was here a short time ago.
> . . . I found Marshall very stirred up and emphatic over it . . . and he proposed

a showdown which I cordially endorsed. As the British won't go through with
what they agreed to, we will turn our backs on them and take up the war with
Japan.

Marshall and Admiral King, another advocate of the Japan first attitude,
presented a plan to Roosevelt five days later for prosecuting the Pacific
War. The President refused to accept it, however, and sent the two of
them to London with Harry Hopkins to appeal again for Operation
Sledgehammer, the name of the proposed bridgehead invasion of Europe.
If Britain would not agree that this were feasible, then they would settle
for an offensive in French North Africa.

Long Anglo-American discussions began on July 18 to decide which of
three possible offensives to undertake: aiding the British forces in Africa
via the Cape of Good Hope route; attacking French North Africa to catch
Rommel from the rear; or launching a limited bridgehead on the Channel
coast of France. The British view—strongly supported by facts—was that
German defences put the Pas-de-Calais out of the question. Marshall
argued for the Cherbourg peninsula, and that even an unsuccessful landing was preferable to inactivity. Eisenhower at that time favoured the
cross-Channel bridgehead too, but subsequently appreciated that the
British viewpoint was wiser. So native caution triumphed over the natural
enthusiasm and eagerness of the Americans to attack in Europe there and
then, despite having landing-craft to carry only one division!

After four days of bitter argument Britain decided definitely against
Sledgehammer, and then, on July 24, the Allies agreed to proceed with
planning Operation Torch, the invasion of North-west Africa. On the
next day Roosevelt cabled his approval of the plan, to take place not later
than October 30. And then, again on the next day, with no time to lose,
in his headquarters at Claridge's Hotel, a few hundred yards down Brook
Street from Grosvenor Square, Marshall appointed Eisenhower
Commander-in-Chief of Torch. This operation was not in fact launched
until early December, but even then it marked an amazing achievement.

And the direct-assault invasion? After he heard of the proposal for Torch
Stalin agitated less than before, but still said that it ought to be possible to
try a Second Front in France. At this precise time the Canadians carried
out the reconnaissance attack against Dieppe, and exactly two-thirds of the
5000 men there became casualties: practical proof for Russia and America
alike of what might have happened to a larger-scale invasion at any time
in 1942. The attack taught the Allies much more than they could have
learned otherwise, and when D-Day came countless lives were saved
through the sacrifice of those Canadians who died at Dieppe.

2

The Mulberries are born

"PLAN for the offensive . . . never think defensively," Churchill told Mountbatten. Combined Operations, now under Vice-Admiral Lord Louis Mountbatten,[1] was gaining valuable experience of offensive landings by raids on places as far apart as Norway and St Nazaire, in France. Mountbatten reported direct to the Premier whenever necessary.

In May 1942 three important ideas for the ultimate Second Front were conceived. First, the Combined Commanders were appointed to overcome the problems of amphibious assault. Secondly, the Wheezers and Dodgers[2] floating roadway, or "Swiss Roll," to link ships with shore by means of 1000-foot sections with rafts floating under each junction, was first formulated. And thirdly, Churchill revealed once more his astounding vision in science as in other things.

Long before the complete idea of the artificial "Mulberry" harbours had been born he sent a minute to the Chief of Combined Operations on the kind of piers which would be needed at such ports. Not only did he predict the shape of these mechanical contraptions, but also the principle on which they must work.

Churchill's minute is dated May 30, 1942, and appended to this technical report on

PIERS FOR USE ON BEACHES

Conditions of Beach
Average gradient is 1 in 200 and beaches are open to the south-west.

Conditions of Tide
Range of spring tides is 30 feet and the strength of the tide parallel to the beach is 4 knots at spring.

Scaffolding Piers
A pier to be of use for unloading ships of 20-foot draught would have to be 1 mile in length and 40 feet in height at the seaward end. The present type of

---

[1] Afterwards Admiral of the Fleet Earl Mountbatten of Burma.
[2] The colloquial title for a small Admirality research group.

scaffolding pier does not exceed 20 feet in height. It is doubtful whether a pier of these large dimensions could be made with scaffolding, but in any case the amount of material required would be prohibitive.

Pontoon Pier

A pontoon pier would have to be similar in length. All floating piers suffer from the disadvantage of having to be securely moored with heavy anchors. Even then they are most vulnerable and will not stand up to a gale of wind. The strength of the tide is so great that the moorings will have to be very large. If large pontoons were moored, 20 yards apart, at least 200 anchors would be required. The seaward end of a floating pier must be particularly well moored and the mooring chains form an obstacle to ships coming alongside. Owing to the poor ratio between the weight of a floating pontoon and the weight they can carry, and to their vulnerability to sea, wind, and tide, they are not favoured in comparison with scaffolding piers on open beaches.

Churchill added his minute to the Chief of Combined Operations:

They *must* float up and down with the tide. The anchor problem must be mastered. The ships must have a side-flap cut in them, and a drawbridge long enough to overreach to moorings of the pier. Let me have the best solution worked out. Don't argue the matter. The difficulties will argue for themselves.

Nothing seemed too small or too large for Churchill's attention, and from the detailed study of piers for the invasion he turned, in December, to the whole offensive outline.

In a telegram to Stalin he said, "We must decide at the earliest moment the best way of attacking Germany in Europe with all possible force in 1943."

Stalin replied that he agreed but could not leave Russia for such a conference at that time. Churchill and Roosevelt therefore decided to go ahead with a Combined Chiefs of Staff meeting, which was held in January 1943. Even now the state of the War did not make it clear whether the Allies should attack Germany or Japan first. But Casablanca did determine by cold facts and figures that the long-mooted invasion could not now be mounted before the spring of 1944. The year or so intervening would be devoted to detailed planning and preparation for D-Day, coupled with redoubled efforts against Germany both in the underwater war with the U-boats and by an even heavier air assault on her industrial power.

Churchill stressed the value of the Mediterranean as a base "to strike at the under-belly of the Axis." An offensive against Italy would deflect Germany both from the Russian front and the French coast, and so soften the northern invasion route when it came to final fruition

Once again the Americans disagreed with British policy completely, thinking more about the current successes of Japan than the ultimate Allied goal. But, as usual, Roosevelt saw more clearly than some of his service experts, in appreciating that the Mediterranean was a necessary prelude and part of the liberation, and agreement was reached to the extent of Eisenhower leading his American force in Operation Husky, the invasion of Sicily. But beyond that the Americans did not commit themselves, and, as Chester Wilmot observes, unfortunately assumed that Eisenhower would not require large numbers of landing-craft after the conclusion of Husky. One last phrase emerged at Casablanca, that the President and the Prime Minister both had as their objective "unconditional surrender" by Germany, Italy, and Japan.

Towards this end Lieutenant-General F. E. Morgan[1] was appointed Chief of Staff to the Supreme Allied Commander— happily shortened to C.O.S.S.A.C.—at the Casablanca conference.

C.O.S.S.A.C. went straight into action on all possible projects linked with the invasion. One of the vital needs exposed by Dieppe was powerful, close support for the assault troops, of such a shattering nature that the enemy defences would be swamped between the time the naval bombardment ended and the moment when the first wave of troops touched the beaches. The brainwave to emerge was for artillery which would float: hence the most ferocious and formidable weapon ever to bombard a strange shore, the "Rocket Landing-craft."

Trials started on April 11, 1943, in the grey watery wastes off the Isle of Wight to see how much concentration of rocket fire could be achieved from an adapted tank landing-craft.

Ten days later, and another trial. The row upon row of rockets, looking almost like lines of troops with their rifles at the "slope arms," stood ready to be fired. Suddenly, in eleven seconds, 759 rockets raced and soared into the sky at an identical angle.

One more week, and a third trial. Then production plans were started to convert thirty landing-craft into Rocket Ships, each able to fire a salvo of over 1000 rocket shells: a withering weapon destined to be devastatingly successful in the invasion—and even earlier, at the Mediterranean landings later in 1943.

Only a year left now, and so much still to be done. May marked the real beginning of this battle against time and a thousand obstacles: a fight for a Second Front in the summer of 1944. On May 1, 1943, the 6th Airborne Division, a new formation, came under the command of Major-General

---

[1] Afterwards Lieutenant-General Sir Frederick Morgan, K.C.B.

Gale.[1] By May, also, all Germans and Italians on the African continent had been killed or captured; Stalingrad stopped the Germans on the Eastern front; and the Allies accounted for forty U-boats in the everlasting minute-by-minute conflict on the seas.

By the end of May another meeting of the Anglo-American High Command, in Washington, fixed the target date for D-Day as May 1, 1944. Operation Overlord—the longed-for liberation—at last assumed reality. There was an actual date to aim at less than a year ahead. All was not yet agreed, however, for the Americans did not favour carrying the North African fight into the "under-belly" by invading Italy. Their eyes remained on France and the Pacific, whichever way round the two were placed. In the end all that the Americans would agree to was that Eisenhower should "mount such operations in exploitation of the attack on Sicily as might be calculated to eliminate Italy from the War."

Churchill got Roosevelt to arrange for General Marshall to accompany the Prime Minister and General Sir Alan Brooke[2] to Algiers to talk with Eisenhower about the extent of the forthcoming campaign. Churchill wanted "nothing less than the capture of Rome." Eisenhower reserved his judgment until he saw the strength of the opposition in Sicily, to be invaded on July 10. Within a week of this date Eisenhower had made up his mind. Italy should be assaulted.

The entire conquest of Sicily took only thirty-eight days, and, apart from its obvious place in the overall plan for victory in Europe, it gave the Allies further vital experience of seaborne invasion. For the success of the operation, considerable credit went to the new amphibious load-carrier, the American D.U.K.W., and equally to the L.S.T. ("landing-ship tank"). The latter was a new design based on British experience, built in the United States, and undergoing its first operational role in Sicily. All major amphibious assaults after this time had the L.S.T. as their foundation and their limitation.

From Malta and many African ports between Bizerta and Benghazi the landing-craft came, but the weather was particularly bad, with a wind blowing and a heavy swell rolling into the Sicilian shores from the Mediterranean. The convoys of small craft met it somehow, and, although delayed, damaged, and scattered, they survived the night's crossing, to find next morning that the wind had dropped, leaving only a swell and surf on the western beaches of Sicily.

How fortunate for the Allies that, as Churchill reminds us, he was "well

---

[1] Afterwards General Sir Richard Nelson Gale, G.C.B., K.B.E., D.S.O., M.C.
[2] Afterwards Field-Marshal Viscount Alanbrooke of Brookeborough.

abreast of all the thought about landing-craft and tank landing-craft."

While the seaborne assault went well, Sicily marked a moment of tragedy for airborne forces. More than one-third of the gliders carrying the 1st Air Landing Brigade were cast off too early by their American towing aircraft, and many of the men they carried were plunged into the sea, trapped, and drowned.... Yet, despite it all, Sicily meant much to Eisenhower, both in terms of contributing to changing his mind about an invasion of Italy, and also for the vital experience he gained before the final D-Day the next summer.

Meanwhile work went on throughout England, and even on the Continent, for D-Day. Some of the earliest activities were by small parties of men who paddled ashore in canoes at night to test the defensive strength of various beaches in Holland, Belgium, and France. As well as reconnaissance, they had to survey the beaches too, and, as they landed literally under the enemy's nose, they could not use any normal surveying methods. Nor could they make the slightest sound.

Combined Operations, who carried out these duties, therefore called for a Beach Gradient Meter, which was created in the form of a small truck, with apparatus to record the slope. This accompanied the paddling parties to many alien shores, enabling them to bring back the contours of each beach they raided. By such strange means valuable help was given towards the final decision about which would be the best areas for invasion.

It is certain that the location of the assault was a prime problem, but when the Seine Bay became the agreed area, in January 1943, the creation of a harbour where none naturally existed became the most vital, and also the most difficult, obstacle facing the Allies. On the flat, open beaches of Normandy even a breeze could churn up the Channel into an awkward surf. And, as Combined Operations H.Q. observed, this would make landing men an operation of great hazard, and delivering stores practically impossible. Without a harbour the whole enormous enterprise would be jeopardized, and might even be doomed. So paramount was the provision of a harbour that a report to the First Sea Lord called it "the crux of the whole operation."

At this stage two things were sure: there were no natural harbours on the beaches earmarked for landings, and no one knew exactly how to make artificial ones. Yet they had to exist before D-Day.

The poor planners working under C.O.S.S.A.C. were worried, with considerable cause. Not only had the enemy had four years to perfect their coastline defence, but as long, also, to plan the destruction of every port which the Allies could conceivably use. Then there was the Channel itself, unpredictable even in May or June. So C.O.S.S.A.C. could not fairly face the prospect of an amphibious assault 100,000 men strong over only the open beaches of the Seine Bay. Five thousand ships would be involved, and bad weather would prevent unloading from landing-craft and D.U.K.W.'s. Everything seemed against an artificial harbour, including a rise and fall of tide as much as 24 feet at spring. So any breakwater based in 30 feet of water at low tide would have to be 54 feet tall to reach the surface at high water. Yet, somehow, the Allies had to create two pre-fabricated harbours—each the size of Gibraltar—in little over a fortnight from the time they were towed over there.

In April 1943 Lieutenant-Commander Robert Lochner, R.N.V.R., was pondering this problem of artificial harbours when he suddenly real-ized that a wall in the sea need not be taken right down to the sea-bed, but only to where the waves lost their power. So the answer could be a *floating* wall.

From his original ideas, three full-size floating breakwaters—or "Lilos," as they became known—were being built in Portsmouth Dockyard dur-ing August, each 200 feet long and 12 feet wide.

Meanwhile the wave formations of possible Mulberry harbour sites were being examined, mooring experts determined the best way of secur-ing long lines of floating objects close together—and Churchill, with his staff, set out aboard the *Queen Mary* to meet the Americans again, this time in Canada. As he crossed towards Halifax, Nova Scotia, many things occu-pied his mind, but principally the preparations for Operation Overlord and the Italian campaign.

The pros and cons of the Pas-de-Calais or Normandy had finally been thrashed out, and it would be Normandy next year. Its defences were less strong, the beaches reasonably favourable, and the immediate vicinity favoured the movement of large invasion forces. The coast between Le Havre and Cherbourg was well fortified with a mass of concrete forts and pill-boxes, but the absence of a harbour there made it unlikely that the Germans would back up the defences with large forces. Little did they dream that the Mulberry harbours would materialize out of open sea and beach, but in April 1943 Vice-Admiral John Hughes-Hallett originated the basic plan from all the various inspirations on the subject.

What was the broad idea?

It was: to build in Britain equipment which could be carried across the Channel in prefabricated form and transferred into harbours to sustain an invasion. On the beaches great piers, with their seaward ends afloat, and sheltered, where vessels could unload at all tides; protecting these, an arc of breakwaters enclosing an area of sheltered water for deep-draught ships. The breakwaters would be built of sunken concrete structures—code name, "Phoenix"—and the revolutionary conception of scuttled block-ships, known as "Gooseberries." And, as well as all these, there was the special scheme of floating breakwaters, which was absorbing so much time and brainpower in London and Portsmouth.

If the Mulberries could be brought into being Churchill felt happy that the Allies would be able to unload at least 12,000 tons of equipment a day—enough to support an advancing army of one million, increasing to two million.

By the time the *Queen Mary* berthed at Halifax he was well satisfied with the prospect of presenting the picture to Roosevelt, which should convince the American authorities that Britain was doing all she could towards D-Day.

So started the "Quadrant" Conference. Suddenly, about the middle of August, the Admiralty heard from Churchill that a team familiar with the floating breakwater were to fly to Quebec at once. Two War Office developers of the "Whale Piers" accompanied the group, which included Dr William Penney.[1]

Up-to-date tidal intelligence, Whale Piers, and floating breakwaters—these three things cast a completely new light on the entire operation. The rapid result was that the Mulberry project took practical shape. On his last day in America Lochner gave a short talk on the breakwater to both Roosevelt and Churchill.

The same night it was settled that Britain would be responsible for Mulberry. The two artificial harbours would be created by sixty block-ships, concrete caissons, floating breakwaters, and Whale Piers. The Mulberries were born.

[1] Afterwards Sir William George Penney, K.B.E., O.B.E.

A wounded British company-sergeant-major is carried back to an advanced dressing-station.

Men of the Royal Electrical and Mechanical Engineers brush up their French as they sail.

(*above*) Two of the first German prisoners to be taken being marched in the tracks of a tank.

(*left*) German prisoners, taken early in the fighting, are rounded up and shipped back to England on a returning assault craft.

3

Trial and Error

EXPLODING enemy minefields on beaches to be assaulted was an important invasion problem. On the same shores of Shoeburyness where Lieutenant-Commander John Ouvry[1] had conquered the German magnetic mine, late in 1939, tests were made in 1941 to find out the effect of exploding charges in the air, or at ground-level, against land and beach mines. In the autumn of 1942 Combined Operations hit on the idea that these charges might be fired from weapons mounted in a special landing-craft.

The result was the "Hedgerow," composed of rows of spiky spigots fitted into an assault landing-craft. One of these was ready in time to be tested amid all the thunder and tracery of the Salerno assault on September 9. As a result of this experience the elevations and projectiles were altered and the mountings made stronger, so that the Hedgerow flotillas could begin to be built for D-Day.

Secretly, steadily, momentum was gathering, and the thousands of general landing-craft began to appear. The invasion force started on a modest scale almost as soon as Dunkirk ended. The first Commandos came from the Royal Navy, Royal Marines, and the Royal Naval Volunteer Reserve, later developing into a combined services corps. The craft themselves, which were used for the early Commando raids, proved unsuitably low-lying and liable to swamp in any substantial seaway. They were really out of date when war broke out, because they had been the craft used at the Inter-Service Training and Development Centre, Fort Cumberland, Portsmouth, where the idea of a combined assault force first blossomed. Most "modern" pre-war developments like these had to be drastically reviewed in the light of conflict in the 1940's. When the Japanese used large landing-craft carriers, bearing fleets of inshore landing-craft in their fight against China, it began to be realized that landing-vessels of every kind would be wanted to convey troops, guns, tanks, and other armoured vehicles.

[1] Afterwards Commander J.G.D. Ouvry, D.S.O., R.N.

Experimental craft went on to a hundred drawing-boards, and then, as they were approved, shipyards and yacht-building centres built them almost in mass-production. Where possible, parts were prefabricated in the safety of inland factories, and sent to assembly points around the coasts for incorporation. Cross-Channel packet-boats of all sizes were requisitioned, converted, and fitted with specially strong davits to carry a number of inshore assault landing-craft. Each of the L.S.I.'s ("landing-ships infantry") could take several battalions of troops to within easy range of their objective, and then lower the 10-ton assault landing-craft into the water. Scrambling nets would also be lowered down the sides of the L.S.I.'s so that the troops could man the L.C.A.'s ("assault landing-craft") .

Literally dozens of different designs took shape between autumn 1943 and the following spring. A type of "flat-iron" gunboat was the L.C.S., the support landing-craft. These were to sail in ahead of the main landing-parties to deal with immediate opposition. Early L.C.S. rather resembled midget submarines, and were equally hard to see from a beach.

L.C.P.'s ("personnel landing-craft") were another development, though less impressive than the two monster vessels, the L.C.T. ("tank landing-craft"), displacing some 300 tons, and L.S.T. ("tank landing-ship"), ten times the size, with a 3000-ton displacement. This was being built to take troops as well as a load of 500 tons in tanks and heavy vehicles. L.C.T.'s could also be converted into rocket, gun, and flak ships, in a similar way to the Hedgerow. And as the whole operation changed from broad aims to detailed development, the need appeared for still further craft: L.B.E.'s ("engineering landing barges"), to do rapid running repairs along the beaches or in a more secluded spot, and L.C.K.'s ("kitchen landing-craft"), floating galleys for feeding the troops on the beachheads as soon as conditions allowed.

The jigsaw still seemed ragged, but at least the pieces were being cut, if not yet in their proper places.

The Commandos were not the only Royal Marines to be preparing for D-Day, for in the late summer of 1943, when the Navy found itself short of crews for the vast fleet of landing-craft, the marines converted their light assault division into men for these vessels. In less than six months over 10,000 marines were trained to perfection, and on D-Day about two-thirds of all the assault craft landing the first waves of the army were manned by marines.

The C.O.S.S.A.C. plan at Quebec proposed a three-division landing and two airborne brigades to take advance positions behind the enemy's coastal defences. During the first fortnight eighteen divisions were expected to be landed, when main American army forces could then be shipped straight from the United States. General Morgan observed that the operation would only triumph if the Germans had not more than twelve reserve mobile field-divisions in France, whereupon Molotov inquired, when told of it, "And what if there are thirteen?"

Operation Anvil was also agreed on as a result of Quebec: a diversionary assault in Southern France around the Toulon-Marseille area.

The plan, the landing-craft, and now the naval commander. In October 1943, Vice-Admiral Sir Bertram Ramsay, back from the invasion of Sicily, became Allied Naval Commander-in-Chief, Expeditionary Force. From Dunkirk to Sicily and now to Normandy. This was to be known as Operation Neptune. One of his headaches was destined to be to get enough ships—a basic problem but not one to be solved automatically. Shipping for five divisions seemed possible: C.O.S.S.A.C. wanted ten divisions!

General Sir Alan Brooke told Morgan, "It won't work, but you must bloody well make it." The same advice might have applied to Ramsay's task.

One of his other headaches was Mulberry, but here the backroom boys rose to the occasion. After the Quebec Conference they had to build and test over two miles of the floating sea-barrier. Yet this was only part of the problem of Mulberry. Fifteen thousand workmen had to be found to build the Phoenix concrete caissons forming the inner breakwater.

That autumn, Ramsay appointed Rear-Admiral William Tennant[1] to co-ordinate the many naval needs for Mulberry. Tennant soon saw that there might not be enough room for all the thousands of small supporting craft inside the sheltered waters, and that extra breakwaters to be formed by blockships would definitely be wanted. These blockships would be sailed across the Channel under their own steam, and then sunk in line. So sixty old ships had to be produced and manned in the next six or seven months to transform Gooseberry harbours from fancy to reality.

The Lilos had by this time been superseded by "Bombardons." Ninety-six full-scale Bombardons were needed for the two Mulberries—which meant 25,000 tons of steel, 1000 tons of nuts and bolts, and 1700 men for the six months from now to D-Day.

The job began in Tilbury and Southampton Docks, and when the first two prototypes were ready they were towed round to Newhaven, where a winter gale off this exposed strip of Sussex shore caused both units to break their backs. Intensive detective work soon revealed the flaws, however, and suitably strengthened new units were towed to Weymouth Bay.

[1] Afterwards Admiral Sir William Tennant, K.C.B., C.B.E.

All this took time, and it was April I before the first full-scale trial started. April came in with a strong sou'-wester, an ideally tough test for the break-waters. Rough, rolling seas swirled in around Portland Bill towards Weymouth Bay, but the Bombardons smoothed the waves so effectively that the next day the Admiralty received a signal saying that the floating harbour had withstood for ten hours a stress twice as great as it was designed to meet, and had smoothed waves 8 feet high and 200 feet long.

4

Enter Eisenhower, Montgomery—and Rommel

ON December 7, 1943, President Roosevelt passed through Tunis on his return route to the United States from Cairo, and Eisenhower went there to meet him. Roosevelt arrived in mid-afternoon and had hardly got into his car with the General before he announced, "Well, Ike, you are going to command Overlord."

And Eisenhower had already learned the lesson which was to win his crusade in Europe—that war is waged in three elements, but there is no separate land, air, or naval war. Air Marshal Tedder[1] became his deputy commander, General Bernard Montgomery[2] was assigned as head of the British forces, and Air Chief-Marshal Sir Trafford Leigh-Mallory as Air Commander-in-Chief. Vice-Admiral Ramsay, of course, had already been appointed. Roosevelt made Eisenhower's appointment known in a Christmas Eve broadcast, naming him Supreme Commander, Allied Expeditionary Forces. Soon after this Eisenhower was asked by Marshall to "allow someone else to run the War, for twenty minutes," and go to Washington. Eisenhower was still busy with the Italian campaign, of course, but agreed.

Until he could establish himself in London in the New Year, Eisenhower asked Montgomery to consider revising the ground plan for the beach assault, which seemed insufficiently strong, with an initial attack on a frontage of only three divisions. He was glad to learn that Monty was working on a plan for a five-division frontage. Meanwhile Eisenhower met Roosevelt once more. The President was indisposed, but insisted that he had not felt better for years. Eisenhower never saw him again.

Eisenhower flew back to London, arriving on the evening of January 14, and almost his first job was to find a suitable site for his H.Q.—Supreme Headquarters, Allied Expeditionary Force, shortened to S.H.A.E.F. Soon he found the spot from which to command the mightiest fighting force

[1] Afterwards Marshal of the Royal Air Force Arthur William Tedder, First Baron Tedder of Glenguin.
[2] Afterwards Field-Marshal Viscount Montgomery of Alamein.

ever to be assembled for one assault. It was within sight of Hampton Court
Palace, with its timeless Tudor associations. So the deer of Bushey Park
were suddenly disturbed from their habits to make way for a miniature
town of Nissen huts to house the H.Q. staff.

Eisenhower found to his relief that Montgomery had the new plan
ready in principle, advocating two or three airborne divisions followed by
the main sea assault of five divisions plus two more immediately. The
coastal frontage of the assault was thus doubled to 50 miles wide, while it
also meant large increases in forces. Desirable as it was, this would be easier
decided than done, for the Admiralty could scarcely meet the original
C.O.S.S.A.C. needs of 3323 landing-craft, 467 warships, and 150
minesweepers. With only a matter of three clear months before the target
date of May 1, it was only too obvious that an extra month at least would
be wanted to get more new landing-craft straight from production, and
also to allow for time in which to divert craft from the Mediterranean to
Overlord. Incidentally, the U.S. Navy allocated a mere 2493 craft to
Overlord out of its strength that year of over 30,000!

Eisenhower endorsed the revised assault plan within a week of his
arrival in England, and two days later notified the Combined Chiefs of
Staff of the month's postponement. None of this was in any way his fault;
rather could it be blamed on the C.O.S.S.A.C. organization and in particular the American members, who seemed always to be fighting for the
Pacific. Even throughout February and March the struggle for landing-
craft continued, and Ramsay had to plan half in the dark during these vital
months.

Luckily, other equipment was not quite so hard to obtain. Montgomery
developed a Joint Fire Plan to saturate the beaches in a climactic crescendo just before the first troops waded in. To achieve this drenching fire the
landing-craft had to have their own floating artillery of guns, mortars and
rockets.

The fire of this floating artillery also had to be magnified by powerful
amphibious armour. Dieppe had taught that tank support would have to
be given from the first moment of D-Day. General Brooke formed an
experimental armoured division in March 1943 to develop tank warfare as
applied to the Second Front, and told its commander, Major-General Sir
Percy Hobart, to see that they had armour for the job. Hobart proceeded
to prepare an imaginative range of vehicles: Bulldozer tanks to tackle
beach obstacles; Flail tanks to hammer a way through mines; tanks to
attack concrete fortifications; the weird, turretless tanks for other tanks to
use as ramps to scale sea-walls; tanks carrying bridges, and others throwing flames against pill-boxes.

Most valuable and vital was the amphibious D.D., Duplex Drive, tank, able to invade on its own. The Admiralty disbelieved that this D.D. design would ever actually swim in an exposed sea, or that it could be launched from landing-craft. Despite demonstrations to the contrary by its Hungarian inventor, it was still spurned since it did not have a rudder!

Hobart took over five of these D.D. tanks, but these were the obsolete Valentine type. The obvious choice for conversion to amphibious operation Brooke saw to be Shermans, so he ordered the conversion of 900. That was in July 1943. By January 1944 Hobart saw that this number would never be available at the current conversion rate, despite Montgomery's enthusiasm for them. Then the Americans began to move. On January 27 Eisenhower saw the D.D. demonstrated. On January 28 an engineer was on his way to the United States with drawings of it. By February 4 American factories had actually begun work on the job. By early April 300 Shermans had been converted.

While Eisenhower was getting to grips with the race against time to invade Europe Rommel was moved, in January, by Hitler to command two of the armies in the West. Von Rundstedt remained the enemy's Commander-in-Chief, but soon Rommel became the real power behind the Atlantic Wall. This meant pursuing a policy of which both Hitler and himself approved—the repulse of invaders as near the actual coast as possible. Apart from moving troops accordingly, Rommel started a scheme at once to impede any forces trying to land along the Channel coast, although he did not really know where the assault would occur.

By March a whole assortment of wire entanglements, jagged spikes, concrete teeth, and beach mines began to be noticed by Commando reconnaissance raids along the coast; posts and wires were planted inland to deter airborne assault; artillery sites were roofed in against attack, and a rash of new pill-boxes appeared. Rommel ordered low-lying areas in the coastal belt to be flooded—a measure which was especially successful in the marshy region around the Carentan estuary—while existing sea-walls were strengthened and extended to try and stop the tanks landing.

Most serious of all, however, were the underwater obstacles located at varying distances below the high-tide mark. With explosive charges attached to them, these were intended to impale or cripple landing-craft before they could reach even the shore. After an inspection by Rommel in March work on these was accelerated, the number of coastal batteries was increased, and the obstacles were observed to be appearing farther and farther out to sea. The anti-air-landing obstacles grew more frequent on our reconnaissance photographs, some being fitted with booby traps.

To man all these extra fortifications Rommel had to risk foregoing depth in defence, but this agreed with his policy, in any case. It started a storm among the German High Command, however, which led, eventually, to a fatal compromise. Rommel wanted to halt a hostile force by amassing a violent volume of fire on the beaches and hammering home the counter-attack by all available reserves near the coast.

Von Rundstedt preferred the crust-cushion-hammer principle: a crust of infantry manning the coastline, a cushion of infantry divisions in reserve in the rear, and a hammer of armoured forces in strategic reserve still farther inland. As it happened, the central Panzer divisions were forced to engage us too soon, and so were unable to strike a co-ordinated blow at the right time and place.

As the underwater obstacles multiplied it became clear once and for all that the invasion could not possibly begin on the beaches at night, and that even by day the risks were likely to be large.

If high tide were chosen as the moment for the first assault many landing-craft would be ripped or blown to bits by the mines and traps. At low tide, on the other hand, the men would be exposed to fearful fire across hundreds of yards of open beach. So half tide was the only answer. To help cover the infantry Montgomery decided to use armour early in the assault: D.D. tanks, then specialized armour, then the infantry. Flails would clear the way for the D.D.'s and others. A complication then arose, though, for some of the beaches had patches of sticky clay well below high-water mark; one of Monty's advisers happened to remember this from a pre-war holiday in the Seine Bay! Aerial photos picked out these patches, and Commandos slipped silently ashore one spring night and brought back samples. These were urgently analysed, and a comparable beach found in England. Tests soon showed that tanks became well and truly bogged. Hobart, as usual, came to the rescue, and an antidote appeared: an attachment which enabled a tank to lay a matting road across the clay over which the rest could follow. Wherever clay was suspected it was arranged that the leading tank should be a "Bobbin," as the device was called.

With Bobbins and Flails the rest of the armour ought to be able to get through.

In February and March two midget submarines, X-20 and X-23, took their place at the submarine base of Fort Blockhouse, Gosport, ready to help survey some of the beaches. It was X-20 which was the one lucky enough to undertake Operation Postage. The little vessel sailed submerged right into the Arromanches area of the invasion coast, and took soundings of depths all along the sector, measured the beach gradients, and found as many underwater obstacles as it was able to in the time. This whole operation took several days, and ended successfully, all the necessary information being acquired. The enemy had no idea that a solitary little submarine had dared to stay so close to the Atlantic Wall for so long, undetected.

After this the two X-craft prepared for their equally secret but more rewarding role of sailing ahead of the invasion to act as navigational marks for the whole armada.

Similar surveys to those made by X-20 had also been carried out a little earlier by small personnel landing-craft towed towards the French coast by motor-launches.

Pluto. Not Walt Disney's famous cartoon character, but the name, in initials, of the equally famous operation for supplying petrol to the thousands of vehicles once they were on French soil: Pipe Line Under The Ocean. Unlike some other invasion projects, this had been developed in good time, and by 1942 1000 miles of pipes were already in position to carry fuel from Stanlow, on the Mersey, and Bristol to London and other southern ports.

Then the problem was how to extend this actually under the ocean. The back-room boys again came forward, and, working under strict secrecy, developed a 3-inch-diameter pipeline. After it passed all its tests sea-trials were wanted as well to see how it would unwind. The Wheezers and Dodgers even had a hand in Pluto, too, on these sea operations, designing special marker-buoys fitted with a mechanism to bring them to the surface at a certain time.

Then began the production of Pluto: four lines of 70 miles each, from the Isle of Wight to Cherbourg, due to be captured soon after D-Day, and later seventeen lines from Dungeness to Calais.

Men of the R.E.'s and R.A.S.C. were trained to work pumping-stations set up at the English terminal points, one of these pumping-heads being provocatively placed in the cliffs immediately opposite Boulogne. Ships were found with holds big enough to house the massive pipeline, and landing-barges earmarked to link up the main lines when it was laid to the battle beaches. Over a thousand naval personnel had the duty of doing this unique job.

All over Britain signs of D-Day abounded. Troops trained literally from John o' Groats to Land's End, and tanks roared through quiet English villages, disturbing the dust of soft spring days. Civilian travel to and from Eire was stopped, to cut down the risk of espionage, and in April the whole coast from the Wash to Cornwall came under strict supervision. No visitors were allowed without reason, and no residents could travel more than a certain distance from their own home.

Since it would be impossible to camouflage the intentions of an armada —even though its ships might be camouflaged— there was a vital need to mislead the enemy about the D-Day goal, or at least conceal it as long as possible. To help do this dummy landing-craft built specially for the purpose were berthed very visibly in Dover and other Cinque Ports, as well as in ports in Nore Command. With these elaborate "blinds" went troop concentrations in Kent and Sussex to suggest preparations for a landing in the Pas-de-Calais area. The skyscraper effect of the tall Phoenix and Whale units at Selsey and Dungeness confirmed the enemy's idea that the Strait of Dover must be our intended location. All this while, too, the Allies made sure that they spread the ships and landing-craft equally among ports of the British Isles, so that no abnormal concentrations could be observed by enemy aircraft over the coast opposite Normandy. All divisions not scheduled for early landing in France were trained and billeted in Kent, and German aircraft over this area definitely reported both the dummy craft and the troops. Proof of this came from Intelligence, who reported enemy reinforcements from ten divisions to fifteen between Le Havre and Calais, while Brittany and the Mediterranean also received some.

Churchill, meanwhile, had recovered from pneumonia and convalescence at Marrakesh, and was back in his old form. He hastened Montgomery's request to have vehicles water-proofed by a special process which would permit them to be driven through a few feet of water without harm on the Normandy shores.

He also kept in touch with Mulberry, especially watching the progress of the twenty-three Whale floating-pier units, which "must float up and down with the tide," you will remember his saying long before they were born. The main Mulberry components were now an inner Phoenix breakwater of huge concrete caisson units which were to be towed across the Channel and sunk by opening release valves; and a series of the Whale floating piers. These ran out to "Spud" pier-heads, also floating, and mounted on great, stilt-like legs, which were designed to adjust themselves to the height of the tide.

The Premier also encouraged the Mulberry project personally at a conference in late January at which it was decided definitely to augment the proposed two harbours with the Gooseberry blockships. At Churchill's suggestion America agreed to supply nearly half the number of these ships.

At a service conference exactly two years earlier Vice-Admiral Lord Louis Mountbatten had said, "If ports are not available we may have to construct them in pieces and tow them in."

He heard the idea jeered at in derision, but, fortunately for the Allies, he was one of the select company whose vital vision helped win the War.

So it went on.

As soon as Intelligence reported the latest tactical obstacles the Germans were preparing for us, the British Army quickly copied them at a secret situation in East Anglia so that troops could be familiarized with them. They built pill-boxes, stone walls, barbed wire entanglements; dug ditches which tanks would have to face; laid minefields; and erected steel obstructions. These were all replicas of enemy equipment. Not only did the Army study them; where possible they designed counter-measures which could destroy them. These were tried out in the field, where new battle techniques also first saw the light.

The Bangalore torpedo, for instance, had been used frequently for firing across a minefield, detonating all mines in its route, and so clearing a path for advancing troops. Now a new way was being evolved, more in tune with the time of armoured warfare. A Sherman tank was covered with a series of pipes, each containing a Bangalore torpedo. These pipes pointed straight ahead, and as the tank advanced it fired these unusual "guns" in sequence. The torpedoes were shot out, and exploded ten yards in front of the vehicle, clearing a continuous track through the mines.

Sea and harbour too could be equally lethal, and plans to clear enemy harbours of mines had to be made, so that when the Allies captured a port it would be workable.

But before this could even be attempted some sort of special suit had to be devised to protect the frogmen, who would tackle these weapons, from the danger of death by underwater blast. In only six weeks these suits must be tested, made, and distributed.

To test them, naval personnel underwent a series of exacting trials at Horsea Island, near Portsmouth. They were lowered into a deep sea-water lake, where they subjected themselves to explosions at varying distances to discover the effects. Often they were taken from the lake semi-conscious and with agonizing aches, which lasted long afterwards. But, by their heroism, a protective suit was rushed into production, and played its role in Cherbourg and elsewhere, when Port Parties had to clear mines from enemy harbours. Many frogmen owed their lives to this suit.

Another underwater development at about this time was connected with the Army's secret amphibious tank. No one had yet devised a way of escape for the crews of these monster vehicles if they should sink at sea. In only three days a lightweight apparatus was created and tested actually under water, by sinking one of the amphibians. This too served in saving lives on D-Day.

5

The Air Onslaught and Enemy Mining

PLANS progressed on land and sea; the tempo quickened, the atmosphere became more electric. But D-Day could come to nothing without the Allied Air Forces. First of all, the ceaseless strategic bombing against enemy centres of industry and aircraft production inflicted such blows on the strength of the Luftwaffe that for each of the five months from November 1943 to March 1944 less than half the planned production of enemy single-engine fighters was actually achieved. At the same time heavy attacks on airfields and in combat cut the enemy's power still more. The full-scale raids on inner Germany allowed the Allies to get gradual control of the air over France, ready for the invasion. This policy was not pursued without heart-breaking sacrifice by both the British and American Air Forces. On the night of March 30–31, 1944, ninety-four aircraft of Bomber Command failed to return from an attack on Nuremberg.

By this time, however, the new American long-range fighters had now mastered the enemy's during the day, and bombers made powerful precision attacks, protected by the Thunderbolt, Lightning, and, later, the Mustang.

Throughout the preliminary period, before the final fling for D-Day, air attacks also had to be maintained on "Noball" targets, the code name for the flying-bomb and rocket launching sites.

Important as all these objectives obviously were, the main aim was to stop enemy supplies reaching the invasion area once the fight was on. To do this the railway bombing plan started in April. For if the enemy's railway system could be hit hard enough they would not be able to supply or reinforce the troops. So the railway centres of Northern France and the Low Countries became the recipients of 66,000 tons of bombs in three months, with the avowed aim of making a "railway desert" around the Germans in Normandy. Secondary targets were the main marshalling yards. Part of the plan, too, covered the destruction of road and rail bridges, including the severing of the Seine bridges, below Paris, and the bridges over the Loire, below Orleans.

Eighty targets were attacked, fifty-one being heavily damaged, twenty-five damaged, four little affected.

The first full onslaught on a rail centre took place on March 6–7, when the R.A.F. bombed Trappes. No less than 190 direct hits exploded on the actual tracks, and the entire electrified line between Paris and Chartres was cut. It still needed repairs two months later. Throughout March and into April the story was the same: at Paris/Noisy-le-Sec the whole railway complex was completely wiped out. A supper-time attack on Charleroi ploughed up the massive marshalling yards, which were still out of service on D-Day. A creeping paralysis extended over the whole northern network, west of Paris–Amiens–Boulogne and South Belgium.

Eastern routes to Paris received similar devastating attention in May, but the attacks were restricted on several occasions because of the danger to French civilians. In fact, the vital junction of Le Bourget was not attacked at all, since heavy loss of life among Allies would have been inevitable. So it was not yet total war.

Fighter-sweeps on a stupendous scale intercepted locomotives all over Northern France. On May 21 over 500 Thunderbolts with 233 Spitfires claimed sixty-seven locomotives destroyed and ninety-one damaged. The Americans claimed ninety-one locomotives destroyed on the very same day.

Lines, locomotives, and rail and road bridges leading into the assault area were also targets for the Allied Air Forces. This bombing of bridges had a double objective: to check troops and supplies from entering the battle, and also to prevent them from making a rapid retreat should this become necessary. Heavy bombers would need about 600 tons per bridge to ensure destruction, but it was realized in time that fighter-bombers could cut this tonnage to 100–200. Leigh-Mallory had to take care not to betray any special interest in the routes to Normandy, and so early on the bridges over the Seine became the targets, together with others which did not appear to commit the Allies to any specific assault area. Once or twice lucky hits detonated the Germans' demolition charges set for future use in a retreat!

So the steady air attacks went on. Forty-nine coastal batteries capable of firing on shipping approaching the assault area were bombed and blasted.

Enemy Radar spanned the entire coast from Norway down to the Spanish border by a chain of stations. The Allies did not need to attack all of them within the assault area, for if some stations vital to the chain could be destroyed the system would not work. These Radar targets had heavy defences, so low-level attacks were carried out by the R.A.F. 2nd Tactical Air Force during the week before D-Day. Many senior pilots died in these missions, but in so doing saved the lives of many invading Allies the following week. Navigational and wireless-telegraphy stations received the same sort of accurate, shattering attack. A mesh of wires fell across the stations in misty smoke and fire. Masts leaned over crazily and crashed down in a maze of metal.

Yet another series of operations was aimed at airfields within a radius of 150 miles of Caen, and during the final three weeks or so between May 11 and D-Day every enemy airfield in that range was systematically bombed, yet without revealing that the Seine Bay would be the area where the liberating forces would land.

Constructive—as opposed to destructive—operations had their place in this amazing Allied air scheme. In fact, members of photographic reconnaissance units were some of the earliest people to be on active preparation for the invasion. For more than a year complex information had been gathered which wanted careful collation if it was to serve its purpose in the overall plan. Damage-assessment sorties after all major bombing raids was an obvious example of reconnaissance of this kind.

Apart from this, however, a patient, painstaking coverage by camera was made of the entire occupied coastline from Holland down to the Spanish frontier, for details of defences. Verticals and oblique angles were photographed of beach gradients, obstacles, coast defences, and shore batteries. Complete coverage from Granville to Flushing helped to hide our specially selected beaches.

Flying three to four miles out from the coast, aircraft took oblique pictures at wave-top height—often hazardously—to give assault coxswains a "landing-craft view" of their area. Then the planes came inshore to 1500 yards from the coast, and at zero feet—waves washing their wing-tips—they took photographs—again at oblique angles—to provide platoon assault commanders with recognition landing-points. Next, climbing steeply to 2000 feet, they took more pictures from the same distance off shore to record views of the immediate hinterland in relation to the beaches.

Day in, day out, the unspectacular work went on, right through the winter of 1943–44 and until the spring. Inland strips (behind the assault areas) and likely advance-airfield sites were photographed for future reference; bridges over rivers were given special pictorial attention. More still: all dropping areas for our airborne divisions had to be accurately mapped from photographs, and, as Rommel stepped up his "defence offensive" throughout March, April, and May, the booby traps, spikes, and so on, came under the all-seeing eye of the reconnaissance camera. Flooding had to be checked for change regularly; enemy supply dumps confirmed; and a mass of other detail noted. Allied equipment, and landing-craft at anchor in our ports, was photographed to test the most effective camouflage. In the fortnight before D-Day *one* R.A.F. Mobile Field Photographic Section alone made 120,000 prints for Army requirements!

While all these diverse air duties were being carried out the actual Operation Overlord received an alarming threat. Reconnaissance reported in the autumn of 1943 that flying-bomb and rocket-launching sites could be detected under construction in the Pas-de-Calais and Cherbourg areas. Part of our valuable air power had to be diverted to deal with them, and on December 5, 1943, sixty-three flying-bomb sites and five rocket sites received their baptism of bombing. The Pas-de-Calais sites were aligned on London, and those around Cherbourg on Bristol. From then on a steady stream of aircraft attacked a total of ninety-seven flying-bomb sites, neutralizing eighty-six. Two out of seven rocket-sites were smashed. Although, as is well known, these secret weapons were to score some serious successes, it is estimated that without the air assault on their sites the fearful flow of 6000 flying-bombs per day might have been aimed at England. Under such a staggering attack the Allies could hardly have begun an invasion. But owing to the Allied bombing raids, the Germans were unable to launch their first flying-bombs until June 13 (after D-Day), nor did they ever succeed in launching them in the numbers originally intended.

The final figures for the two-month softening-up operations of April, May, and June (up to the 5th) were 200,000 sorties by the combined Allied Air Forces. So it was a question of offence and defence. As the spring sped on more and more craft of the D-Day armada were gathering, inevitably very vulnerably, around the coast. All this time protection against attack by air had to come partly from the Allied fighter force. For over 6000 craft were to be employed during that first week after D-Day. Not only were the craft good targets, but equipment and troops too had to be assembled. Leigh-Mallory knew that Germany had 450 heavy bombers still on hand to hammer the preparations for invasion, but for some reason this scale of raid never materialized. Three phases of enemy air attack by night during April and May revealed that they knew of the general activity for invasion, for all were directed at the South Coast.

On April 25–26 forty aircraft attacked Portsmouth and Havant; on the next night eighty aircraft repeated the Portsmouth target, and operated within a triangle of the Needles, Basingstoke, and Worthing. Two nights later came Plymouth's turn. The second phase, in mid-May, made by forces of 100 and 80 aircraft respectively on successive nights, concentrated on Southampton and Weymouth. And the third phase at the end of May took the targets south-westward to Dartmouth and Start Point.

Apart from these efforts, the enemy's reconnaissance sorties were restricted to only 125 in the six weeks before D-Day. So strong had the Allied Air Forces grown by now that these fleeting flights by Luftwaffe recce rarely got farther than mid-Channel—probably deterred by our permanent patrols flying as far out as 40–50 miles south of the Isle of Wight.

This was just as well, too, for a considerable part of the initial invasion force was gathering in the Solent. This armada of unprecedented size swung at anchor, the vessels scarcely able to clear each other as they moved with the tide. Here was an amazing chance for the fading fortunes of the Germans, but, as usual, they muffed it. If they had showered only a comparatively small number of mines among these vessels remarkable results would have been obtained. Minesweeping in waters so tightly packed as these would have been almost impossible, so the ships could not have weighed anchor safely, or even swung to the Solent tide.

Twice the Germans did try to mine the Solent area, on April 28 and May 15, but the raids caused no casualties, no inconvenience. The first time white-flare markers were dropped in the Needles channel well clear of any anchorage, while a strong tide was running. Mine-laying aircraft came over afterwards and released their missiles on the flares, which by then had drifted into shallow water. Most of the mines thus exploded quite harmlessly owing to the lack of depth of water, for they were set to fire in these conditions so that they should not be taken intact. But, to make matters easy, two of them did actually drift down without exploding at all, and landed on good Hampshire soil at Milford-on-Sea. These gifts were promptly photographed and stripped at once by officers of H.M.S. *Vernon*, the Navy's Portsmouth base, famous for rendering enemy mines safe. Their whole war was one long chronicle of courage.

The May mine-laying raid was attempted at the other end of the Isle of Wight, on the eastern Solent, but it was frustrated by fighter aircraft, aided by a ship's smoke-screen. The only observed mines fell on land! So the armada grew daily, packed so tightly that it spread southwards into St Helen's Roads, near the area of this second mine-laying effort. That was all: one more opportunity lost.

Yet another lost chance concerned mines as well. By early 1944 the Germans had become very aware of the imminence of invasion, but of course could not guess where it would take place. So, as a protective measure, a large defensive field of moored mines was laid parallel to the coasts of Holland, Belgium, and all Northern France. They reckoned for certain that the Allies would invade during the first five months of the year. They could not leave so widespread a minefield indefinitely as it would interfere with their own vessels around those coasts, so every one of these mines was fitted with a flooder set for the end of May. The weeks went by—and still no invasion. Then, at various times throughout the day of May 31, each of these thousands of mines in the great field flooded according to schedule and sank harmlessly, and with complete futility, to the bottom. What a waste of material, and what a major mistake! The mines would not have saved the Germans, but they would have meant more losses for the Allies. As the legions of lost mines sank silently to the sea-beds around the north coast of France the tension grew tauter in England, and only 144 hours later came D-Day.

Bomber Command had its own silent mine-laying duties too. As if to show the Germans how to carry out offensive operations, they laid over 3000 ground mines in areas along the Dutch, Belgian, and French coasts, east of Texel, and in Baltic and German waters. The aim was to try to bottle up as many naval outlets as possible, so that the enemy had few ships free to intercept the invasion fleet. The operations were highly successful.

Some of the credit belongs to the brilliant scientists attached to H.M.S. *Vernon*, who devised the complex acoustic and magnetic mines, and combinations of both, that defied sweeping by their ingenuity. Throughout that spring mines were assembled, their circuits being constantly changed to mislead the enemy's sweeping-plans. A special section—MX—was set up actually at West Leigh House, near Havant, where mines went straight from test to assembly and laying: a streamlined plan scarcely similar to our peace-time procedure of Admiralty organization! Parts were dispatched to, or collected from, the most unlikely spots in England, for these mines were a mass of relays, clocks, and other highly technical components which could, more often than not, only be made at one factory in the country. So urgent did the overall operations become that components had to be fetched literally off the factory floor by hand and rushed down for assembly. One *Vernon* officer had to fit in a weekly courier service for several weeks. His routine was wonderfully secret. He left H.M.S. *Vernon* during the afternoon empty-handed, took the Waterloo train and then a taxi to a temporary Admiralty address at Fitzmaurice Place, just off Berkeley Square. This was merely a convenient spot for a firm supplying some essential part of a component to leave a large supply for him to pick up. From here he caught a naval car, driven by a dark siren, to King's Cross, where he caught the night-train north. The sunset streets of London wore an air of expectancy, excitement, and held that *Warsaw Concerto* mood of magic too. Then the night, crowded trains, and the ghostly gloom of Wakefield in the early hours of morning. Chill wind, crates on the platform, the wait for the Dewsbury train. A filthy carriage, another hour, and Dewsbury at dawn. Tea and a currant bun, the car uphill to the factory, delivery and collection, the rows of Yorkshire girls in the morning shift and the day-train south. A strange interlude, remote from war.

Meanwhile one other evening air attack was aimed at the battleship *King George V*, in Plymouth. The Germans used a new type of radio bomb, which was controlled by the observer in the aircraft making the attack. Luckily this proved just as unsuccessful as the mine-laying raids in the Solent.

The armada advances.

In an English port, landing-craft await the men and materials which they will transport to Normandy.

The D.U.K.W.s, launched from larger craft, were invaluable for amphibious support.

This landing-craft in the chilly dawn waters symbolizes Operation Overlord.

6

Monty's Master Plan

ON New Year's Day 1944 Montgomery handed over his command of the Eighth Army, and took off from the Sangro river airstrip, in Italy.

He was flown to Marrakesh, where Churchill—recuperating from pneumonia—confronted him with the C.O.S.S.A.C. plan. Montgomery's reaction was that the assaulting forces would not be powerful enough. Arriving next day in England, he at once started studying the plan in detail, which confirmed his opinion, both of the lack of strength and over-narrow frontage of the proposed assault.

Montgomery established his H.Q. at St Paul's School, in West Kensington, while the Allied Naval and Air Forces H.Q. were at Norfolk House, in St James's Square. Eisenhower had yet to arrive and begin building the Bushey Park community.

Basically, Montgomery's invasion plan was to assault the Normandy coast north of the Carentan estuary, and also between the estuary and the river Orne. This would yield a base for further operations, to include taking airfield sites and the port of Cherbourg.

Once ashore and firmly footed in France, Montgomery's idea was to threaten to break out on the eastern flank, in the Caen sector. This would draw the main enemy reserves into that area, where the British and Canadian armies would keep them fully occupied. Once these reserves had been committed to the east, he would break out on the west, with the American armies under General Bradley and pivoting on Caen. This break-out attack would be delivered dramatically southward down to the Loire and then swing east in a wide sweep up to the Seine about Paris. This would cut off all enemy forces south of the Seine, leaving them without bridges back over the river—destroyed by air action. The two keys to the entire situation were the rapid advances necessary in the west and the immense importance of Caen in the east.

Before Montgomery went into detail he naturally considered the exact enemy situation in northern France and how it would influence his strategy. The German army groups finally opposing him on D-Day numbered some sixty divisions, but these varied from S.S. and Panzer formations down to low-quality static coast-defence forces. Montgomery received all the reports of the elaborate defence measures, including the formidable Element C: the underwater obstacles with Teller mines on the forward face. And he had a shrewd idea of the conflicting conceptions of Rommel and von Rundstedt.

Another handicap to the Germans proved to be the existence of a third army group in France, called Panzer Group West. This administered the Panzer formations, which were operationally commanded by the other army groups: a system which not unnaturally led to some confusion in the overall operation of enemy armour when the invasion was launched.

In the assault sector itself Montgomery anticipated the enemy garrison to be three coast-defence divisions supported by four reserve divisions. He constantly reviewed both the build-up of possible enemy forces in the area and also their strategy. By D + 60 the enemy could concentrate up to twenty divisions in the Normandy area; by D + 20 Montgomery might expect twenty-five to thirty; and by D + 60 up to fifty divisions.

Intelligence kept him posted with regular appreciations of strength, and in April and May they reported encouraging signs. Whereas in January 1944 they had estimated that by D + 60 the enemy would be able to move as many as fifteen divisions into the West from elsewhere in Europe, the level in April dropped to six as a result of the Soviet successes and the turn of events in Italy. The picture brightened even more in May as the Germans stood on the threshold of a three-sided siege: Russia, Italy, and—soon—France.

Meanwhile Montgomery pored over maps of France, especially the Varreville sector. One of his hundreds of problems was the inundations behind the beaches of Varreville, which made the vital exits from beach to hinterland awkward. Here, for instance, he had to be sure the Allies would capture the causeways across flooded areas, or else they might be liable to be pinned down to the beach strip by small enemy forces.

The land behind the beaches generally favoured defence, and was not suited to shifting large armoured forces. But Montgomery had to try and overcome this. Apart from the open, rolling plain south-east of Caen, the whole region was covered to a depth of 30–40 miles inland by *bocage*—that peculiar pastureland split up by high hedges, banks, and ditches into small fields and meadows: ideal for infantry and sniping, but bad for tanks.

As Montgomery prepared his plan the assault on Europe had really already been begun—by the devastating air attacks which were slowly strangling Germany's economy. Then came the road and rail bombardments, which were to be rewarded on D-Day by the remarkable report

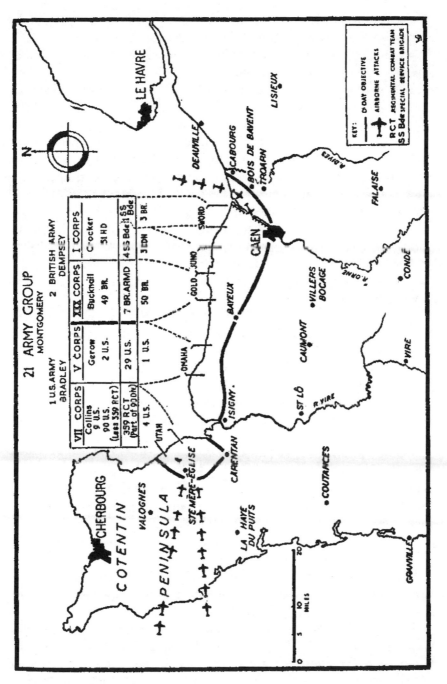

THE PLAN OF ATTACK

that every railway-bridge over the Seine between Paris and the sea was impassable to the enemy. And all the time the victory at sea, in the Battle of the Atlantic, enabled the vast volume of American and Canadian men and materials to assemble in Britain.

What was this amazing assault to be? The invasion of a continent by 130,000 men and 20,000 vehicles, unheard of in the history of war. Their aim: to burst the barrier of the Atlantic Wall and free Europe.

Simultaneous landings would be made by eight brigades— three British, two Canadian, three American, with the U.S. Rangers and British Commandos. Airborne troops were to be thrown in on both flanks: the American Airborne Divisions at the base of the Cotentin peninsula to help the battle of the beaches and then isolate Cherbourg; and a British Airborne Division to seize the crossings over the Caen canal, on the extreme left.

The 1st U.S. Army was to assault astride the Carentan estuary, capture Cherbourg as quickly as possible, and then extend south to St-Lô with the advance of the British Army.

This 2nd British Army assault would develop the bridgehead south of the line St-Lô − Caen and south-east of Caen, to take airfield sites, and protect the eastern flank of the American army aiming at Cherbourg. The U.S. attack would be on Utah and Omaha beaches, the British on Gold, Juno, and Sword beaches.

During the night before D–Day, as the armada made its silent passage, intense air action against enemy defences would begin, while airborne forces were dropped on two flanks in advance of the mass assault of the following morning. At H–Hour the leading waves of liberation forces would land under the stupendous support of naval bombardment, air action, and the guns, rockets, and mortars of close-support craft. So eight brigades, combat forces, special assault engineers, amphibious tanks, and much more would beach on the first three tides.

Airlift priority went to American airborne troops whose vital job would be securing the beach exits from the Utah sector. Main bodies of them were to land near Ste Mere-Église on the night of D—1 Day, some to help the seaborne assault on Utah, others to intercept any movement of enemy reserves into the Cotentin peninsula.

The last lift was for British forces due to land before H–Hour east of Caen, east of which they were to dominate with the aid of the Commandos. American Rangers were to land in the assault on the west of Omaha beach to attack defences on the east side of the Carentan estuary.

One British Commando brigade was earmarked by Montgomery to link the assaults on the Juno and Sword sectors. Another would land behind the assault on the Sword sector, and while part dealt with the village of Ouistreham the rest would cross the Orne and attack enemy coast defences of the river up to Cabourg.

The Allies had studied assault technique now for a long while, with the visible result of all the special equipment being hurried into quantity production. They had the weapons, but what was the best way of using them?

Montgomery's answer was the Joint Fire Plan. The resources of all three services must be mobilized to see that the army got ashore: this was the first essential of D-Day. To do this the plan proposed to destroy or neutralize the enemy coastal artillery batteries, which might attack the approaching naval convoys or fire on the anchorages, and wipe out all strong points and other localities sited for the immediate defence of the chosen assault beaches.

Already air attacks would have been delivered against the coastal defence batteries. The Joint Fire Plan proper was timed to start on the night preceding the assault, when Bomber Command would pick out the ten most important batteries and attack in saturation strength. Medium bombers would then take up the theme on a further six similar targets, the operation being due to start soon before first light—the same time as bombardment began from armoured assault craft. After this naval gunfire, directed by spotting aircraft, would explode into the assault. The specially fitted craft had withering weapons at their disposal: 4.7-inch guns, 4-inch mortars, barrages of 5-inch rockets, Centaur tanks fitted with 75-mm. howitzers, and 17-pounder anti-tank guns, as well as ordinary field guns.

And then, half an hour before H-Hour came the holocaust created by heavy bombers of the 8th U.S. Air Force and medium bombers of the 9th U.S. Air Force. These were timed to go into action against the coastal defence artillery and enemy beach localities as late as possible. In fact, the whole Joint Fire Plan aimed at building up this barrage in a tremendous crescendo which would reach its climax only ten minutes before the first troops waded ashore. Then, from H-Hour minus ten minutes, the fighters and fighter-bombers would take up the offensive inland. The enemy would have hardly any time at all to recover before the invasion was on.

The strategy took shape at S.H.A.E.F. One of the last two decisions to be made was the actual selection of D-Day and H-Hour—the time the leading assault craft hit the beach. Night was ruled out first of all. So it should be daylight, and with a moonlit night for the passage. Daylight was vital for accurate siting of bombardment and also for the landing itself H-Hour had to be as early after first light as possible, to give the enemy least time to notice; and to give the Allies the maximum hours of light in which to consolidate, and then land the follow-up forces on the second tide before nightfall.

The precise time for H-Hour was fixed by taking into account the period before sunrise when aircraft, spotting from high up for naval guns, and heavy bombers, also at a considerable altitude, could see sufficient—but before the coast defenders at sea-level could claim the same. The time required for bombardment from sea and air was whittled down as much as was advisable, the duration decided on eventually being from the first sign of morning light to forty minutes later.

From this it was settled that H-Hour should be fixed for the moment when the bombardment stopped—forty minutes after first light—and on a day when the tide at this time was three hours before high water. As these conditions could not be obtained on all assault beaches at once, due to the whims of the English Channel, a separate H-Hour for each beach had to be used instead. This meant a compromise, as the Joint Fire Plan could not be divided into separate sectors. Ultimately H-Hour varied from 0630 in the west to 0745 on the east sector.

Time and tide wait ...

Finding the right time to coincide with the right tide on a moonlit night meant only three possible dates every month. The target date was still set for May 31, 1944, but an alteration by a week or so one way or the other was obviously inevitable since so few dates could be considered. After May 31 the next trio of dates to give the vital conditions were June 5, 6, and 7.

Along with Montgomery's plans went the Cover Plan too, to point to the Pas-de-Calais as the goal. Two ideas further to those mentioned were full-scale embarkation sign-posting in the Dover-Folkestone area and the aim to keep invasion preparations to proportions which would suggest that the attack was still some six weeks off at the time it finally happened.

With the Cover Plan went several diversions to distract the enemy about the real intentions of the Allies and the area of main assault. These will be noticed at the D-Day stage.

By the end of D-Day all eight Allied divisions would be well ashore, with Commandos, Rangers, and fourteen tank regiments. Within a week basic divisions would have risen to thirteen, and by D + 20 two dozen divisions would just about comprise the strength.

As well as detailed planning, Montgomery had an overall date aim and general principles for the troops to adopt to meet this. Sustained energy and drive was paramount. Beachheads had to be linked, and then the troops would have to push on and penetrate inland before opposition crystallized. Leading formations were being told to bypass major centres of resistance and peg out claims farther on. Determined leadership must be maintained to retain the initiative of invasion and resist counter-attack.

Montgomery was aware of the normal procedure of producing "phase lines" on a map, to indicate target positions to be reached by leading troops every few days. A phased map was drawn in April, but he did not feel too happy about the actual lines displayed there. Montgomery always had in mind reaching the Seine and the Loire by D + 90, but felt that interim estimates would only be misleading and unreal in an operation of this massive magnitude. In fact, his Seine-Loire target date was reached on D + 75, with a fortnight to spare.

So the planning progressed. Maintaining the 2nd British Army for the first few days might prove to be a headache, so Beach Maintenance Areas came into existence. In the overall administration and estimates the weather was expected to be "reasonable" during June, July, and August, but plans had to be made against the proverbial rainy day—which more or less coincided with midsummer, and might have wrecked the entire invasion.

Montgomery, like Eisenhower, only had a bare five months in England before D-Day, and most of that had to be occupied by planning. But training the troops was just as essential, and most of the forces available for Operation Overlord lacked battle experience. Montgomery saw that they got as near the real thing as possible in that spring's training, and travelled all over the country encouraging them by his example.

On April 7–8 all the general officers of the Allied armies in the invasion gathered at St Paul's School to hear Montgomery's planning, and Churchill also addressed the conference briefly.

Shortly before this Churchill had told Eisenhower, "If by the coming winter you have established yourself with your thirty-six Allied divisions firmly on the Continent, and have the Cherbourg and Brittany peninsulas in your grasp, I will proclaim this operation to the world as one of the most successful of the War."

Eisenhower replied, "Prime Minister, I assure you that the coming winter will see the Allied forces on the borders of Germany itself"

And the training went on. On April 2, with only two months to prepare, Lieutenant-Colonel T. B. H. Otway received his invasion orders: to take the 9th Battalion, Parachute Regiment, on the most dangerous mission imaginable—the destruction of the coastal battery near Merville. This vast emplacement was a fantastically formidable proposition. Its guns were said to be of 150-mm. calibre, mounted in concrete constructions 12 feet high and 5 feet deep. More concrete, earthworks, and steel doors all added to the battery's solidity, while machine-guns defended the garrison. Twenty weapon-pits appeared on aerial photographs, the whole position was surrounded by a cattle fence, a minefield, and a barbed-wire fence.

Near Newbury, Otway got the sappers to build a scale model of the battery, complete with obstacles. Day and night rehearsals continued

throughout April and May, more often than not with live ammunition to
resemble real life—and death. By the end of May each one of the thirty-
five officers and 600 other ranks knew precisely his part in the operation.
Then there followed an intensive five-day briefing, with every man sub-
mitting his own sketch of the position he would occupy. Then they reckoned they were ready for Merville.

The final figure for manpower to be moved across the Channel in two
days—D-Day and D + I—was 176,000. Behind those men were the supplies and staffs in England, and carrying the forces to France were the
crews of 5000 ships and craft.

Five thousand vessels.

This was what Admiral Sir Bertram Ramsay had to command. And taking part in the whole operation would be no less than 2,000,000 men. To
summarize: first, Ramsay, together with the other Services, had to break
the strong crust of coastal defences by bombardment, and secondly, he had
to commence and continue reinforcing the fighting forces without a pause
for five or six weeks. The amount of organization involved need not be
stressed.

But before the day came exercises on a large scale. These were very vital
to many of the assault forces, yet the danger existed of the enemy discov-
ering them, and attacking the vulnerable craft involved in such an operation. Luckily all rehearsals prior to Exercise Tiger escaped any enemy
notice. Tiger, however, was the final exercise for Force U. This assault
force was an American formation making up the western flank of the U.S.
area, the Utah beach (U for Utah) . With its assembly ports of Torbay,
Brixham, Dartmouth, and Salcombe, it was part of the Western Task
Force. On the night of April 27–28 it was exercising in Lyme Regis Bay
when three groups of fast-moving E-boats penetrated the patrols covering the assault craft. They caught the last convoy to sail on this exercise,
consisting of eight tank landing-ships, and pressed home a sudden and
successful attack. In the dark waters off Lyme Regis, while its fishermen
slept, the E-boats sank two of the L.S.T.'s and damaged a third. American
assault troops were flung fully laden into the water, and before the attack
could be beaten off many of them were drowned. The naval defensive
patrols were on the weak side during this exercise, and if the episode was
tragic it taught every one the need for as many protective warships and
craft as could humanly be mustered on D-Day. This had been an exercise.
The real thing would be worse.

Before the final rehearsals for the other four assault forces were held
came the gradual concentration of troops into their particular areas. From
these areas they would move on to marshalling zones and, ultimately, be

brought forward to the embarkation points. And these ports, remember, reached from Felixstowe to Plymouth and round to South Wales.

Vehicles and equipment had to be waterproofed for landing from craft into the sea short of the beach itself. Rations, French currency, security, and dozens of other details could not be overlooked, nor could the possibility of postponement, due to weather, otherwise the feeding and billeting of the advance waves of troops would be chaotic.

Production of certain craft and equipment was still short in early May, but by now preparations were advanced for Exercise Fabius, to test the basic embarkation arrangements. This involved actually moving and "shipping" thousands of the forces who would be repeating the experience in a month's time under conditions of active service. This was far from inactive, however, and involved the assault forces O, G, J, and S. The first of these formed the Weymouth, Portland, and Poole contingent of the American Task Force and was destined to land on the eastern flank of the U.S. area on the Omaha beach. The other three forces, G, J, and S, were to sail from the Hampshire and Sussex waters, the first two from Southampton, the Solent, and Spithead, the third from Portsmouth, Spithead, Newhaven, and Shoreham.

The exercise tested out the simultaneous sailing of the three forces based there, and also checked the naval Commander-in-Chief's control of all Channel movements. The Navy's side of Fabius went well, but a freshening south-westerly wind blew up in the afternoon of the first day. If the exercise had proceeded according to plan some of the landing-craft would undoubtedly have been damaged, so the programme was curtailed. The Allies had not enough for D-Day to risk losing any in advance of it. By this date, May 4, the Allied air superiority had become so strong that the only enemy interference with this substantial rehearsal was an aircraft attack on a destroyer in one of the covering forces.

In the same week as Fabius the various higher headquarters of the invasion forces moved nearer the scene of Operation Overlord. Portsmouth was the nerve-centre of communications to the main embarkation areas, so a stately home in seclusion and safety near by was found for Eisenhower's H.Q. Its name—Southwick House, and it nestled in its own grounds behind Portsdown Hill, well out of the way of intruders. Montgomery and Ramsay were on hand too, while the Allied Air Force placed its H.Q. in the Stanmore-Uxbridge area.

Then, on May 15, Montgomery and Ramsay returned to London for a final conference at St Paul's School. Every one was there, including H.M. King George VI, Field-Marshal Smuts, Churchill, and "generals by the score," as Eisenhower records. Churchill made a much-quoted comment:

"I am hardening on this operation."

This did not mean that he had been opposed to it previously, but merely that now he wanted to strike even if the conditions laid down for it were not exactly fulfilled.

Churchill questioned what he considered an excess of motor-cars and non-fighting vehicles, and also made a mental note of the staggering number of 2000 officers and clerks who were to accompany the invasion to keep records. This reminded him of Admiral Andrew Cunningham's story that dental-chairs were actually landed at Algiers in the first flight of Operation Torch! The calculation on which Churchill's contention was based was that by D + 20 there would be in Normandy 189,000 vehicles and 902,000 men—one vehicle for less than each five men.

Still on the subject of vehicles, Churchill had been endeavouring to include a French division in the invasion, for reasons of significance as well as sentiment, but this (General Leclerc's) division seemed to be short of vehicles. Churchill asked Eisenhower for his help, and was assured that deficiencies would be made good from the large American supplies.

Yet another decision—for Ramsay this time—was the actual percentage of available landing-craft which Ramsay could budget for in the operation. Getting and keeping these craft in operational order called for great effort, and he was reluctant to expect more than about 90 per cent. of all craft to be available. In fact, however, the proportion reached the amazing figures of 99.3 per cent. for U.S. landing-craft and 97.6 per cent. for British. Amazing, since most of these craft had already been used extensively in training over the previous months.

Two days after the S.H.A.E.F. conference in London, and with the results of a special photographic survey of underwater obstacles in his hands, Eisenhower decided on June 5 as D-Day, provided that the weather was satisfactory. But even if the time, tide, and moon were right, other conditions were needed to make it possible. It had to be a quiet day with little wind, a cloud base above 3000 feet, cloud maximum 5/10ths and at least three miles' visibility. The chances of getting all this on a specific date were surprisingly slim for June: thirteen to one against. If June 5 were unfavourable the next two days would be considered. If neither of these were satisfactory there would have to be a delay of a fortnight.

Meanwhile May proceeded in idyllic weather, with a calm Channel sprinkled by quicksilver sunshine. Twice a week throughout the month the Supreme Commander conferred with his weather-men to test their forecasts. On the basis of these predictions Eisenhower made dummy decisions for or against a supposed invasion a day and a half ahead—the time in which he would have to come to his final, fateful order. These helped him by experience to acquire the frame of mind which he would eventually need. And the forecasts also gave him the chance of judging the qualities of the Chief Meteorological Adviser, Group-Captain J. M. Stagg of the R.A.F.

Yes, the suspense started to mount now, to catch hold of every one who already knew the approximate D-Day date. Less than three weeks off. The secret of this date was being well kept, too, just as was the location of the actual assault. The Germans would have given anything to have known the place and date. As it was, although they reacted slowly to the general preparations apparent all over Southern England, they did step up naval activity. Apart from the intrusion on the invasion exercises, on April 29 enemy destroyers engaged two Canadian destroyers which were covering a mine-laying operation. Each side lost one destroyer in the action.

During May enemy E-boats roamed more freely in the central English Channel, and air reconnaissance revealed that more moved to Cherbourg and Le Havre.

Three days after the D-Day decision the first enemy U-boat was reported in the western Channel. This forced the Admiralty to revise the disposition of some covering forces and, by co-operation with Coastal Command reconnaissance and armed aircraft, they managed to counter-act possible danger to the armada from underwater attack. Hardly any U-boat activity occurred on the day itself.

Apart from the earlier April and May mine-laying sorties in the Solent and Spithead, the enemy did not penetrate this vital Isle of Wight armada area. Right up to D-Day, however, Ramsay continued to worry over the outcome of any last minute large-scale mining operation. For six weeks enemy mine-laying had been intensified off the South Coast generally, and two new types of mine were introduced. These operations involved air-craft on a scale not attempted for over two years, but by not managing to mine the main assembly waters Germany lost a great opportunity.

7

Sixty Blockships and Two Midget Subs

THE days of May were running out amid a blossomy blaze of sun. Eisenhower had little time to admire the grounds of Southwick House, however, and his sole interest in the weather was its effect on the enterprise under his command. Late in the month Leigh-Mallory was still unhappy about the decision to drop two airborne divisions on the Cherbourg peninsula. He foresaw 50 per cent. or higher losses if this part of Operation Overlord was allowed to take place. Eisenhower's expert adviser did not share the Air Chief Marshal's pessimism, and so it remained for the Supreme Commander alone to make a decision. Eisenhower went to his tent to think it all out, and finally followed the plan as already prepared. He telephoned the news to Leigh-Mallory, and then resumed his urgent work once more.

All over England the camps lay pitched. Now a fever began to grip the forces. After a spate of rumours groups left distant places, where they had been stationed all the spring, and headed south. Fresh transit camps sprang up; trains tore through the night to take the men towards their destiny; and tanks, motorcycles, even D.U.K.W.'s, roared along the English roads. Another wait, till at last, on May 28, subordinate commanders learned the vital date. From this day on every one committed to the invasion was suddenly "sealed" in their ships, camps, or wherever they were. No one came or went; no mail went in or out; barbed-wire lay all around, as if the camps were concentration camps.

Southern England became one vast camp, crowded with forces and crushed with equipment. Every encampment, barracks, vehicle-park, and unit was precisely charted on master maps. The schedule for movement had been so wonderfully worked out that each unit would reach its vessels at the exact time they were ready. As the last day of May dawned "the whole mighty host was tense as a coiled spring," as Eisenhower says, just waiting for its release, to be sped across the Channel in the greatest amphibious assault in history. Now the briefing was over. They all knew from maps and photographs the beach they would assault. Officers had even earmarked houses near Caen for their platoon H.Q.'s, The men relinquished all their personal possessions, and donned new anti-vermin battledress. From camps to transit areas they travelled, soon to be in boatloads.

Before June and D–Day Winston Churchill wanted arrangements to be made for him to watch the pre-H-Hour bombardment from a suitable escort cruiser. Ramsay drew up a plan for this, but felt bound to tell Eisenhower, who could not countenance such an unjustified risk. When Churchill took his weekly luncheon with the King on Tuesday, May 30, he was asked where he would be on D–Day. Churchill told the King, who expressed a similar wish. The next day, however, the King wrote to the Prime Minister explaining that, on reflection, it would not be proper for either of them to be there. After a further exchange of letters this was reluctantly agreed to by Churchill.

The King ended up, "Your very sincere friend," while Churchill felt no ill-will in signing himself, "Your Majesty's humble and devoted servant and subject."

Now the No. 1 question was the weather. In May more than half the days would have been good enough for Eisenhower to launch the liberation. But, ironically, Thursday, June 1, dawned a dull, difficult day. The tents pitched all over the southern counties cast no shadow as the sun rose. Stagg found the whole situation marginal. No foolproof forecast could be given with these conflicting indications. From June 1 onward the Supreme Commander held meetings twice a day solely to consider the weather reports. Not at conventional times were these convened, but at 9.30 P.M. and 4 A.M. Four in the morning at Southwick House. Hampshire villages slept all around in the hush before dawn. Hambledon, Fareham, Southwick, Wickham, and—over Portsdown Hill—the old castle town of Porchester. Then, beyond it, Portsmouth Harbour and the Solent crowded with craft, with the muted outline of the Isle of Wight rising from the sea, blurred against the southern sky. Only the sound of the power-station and the creak of cranes in the dockyard disturbed the night.

The Anglo-American committee, headed by Group-Captain Stagg, examined and analysed every scrap of meteorological information which poured into the house from many sources. To help the forecasts further, two U.S. and two British warships were stationed specially in the Atlantic to transmit reports of the weather which would be likely to head in the prevailing westerly way towards England, the Channel, and Normandy. They had already gained extra experience from a similar service to the Fabius exercise.

Many things were already happening elsewhere; ships were actually on the move, but, in the final analysis, it was Eisenhower's decision when to start the assault which would affect them all. The Gooseberry ships sailed, with Lieutenant-Commander J. E. Taylor, R.N.R., aboard the liner

Durban, one of these sixty blockships soon due to be scuttled off the Arromanches beaches. At last it had taken shape. How long ago was it when Taylor had attended that first meeting at the Gooseberry H.Q. near the Mall? When he heard for the very first time of all those mysterious Mulberries and Gooseberries; "Corncobs," Phoenix, Whales, and Bombardons; "Spud Pierhead," "Beetles," and "Dolphins."

A for American, B for British. So the two artificial harbours were designated appropriately A and B, with Mulberry A at St Laurent and Mulberry B at Arromanches. But the breakwaters alone would not be enough, hence the five Gooseberries, one each at Varreville, St Laurent, Arromanches, Courseulles, and Ouistreham.

Just how important the Mulberry and Gooseberry idea was considered may be gathered from an official memo to the First Sea Lord, which put the matter in these words:

"This project is so vital to the success of Overlord that it might be described as the crux of the whole operation."

Rather a frightening thought. Frightening too was the model room at Plans Division H.Q., with its sandy scale model of the chosen D-Day beaches: just a small affair, but, discovered by the wrong person, it would have ruined the whole invasion. Although, on the surface, no one would ever guess the truth, London was full of such secrets at that time.

Taylor had headed north on a preliminary trip and met an H.M.S. *Vernon* officer whose job was to set the explosive charges to scuttle a dozen of the sixty blockships, which were already lying unobtrusively at anchor in out-of-the-way northern harbours. It seemed strange to be aiming north to prepare for an invasion to take place due south of England. But this was to be a many-sided assault.

The necessarily complex plans for adapting the blockships for their role pushed ahead slowly. Methil and Oban were picked as ports suitable for them to await their last voyage, and as each conversion was made and the charge machinery installed, one by one they made for their respective port. The dozen which the H.M.S. *Vernon* officer had prepared were already in a near-by harbour, so needed only a short trip. Taylor and this officer, their immediate work finished, returned south, Taylor soon to join his particular Gooseberry ship, the liner *Durban*.

It was past mid-month now, as the *Durban* vanished out of Portsmouth harbour into the May morning Channel mist, accompanied by another one of the sixty, *Sumatra*. While Eisenhower was starting his "dummy runs" on weather forecasting, to see just how accurate his advisers could be, these two dissimilar ships—one slim, one stouter—clung to the coast up to Oban. At Loch Linnhe they found a score of other ships already assembled, all with comparable numbers painted large on both port and starboard sides. Although they still did not know it for sure, invasion was less than a fortnight off now. Two more days ticked by, and then they slipped out of Oban as inconspicuously as such a force of ships could do, and reached one of the two final assembly ports—Methil.

May 26. D - 10, by the original reckoning. The order came to sail, so the twenty-two ships composing the British and non-American Allies' contribution to the Gooseberry plan began the next long stage of this prolonged final trip. Some escorting minesweepers plied a course calculated to clear a way through an imaginary minefield; mines might not always be imaginary, so it was as well to be prepared. Night, and the light from Kinnaird Head seemed something to catch hold of in the enveloping dark. Day, and night again, off Cape Wrath, the extreme edge of Scotland. A long way from Normandy. Then with a week to go, they were back at Oban.

D - 7 now. Duffle coats issued all round. The men would be living and sleeping in these soon. Once the invasion was really on, and until they had safely scuttled their vessels, anything might happen. But one thing was certain. They would not see bunks for several days or nights. Wherever they were, they would be sleeping in these all-purpose coats. And, as if to bring home the imminence of the whole operation, with the coats came their forty-eight hours' emergency rations and the basic gear of knife, fork, spoon, tin plate, mug, and toilet paper. The better to remind them that there was a war on they were also given a lifebelt, gas-mask, steel helmet, identity disc, and paybook.

Then, as June came in, the ships went out.

The naval officer in charge sailed in *Sumatra*, as the whole sixty vessels set their bows for the Bristol Channel, the next point in this strangest voyage in history. They made a magnificent motley, a really remarkable convoy in three groups. The twenty-two British and Allied ships took the lead, followed by sixteen from the United States, and then another score or so.

"Speed 5 knots—keep closed up." This was the signal from the flags in *Alynbank*, and it was obeyed as nearly as possible. But by evening the first trouble had occurred—not surprisingly, since the combined age of the sixty ships must have run into a couple of thousand years! *Dover Hill* and *Empire Tamar* caused a delay by stopping for a while. And soon after they had restarted another *Empire*-class vessel, *Empire Defiance*, had to be towed for seven hours until a breakdown in her aged system had been mended. It was clearly going to be all that the ships could do to get to their destination. Without further mishap they did reach the Bristol Channel, however, and fringed the Cornish coast to Land's End, rounding it by the end of an uneasy night. To the people of Penzance who saw some of them, the convoy might have looked like a normal one from across the Atlantic. But it was not.

They had two operational orders sealed on board, each giving the date and time of D-Day and H-Hour. One was Serial 10 and the other Serial 1.

Serial 10 gave June 5, 0640. Serial 1 gave June 6, 0720.

Which would it be? A good question, and the only man in the world who could know the answer when the time came for a decision was Eisenhower.

Friday, June 2. A day of suspense, with the weather still sluggish. The outlook for D-Day—then provisionally fixed for Monday, June 5—was about the same as for Saturday and Sunday, and continuing likewise. In the evening the first warships sailed from Scapa, Belfast, and the Clyde, and down through the Irish Sea. That day, too, the two midget submarines charged with the privilege of marking the assault areas for the first craft set sail from Portsmouth Harbour, or, more accurately, from Fort Blockhouse.

Five men could be accommodated in both X-20 and X-23, the former being the submarine which had carried out the beach reconnaissance off the Arromanches sector earlier in the year. As well as the commanding officer and first lieutenant, they carried an engine-room artificer and two C.O.P.P.'s—Combined Operations Pilotage Parties.

On these two midget submarines the initial accuracy of the entire assault depended, for they were to be the X-craft marking the spot!

All morning and afternoon of June 2 the two little craft could scarcely be seen for the activity around them. The mass of gear for the operation had to be stowed compactly, and special stowing-bags were designed. Twelve oxygen bottles were stuck down the main hatch, to guarantee an extra day's supply, in addition to the craft's ordinary built-in cylinders— in case of accidents. Into the small space below went three R.A.F. rubber dinghies, two small portable Radar beacons, some Sten guns, lightweight diving-suits, and three flashing-lamps with batteries and 18-foot telescopic masts. With all this general and special marking-gear were included revolvers and ammunition too.

This was all carried inboard. Outside, either carried or fitted, extra buoyancy chambers had been built, two small special anchors were stowed for'ard; bollards were incorporated fore and aft, while an 18-foot sounding-pole was secured on as well. Into the hull went an echo-sounder, and an upper-deck repeater was rigged from the master gyro-compass. In fact, each submarine was a floating store. The C.O.P.P.'s first job was to make certain of the crafts' navigation, as an accurate position was the crux of the initial impact of the invasion. All this preparation went on while the dumpy little ferry-boats from Portsmouth to Gosport steamed within a few yards of the X-crafts' berths at Blockhouse.

At half-past nine on Friday evening, June 2, X-20 and X-23 slipped silently from their moorings and set course to make the East Gate in the Portsmouth boom—the boom which was a reminder of defence against attackers and invaders in another war.

Operation Gambit was on.

Past the grey stone walls of old Portsmouth, glinting gold in a fitful sunset, they moved at a slow speed. The weathered red brick of Blockhouse faded from view, and three-quarters of an hour later the two tiny craft passed through the boom gate and met their escorts.

Now night fell, with clouds rolling in from the west. X-23 was astern of H.M.S. *Sapper*, and the two found it hard to join company. An awkward swell lifted and lowered the X-craft, and it took another three-quarters of an hour to pass the tow. Communications were so bad, in fact, that the craft stayed on the surface so that all signals could be made visually. Yet, in spite of the sea, a steady speed was being maintained. X-20 followed, and the two teams kept company.

Lieutenant Ken Hudspeth was commanding X-20, and Lieutenant George Honour, X-23 both R.N.V.R. officers. No snags until early Saturday morning, when the little fleet had to stop to allow Hudspeth to clear a dan-buoy mooring-wire, which had fouled X-20's idle screw. Just before dawn the time approached for the two midgets to be left alone. Their two escort-trawlers began flashing final signals with subdued lights. Last-minute checks were made.

"Good luck" messages were flashed from each large ship to its tiny ward. Then the X-craft slipped their tows and parted from their escorts—and from each other. They were really on their own now. Five men in each, with a load of responsibility.

Honour's voice came, crackling and distorted, over the phones from the wet and cheerless casing up aloft.

"Full ahead main engine, course 172 degrees."

As the early light lanced the sea they dived to avoid any chance of being spotted. They caught a trim and kept to a steady 30-foot depth, half speed ahead on the main motor. On and on exactly like this for the whole day of Saturday, June 3, and the same course of 172. Honour hoped to reach the French coast without using any of his precious oxygen, and to do this he had to raise the induction once every five hours and run the engine for a few minutes to draw a fresh air supply through the boat. This process of "guffing through" demanded a careful inspection of the surrounding sea through the day-periscope, followed by a short spell of accurate depth-keeping while the induction was raised.

By the later hours of evening the boat had been ventilated three times without breaking surface. Then, as soon as darkness fell, the craft came up to the surface to charge the batteries, while the same course was continued.

Sunday, June 4, three o'clock in the morning, and the speed went up to full ahead. Another hour, and a dead reckoning placed the craft quite near its final position. Nothing now except to wait for morning, when some accurate periscope navigation could be executed. So the main ballast-tanks were slowly flooded, and X-23 sank and settled happily on the bottom. Four of the five men aboard slept soundly for four hours till about 0800. A quick breakfast, a few pints of water pumped out of the compensating tank, and a slow rise to periscope-depth.

It took only a minute or two to ascertain that they were the right distance off shore. Through the day-periscope Honour saw a bare and flat coastline, rather like East Anglia, except for the absence of creeks and inlets. Trees were few, and no semblance of a cliff seemed to be visible. But away to port there was a river-mouth, or what looked like one, and a couple of church spires pointing heavenward on this early Sabbath morning. Could they have landed dead on position, just off the estuary of the Orne? It seemed too good to be true.

"Course due east. 650 revs. Keep her at periscope-depth."

Honour peered through the periscope continually; sure enough, they were off the Orne. They were able to identify both the churches (which stood exactly where the map marked them), while a cross-bearing on another conspicuous eminence fixed the position beyond doubt. A hum of excitement hung in the air of the submarine.

Honour kept her at periscope-depth, or just below, until 1100, taking periodic peeps at the land. But there was nothing at all to see—no traffic, people, or any activity at all.

"Complete picnic," he announced.

But they still had to wait. At tea-time they rose to periscope-depth again, and confirmed their position by fresh fixes. Then they bottomed for a few more hours. Silence, supper, sleep, games of liar dice, just off the invasion coast!

A last check over the equipment. Next day was due to be D-Day. Only a matter of hours now. Promptly at 2315, after the last summer light had dropped west, they surfaced and switched on their checked and re-checked wireless receiver. The right wave-length, the right programme, the right time. But no message yet. They knew that it would come within a few minutes. The weather was bad. The invasion might be on—or it might not.

This photograph, taken before the invasion by a reconnaissance aircraft, shows the sort of beach obstacles which had to be overcome.

British amphibious tanks land; one is set on fire.

(*left*) Horsa gliders in the fields near Caen. The rear part of the fuselage is detached on landing for quick unloading.

(*below*) British paratroops embark on the night of D-1.

8

The Weather worsens

SATURDAY, June 3, and precious little encouragement in the weather. A westerly wind was blowing inland, past the Needles and all along the Solent, whipping up its waters and rocking the landing-craft. Heavy cloud was due to drop still lower, and the outlook for Monday, D-Day, was not good. Two of the stations from which forecasts were forthcoming gave completely opposite versions of what was likely to develop! Scarcely the sort of start Eisenhower wanted.

He still had until the early hours of Sunday to decide. Meanwhile Churchill drove down to Portsmouth with Ernest Bevin and Field-Marshal Smuts, and saw some of the troops embarking for Normandy. Stokes Bay, a peaceful peace-time haunt of Gosport people for bathing and beach picnics, was a mass of barbed-wire and landing-craft. Churchill visited one of the headquarters ships and then sailed down the Solent, boarding one ship after another, and meeting the men.

Elsewhere the loading went on. In the harbours all round the coast the infantry and tank landing-craft lay six deep out from the jetties. Everything was covered with camouflage-netting to stop recognition from the air. Six deep for literally as far as the eye could see. L.C.T. 7008, L.C.H. 317, U 23—they all had a magic meaning in the stupendous scheme about to begin.

Then the troops, split into boatloads, saw their craft for the first time. Loudspeakers told them which one was theirs, and they humped their kit on bent backs and marched across wired-off promenades and beaches to the boats. Down the gangways—often with folding bicycles, if they were Commandos. And the armour went aboard as well. Cranes dangled great lorries over the gap between wharf and ship, then swung them aboard, camouflage-roofs and all. The jaws of a tank landing-ship opened beside the quay, and a Sherman tank, gun pointing perilously, nosed aboard. Others drove directly on from beaches, up the special ramps.

G.I's filed singly over the sand of a West of England shore, their tin hats rounded, ready for action.

"Why are we waiting?" sang a boatload of British.

Back to Portsmouth, and carrier crews waited about on board beside their supplies.

"Return empty to R.A.S.C.," was marked on one sack of something. They would be lucky. But probably it would be back at the Hilsea depot within a few days. Life did not just stop once D-Day dawned. It would go on, and there must be supplies. In the background stood the tall landmark of the H.M.S. *Vernon* mining-tank and the power-station chimneys.

Along the coast, at Dungeness and Selsey, the fantastic Phoenix creations were taking final form. Until wanted they sat on the bed of the sea, which had to be perfectly flat and shallow. The Phoenixes, as Rear-Admiral Tennant said, looked as if "some one had picked up Chicago and put it down on the Sussex foreshore."

Extra parking areas were found for about five miles of pier roadway at Peel Bank and Marchwood, opposite Southampton, so that, with towering pier-heads suggesting some factory risen from the water, the scene in the Solent was equally bizarre!

But, strangely enough, days passed without von Rundstedt even receiving a report of this amassed armada. Neither was Ramsay's H.Q. at Southwick House detected from the air. There was parkland surrounding the Georgian residence, and security went to great lengths to keep it secret. No one was allowed to walk in the fields, as trodden grass would have been revealed in aerial photographs.

In the library—also Ramsay's mess—that Saturday evening Eisenhower again met his meteorologists. Stagg was far from happy now. Admiral Creasy[1] called him "Six feet two of Stagg, and six feet one of gloom." A high-pressure area over the Azores was giving way, and three depressions seemed to be headed up the Channel. His four-day forecast, embracing all three possible invasion dates, spoke of high winds, low clouds, and even fog.

Postponement seemed more than likely, but Eisenhower decided that Force U and Force O should sail from Devonshire and Portland as planned originally, in case the weather should unexpectedly improve. Stagg, however, found the conflicting reports from the weather-ships and stations the most uncertain of the whole year. Rotten luck right at the start.

The evening meeting started at 2100 and lasted until after midnight. They all reassembled at 0315 on Sunday, June 4, within two hours of the time when the main assault force was due to sail. Stagg now had to speak of rising winds and low clouds. Ironically, as Ramsay looked out just before the meeting began, the sky seemed clear and the wind low! But Stagg was adamant. Waves would be high, air support almost impossible,

[1] Afterwards Admiral of the Fleet Sir George Creasy, G.C.B., C.B.E., D.S.O., M.V.O.

naval support bombardment inefficient, and the whole operation highly hazardous—as it would be even in fine weather. Although Montgomery would have agreed to go ahead, the difficulty of air support forced the Supreme Commander to postpone D-Day for twenty-four hours.

One decision, and another one to be made within a day.

All Force U was at sea by now, and part of Force Orders went out within minutes to tell them to reverse and return to harbour. There were instructions for this emergency already worked out, of course, but it was not easy. Force U 2A failed to receive the recall signal. This was a large and slow assault convoy, composed of 128 tank landing-craft with their escorts. By 0900 on Sunday the force was 25 miles south of St Catherine's Point, Isle of Wight, and still steering due south. Two destroyers raced out of the Portsmouth assembly area with a Walrus aircraft overhead to intercept it, otherwise the force would before long have been detected by enemy Radar, if not by reconnaissance.

Force U ran into rough sea on their return, and although the whole force was ordered back into Weymouth Bay, some never reached it and were still punching towards it when the next decision was due. Throughout June 4, too, there was doubt about whether Force U would be fit to go ahead without returning to reform. This would almost certainly have meant putting off D-Day for a fortnight, so Eisenhower heard with relief that Rear-Admiral Kirk was ready to proceed.

The other ships already on the move found the stormy Irish Sea difficult for the manoeuvre, yet somehow they managed to regain port, refuel, and be ready to resume operations a day later. A silent but brilliant Service.

So no harm was done to D-Day. And as the false starters staggered back for the gun again other second line forces were still surging to the South Coast by road and rail.

"Home, home on the range," wafted over Portsea Bridge as a lorry-load rumbled across, "Where seldom is heard a discouraging word." Some would never see home any more. They had only two days to live.

The armada lay uneasily at anchor as the troops passed the time. They smarmed grease on their faces for camouflage, and then waited for the word.

Over in Operations Room at Southwick House the whole picture was seen spread on the wall. A long, lofty room, here was the very heart of Operation Neptune—as the naval aspect of Operation Overlord was called. In the room were usually about forty people, mostly naval officers or Wrens plotting positions on charts and attending to the streams of signals borne in by an endless belt appearing through a hole in the wall from the cypher-office. Air liaison officers, military liaison, and American officers made up most of the remainder.

The walls of this high room were papered in white and gold, in the manner of Adam, and reminiscent of the house's past, when all these cryptic references would have been quite without meaning. At one end the wall was covered by an enormous blackboard chart of the Channel, and up and down in front of this moved a travelling step-ladder, used by the Wrens progressively more and more for plotting on the map the hour to hour position of all units at sea—or base.

In front of the big blackboard wall-map, and to one side, sat the signal officer. Level with him, but near the centre of the room, sat Admiral George Creasy, Chief of Staff to the Naval Commander-in-Chief, Admiral Ramsay. These two desks marked a line across the room about four yards from the wallmap. That space was the "holy of holies," reserved for Ramsay and his immediate staff. And there the Commander-in-Chief spent many long hours—particularly after the assault began.

But now it was still only Sunday, June 4. When Stagg awoke at 1000 that morning after advising a postponement he was surprised to see a sky almost bright, with only a light wind, but by 1100 the Admiralty had issued a gale warning to all shipping in the Irish Sea. The weather which had been forecast seemed to be on its way. But would the clearer conditions coming from the east coast of America reach here in time?

Churchill and Smuts had returned to London by train at a late hour the previous night, and the Prime Minister did not get to bed until half-past one. By five-thirty he was awake, and sent for General Ismay[1] to hear for certain of the postponement. Now he was waiting again.

So Sunday passed somehow. The storm gathered and grew, and a strong west wind rolled vicious breakers up Channel. Many of the men herded in small landing-craft, unused to the sea, were taking their anti-sickness pills before the craft weighed anchor. A day in a craft in these conditions can seem eternity to the stomach and nerves. So the squat craft rode out the storm somehow, while the wind tore at the silver-grey barrage-balloons overhead—protection against enemy air activity, which fortunately could not possibly exist by that time.

The wind and the rain reached the panes of Southwick House, too, rattling the window-frames. Eisenhower ate an evening meal and then moved into the library for the 2100 weather conference. Every one was there: Eisenhower, Montgomery, Tedder, Smith, Ramsay, Leigh-Mallory, and others. Yet it did not look like the most momentous meeting of war in history. They sat easily in a casual group of armchairs and leather sofas, with their notes in buff files. They all knew what was at stake. Before dawn

[1] Afterwards Baron Ismay of Wormington, K.G., P.C., G.C.B., C.H., D.S.O., D.L.

the decision had to be made. To invade now, or not for a fortnight at least. And keeping security for that time seemed too much to expect. In fact, so complex was the organization that it really could not be put into reverse. And the Russians were timing their offensive with the Western invasion.

Eisenhower presided, and asked Stagg for his appreciation. Stagg reported a depression over Portsmouth, to be followed by fair conditions: 5/10ths cloud, 2000–3000-feet base, lower wind, lasting until Tuesday morning. Then the cloud would increase to 8/10ths—10/10ths, followed by variable skies. The general inference was disturbed, but Stagg hoped for some improvement.

Leigh-Mallory queried whether this agreed with the R.A.F. meteorological men. Stagg said that it did. There would be almost perfect visual bombing weather from Monday evening to early forenoon Tuesday. Then good and poor periods from Tuesday afternoon till Friday.

Although they were all lounging, the discussion was dramatic as Ramsay observed that Admiral Kirk must be told within the next half-hour if Overlord were to take place on Tuesday. Amid all the storm, and stress, and wind and rain, this break in the weather seemed to be a "break" in every sense of the word.

"It's a helluva gamble, but it's the best possible gamble," said Bedell Smith in a picturesque martial phrase.

Leigh-Mallory wondered whether the heavy bombers might find the conditions prejudiced by low cloud on their second mission—if not on the first. But Eisenhower countered by referring to the force of fighter-bombers which the Allies had on call. Turning to Montgomery, Eisenhower asked, "Do you see any reason for not going on Tuesday?"

Monty replied, "I would say— Go !"

Ramsay agreed.

Eisenhower went on. "The alternatives are too chancy. The question is, just how long can you hang this operation on the end of a limb and let it hang there?"

The decision became increasingly clear-cut as each hour passed. For now it was no longer possible to consider Wednesday, June 7, as some of the warships and convoys already at sea would not have enough fuel to last until then, nor time to put into port for fresh supplies. Thursday would be too late, since on that day the second high tide would not occur until it was almost dark.

"Well, boys, there it is," Eisenhower concluded. "I don't see how we can possibly do anything else. I'm quite positive we must give the order. The only question is whether we should meet again in the morning."

As the air programme still seemed doubtful he decided to defer the final

order, but he had to let Ramsay go ahead with the early warnings to the
Americans, who needed the time for the extra distance from the West
Country waters, where they were unhappily anchored after the false alarm
of the previous day.

At about midnight the meeting adjourned for four hours. Eisenhower
ran into Stagg, waiting outside the library, and begged him not to change
the forecast during the next few hours! Eisenhower hurried into his staff
car through heavy rain to return to his own camp, a mile away from
Southwick House, for a bit of rest.

At 0330 he was up again, to feel the camp "shaking and shuddering"
with the wind. As he was making the return trip by car, the rain slashed
the windscreen head-on, and the wheels slipped in the mud of the makeshift road.

The final meeting, climaxing all its forerunners, real and rehearsed, lasted
from 0400 to 0430. It seemed surprising to be even considering invasion
with the weather still so stormy, let alone to have half committed
themselves to it already. Stagg said that the adverse conditions predicted
previously for the French coast at dawn, June 5, were actually operating
there now, which was in one way a relief—to know that these had been
avoided. Then, even as he spoke, the sky was starting to clear a little, and
the rain which had greeted Eisenhower earlier eased steadily. The only
change since the last forecast was for the better, Stagg was glad to be able
to reveal, and the fair interval clearing Southern England at that time would
probably last for well over twenty-four hours and into Tuesday afternoon.
The long-term outlook was still not what might be desired, but the good
period came as a blessing out of the blue—or rather, out of the grey of the
preceding days. Eisenhower balanced the danger of delay for a fortnight
against the later bad weather stopping the build-up forces. But despite all
this, as soon as Stagg finished speaking an air of relief spread round the
room. Tedder and some others asked one or two questions, and then Stagg
and his men left the library to allow the commanders to make the decision.

Leigh-Mallory still thought that air conditions would be below the
planned acceptable minimum, but realized that this applied equally to the
enemy. So even the cautious R.A.F. commander agreed that there was no
other way. Airborne operations would be practicable, anyway; that was vital.

Eisenhower cocked his head to one side in a characteristic way while
hearing their last comments, then he said, quietly but confidently, "O.K.
We'll go."

Five hours earlier X-23, one of the two midget subs off Normandy, had
surfaced and was waiting for the word. It was to be a coded wireless message mixed up in an innocent broadcast, and without it they could not

know whether or not the whole procession of landing-craft, and its accompanying bombardment was due at dawn. George Honour gave his quiet helm-and-speed orders to get her back to the waiting position. But this quiet voice belied the inevitable excitement which all of them felt.

Looking at the coast, they could see enemy aircraft landing not far inshore. The airfield must have been dead abeam. More useful still, a fixed red light burned above the entrance to the Orne river, which they had located earlier. "A hospitable aid to navigation," Honour thought.

With their position confirmed from soundings, the shore light, and previous fixes, they commenced the final run-in, measuring the distance with the taut-wire gear. Very close in to the enemy shore they let go the special anchor, which held first time. As the cable was made fast on the for-'ard bollards the time was nearly midnight. Still the suspense about the whole operation continued.

0055, June 5. At last, after an hour's waiting, they received a faint wireless message about the twenty-four hours' postponement.

"Weigh anchor—slow ahead—course 011."

Monday was much the same as Sunday. The tension eased as X-23 sank to the bottom for twelve hours. They slept and even found time to be a bit bored. But gradually the day passed, and their excitement returned.

Twenty-four hours had now elapsed since they surfaced before, and the log read:

> 2315. Surfaced and commenced wireless watch. Message received operation taking place, but reception was very difficult and master gyro had to be stopped during the period the message was coming in. This unsettled the compass and caused it to be unreliable. However, during the period of wireless-watch the craft had already reached and anchored in her marking position, so the compass defection did not prove as serious as it might have done.

Soon after midnight Honour was able to have the craft flooded down below the surface, to remove any risk of last minute spotting. Then at 0445, June 6, D-Day, she came slowly back "up top." In a few minutes they had rigged the telescopic mast and made all connexions, and the signal light—screened from the shore—was flashing away to sea. X-20 was in her correct position too, having had the same experience. Each craft had spent sixty-four hours out of their seventy-six submerged. Now they sat on the surface, sitting targets, as beacons beckoning the invasion fleet inshore. But all was still quiet, uncannily so. Any minute now, and the invasion would be on, guided by the two tiny craft.

9

D–I: the Armada sails

D – I, and sunrise silhouetted the 3000 landing-craft and 500 war-ships as they started out to sea. Some were already on their way. Force U for Utah, Force O for Omaha, and Force G for Gold, from the West. Force J for Juno, from the Portsmouth area. And Force S, from east of Portsmouth. From Falmouth, Fowey, Plymouth, Salcombe, Dartmouth, Brixham, Torbay, Portland, Weymouth, Poole, Southampton, Solent, Spithead, Shoreham, Newhaven, Harwich, and the Nore. All with one purpose: to liberate Europe.

But first came the Channel. Still the wind gusted and whipped the waves to five feet and more. Men gripped their stomachs, gritted their teeth. The wind stood at w.s.w. with a force of 16–20 m.p.h. It decreased at times, but then the gusts returned.

The Red Crosses of a field ambulance unit brought reality to a scene described by Ramsay as unreal through the absence of enemy activity. Some one would need these on the next day. Meanwhile the barrage-balloons fluttered over the convoys. Tank landing-craft ploughed a line-astern course, escorted by a bevy of larger ships.

From the west, north, and east they sailed, all through that morning. The first goal? Area Z. This was a circular zone, 8 miles in diameter and 25 miles south of Portsmouth and Hayling Island, chosen as a rendezvous. From here on they would follow one of ten swept channels in a southerly direction. Area Z was at once christened Piccadilly Circus by the whole Navy, while the Army occupied itself by playing cards in the cramped craft or polishing, not their dress, but their French from phrase-books. It might come in useful, one way or another....

So that the northern ends, or the start, of the ten approach channels should be precisely positioned, ten special buoys had been laid by three motor-launches of Force J at the dead of the night, May 31–June I. These buoys were timed to transmit signals between 1400 and 2200 on six suc-cessive days from June 4. In the afternoon of June 5 ten motor-launches took up position to point the buoys for the following forces, and the sys-tem proved to be completely successful. A large number of ships, too, were fitted with receivers to obtain positions from the Gee and Decca radio navigational systems, so accuracy, of course, was never in doubt. As the ships assembled at Area Z the men ate stew, followed by plum-pudding. And the flat-bottomed tank landing-craft pitched and rolled to the tide.

After lunch began the biggest, most majestic minesweeping operation of the War. For weeks now numbers of sweepers had been sailing home from the Mediterranean, where they helped pave the way for the invasions of Sicily and Italy. From northern and east-coast bases they sailed in good time to be, as usual, the vessels in the van of any operation which was to be conducted through dangerous waters.

As many as 300 sweepers moved south in perfect order. Twelve flotillas of large minesweepers and many more smaller ones literally swept before them in a broad twelve-channel front, 15 miles wide at the start and 30 miles wide at the southern end. These sweepers had had little preliminary practice for such a specialized and important operation, and they also had the extra burden of having to change sweeps during the passage in order to avoid sweeping with an unfavourable tide. Some flotillas had no time to rehearse this tricky manoeuvre at all, yet it all turned out well on the day.

In their correct formations, and at the moderate speed required for effective sweeping, the ships headed straight towards enemy guns not yet silenced by any naval or air attack. And the danger from the air, E-boats, and U-boats was always present too. This applied equally to all the armada, but the crews of those craft who could move with more freedom and take effective evasive action if attacked found this magnificent manoeuvre inspiring. The crews of destroyers, corvettes, and others watched fascinated as the groups of sweepers, in immaculate drill-like lines, moved back and forth down the vital channels. Cold-blooded courage accompanied the crews of the sweepers, and the periodic punctuation—or underlining—of their purpose by vicious, violent explosions seemed detached from the peaceful pattern of ships on sea, and an impertinence to their progress!

Hazardous as this was—both because of their vulnerability to attack and because of the deathly danger of the mines—the sweepers found fewer fields than they expected. There was reason to think that the Germans would have laid a line right across from the Cherbourg peninsula to Le Havre, but this did not materialize. The credit for foiling the enemy's definite intention was due to the air forces—who had, without knowing it, delayed the arrival of the mine supplies by their blanket-bombing of French railways—and also to the Navy. When the mines finally reached Le Havre the Royal Navy and Coastal Command intercepted the flotilla of ships sent specially from Brest to lay them, and dealt with all except one.

As the sweepers encountered less interruption than was anticipated they

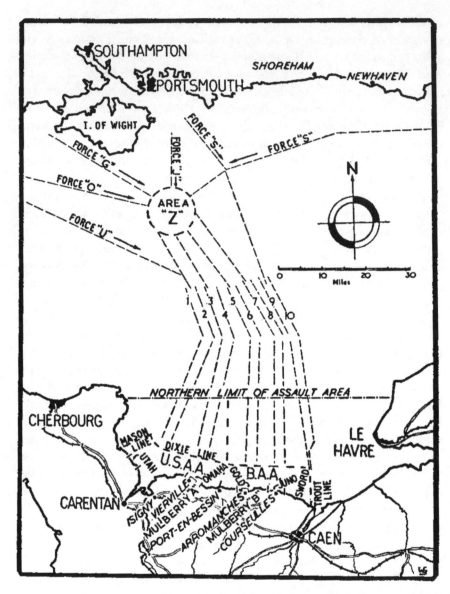

OPERATION NEPTUNE

went ahead of schedule and were actually within sight of the invasion coast long before dark. Two flotillas were level with Le Havre by sunset, and so close inshore that some of them could see individual houses on the Vierville coast—destined to be the location of the Omaha landings, now less than twelve hours off. Yet, for some inexplicable reason, no guns fired on them. Although the enemy was prepared for invasion, they discounted this week in view of the weather, but this lack of identification still seemed amazing. In any case, even if the sweepers were spotted, General Richter did not hear of it in Caen! On this day of all others the Luftwaffe flew only a single reconnaissance mission in the West— and this was far from the invasion scene, off the Dutch coastline, with its dykes and dunes! Eisenhower could hardly have hoped for such luck and sense of surprise.

But it was not all due to luck. While the fleet was still assembling at Area Z, the elaborate cover plan, Operation Fortitude, went into action. For five days now the Allied Air Forces had been hammering the French coast, apparently indiscriminately, from Cap Gris Nez to Le Havre. Even until D–1 twice the tonnage of bombs was being dropped in the Pas-de-Calais area as in Normandy. There is no doubt now that this deceptive bombing did its job of diversion wonderfully, so that by quite late on D–1 the enemy had no idea that invasion was imminent, and, even if they had, all the signs pointed to the Pas-de-Calais. To underline this, dummy paratroops were dropped in three main areas, to cause confusion about the real destination of our airborne forces, soon to be on French soil.

But the main diversions were over the sea near the Strait of Dover. The Allies wanted to conceal the ultimate direction of the fleet moving mainly eastward up the Channel. This force would not reach Area Z till dark, when its change of direction south would not be noticed. This was accomplished by an amazing Radar operation, designed to deceive the enemy into believing the assault to be aimed farther east. The twofold task was, first, to jam enemy warning-stations in the actual area to be invaded—Cherbourg and Le Havre—and, secondly, to mislead the Le Havre to Calais stations into reporting that the fleet was sailing towards this sector.

Thirty-four small ships and over a hundred aircraft undertook this strange mission. Following in the wake of the minesweepers, the vessels aimed for Cap d'Antifer, north of Le Havre, towing as many barrage-balloons as they could to simulate big ships on enemy Radar screens. Then, when they were within Radar range, they sailed slowly up towards Calais. Bombers then flew round and round overhead, dropping tinfoil by the bundle, one each minute. These strips of metalized paper would give the Germans false Radar readings. The aircraft made endless orbits, slowly nearer the coast, to suggest a convoy of big ships sailing across the Channel to the north of the actual D-Day beaches. Similar diversions off Boulogne also helped towards the eventual state of surprise achieved. What with a phantom fleet off Dover, craft ostensibly sailing on obscure courses up the Channel, dummy paratroops, and jamming on Radar sets, the confusion was complete before the end of D–1.

As soon as the sun set on D–1, too, came co-operation with the French Resistance. Arms and equipment had been delivered to them by air for a long time now, and a network of wireless communications operated over a wide area. Agents in the Special Air Service found themselves being flown in unescorted aircraft, to be parachuted down quite alone through the dark and unknown air to blow up strategic points—by themselves or acting with the Resistance. Already our bombs had torn a line of destruction in the roads and railways leading to Normandy. The agents' job was to get at the inaccessible vital places. No massive raid, with a smoky pall of death as its aftermath. Theirs was the silent strike, then the explosion, and escape—if they were lucky.

All the day of D–1 the armada assembled. The only sound of war as yet was the deep, dramatic eruption of depth-charges from H.M.S. *Holmes*, after the possible presence of a U-boat was reported. Then the spray settled, and only the waves and wind spoiled the scene. Spaced out to avoid attack on more than one, the ships slowly turned their bows south, and the men got their last look at England as St Catherine's Point, on the south-east tip of the Isle of Wight, merged into the misty horizon. Nothing now but ships till the next day. And no one knew what that held for himself or every one.

Darkness, and, exactly as planned, all the forces moving east from Devon and the West generally veered round to starboard. Every ship and craft seemed to be on the move at last. And, apart from the thousands of landing-craft themselves, Neptune needed eight battleships and monitors, twenty-two cruisers, ninety-three destroyers, 450 escorts and minesweepers, and 360 M.L.'s, M.T.B.'s, and kindred craft.

Past were the days of camouflage and concealment. Pluto and Bombardon had been hidden successfully; landing-craft had emerged from their rivers and creeks; and the first sections of the floating breakwater were on their way from Portland, round to the south of the island to Area Z. The Green Howards sailed out of the Solent in a high wind, but the evening kept clear—so clear that they saw people and cars moving in a different world on the Isle of Wight.

One of the earliest casualties—soon recovered—was L.C.A. 712. The rising seas battered her badly, and she had difficulty in slipping her tow.

Lieutenant R. Murray, R.N.V.R., persevered, however, and she took her place in the line southward. Another L.C.A. shipped a lot of water as soon as she started south, yet despite this and a broken tow-rope, she met her deadline off Normandy—with assault troops soaked to the skin. The weather was keeping to Stagg's promise of rough on Monday and better on Tuesday for D-Day. Force U—the unlucky Americans affected by the postponement—still met stormy seas, and their commanding officers battled on through them all, spending a total of seventy hours on their bridges continuously: nearly three days and nights without sleep. Out of the 128 tank landing-craft in the Group U 2A of this famous force only seven failed to take part in the assault, owing to engine troubles as well as the weather. A phenomenal percentage of 95.

But still all was anticlimax. The quiet before the storm. As dusk fell a reconnaissance aircraft saw the parallel wakes of craft as they plodded and plied on—on into the night.

Long before the day dawned, the realization slowly came to Admiral Ramsay that complete tactical surprise was being achieved. And because of it the whole operation began to assume an air of unreality. Was it really possible that 3000 landing-craft and all their attendant ships could cross the Channel without the normally efficient Germans knowing—either by agents or observation?

The sullen oily sea of the grey day turned into a black mass of surging liquid. But by 0200 Force U, nearly 1000 ships strong, was arranging its order undetected off the Cotentin peninsula, only 12 miles north-east of the Utah landing-beaches. Overhead they heard the familiar, friendly drone of aircraft carrying airborne troops to precise points on the peninsula. Gradually the 30,000 men and 3500 vehicles approached the shore. Still no sign of awareness. E-boats due to patrol the Seine Bay turned back to Cherbourg because of the bad weather. The Radar jamming of enemy stations was succeeding, for even as they got nearer inshore the coastal batteries were still silent. Perhaps they had been hit by the hail of bombs from Lancasters which drenched batteries all along the coast during the night without revealing the invasion area.

Also 12 miles off shore, in channels 3 and 4, Force O halted at 0300 to lower their landing-craft from the parent vessels which had borne them across so far. The sea swirled below the craft as they hit it with a jolt and a shower of spray. Many of the men were sick long before the assault. The sea swamped some of the craft almost as soon as they were on their own, and several sank. Men drowned, dragged down by the weight of the gear and the rough rollers. Others were hauled to safety. Luckier landing-craft shipped gallons of water, and only baling by tin hats saved the men from the fate of the drowned. One battle against sinking, the next to beat seasickness, and soon the Germans to be faced.

Casualties were light in the assault craft, but the special D.D. tanks met a mass of tragedies. Because of the sea one battalion of tank landing-craft could not launch these amphibious vehicles. The other battalion risked twenty-nine, but a number of these sank at once to the bottom 4 miles out to sea; some were swamped during this long run in; and of all twenty-nine only two were to reach the shore. Men struggled to get free from their amphibious coffins, choked with water, died.

Even the troops in ordinary landing-craft were chilled, cramped, and weakened by seasickness: the worst way possible to await an assault which was to many of them a baptism of battle. Shivering, they lived through the ordeal in advance many times that night.

Because of the danger of enemy shore batteries the "lowering positions" from the mother ships had been fixed for the Western Task Force at 10–11¼ miles from the shore, so that they would be beyond range if discovered by the defences by the time of transferring forces to the landing-craft. The distance also put them outside the area known to be mined. This long haul to shore, coupled with the relentlessly rough sea rolling around them, contributed to the tragic losses sustained by the Americans.

Proceeding in parallel along channels 5 to 10, Forces S and J stole still farther inshore before reaching their agreed lowering-positions. Seven to eight miles out they prepared for the final assault. Over to the left Le Havre still slumbered. The waves were four feet now, and the 15 m.p.h. wind helped to drown any sounds of the approaching invaders. Clouds thickened through the night. Now they were within range of the heavy guns of Le Havre. Force S, the 3rd British Division with all its supporting units, anchored uneasily at this assembly point, not knowing for sure if the enemy Radar were working or not. In fact, it was not—nor one of the batteries—due to a recent raid by Bomber Command. To craft near enough to notice were the reassuring silhouettes of their escort warships, *Warspite* and *Ramillies*.

The first, false dawn etched a mast and funnel in the sky. Then, as faint light fell over the fleet, a squadron of aircraft flew low over the area, laying an enveloping smoke-screen to the east. The black fog blanketed the whole force from the Le Havre coast just at the critical moment before bombardment.

Dawn now—and the first fighting. Four E-boats and some armed trawlers headed out of Le Havre at about 0515, just as Bombarding Force D arrived in position on the eastern flank. They were spotted indistinctly against the land, and the order went at once to our aircraft overhead:

"Make smoke."

The aircraft flew in low over the sea, and laid their smokescreen in seconds, but from behind it the enemy fired a group of torpedoes. *Warspite* and *Ramillies* were able to track these, although two tore right between the warships, uncomfortably close. Suddenly an unmistakable sound: the shattering crack of a sudden explosion. And in the dull dawn flames were licking and lashing the deck of the Norwegian destroyer *Svenner*. The Allies opened fire, and soon sank one of the trawlers and damaged another. The attack was not renewed. So this hit-and-run raid was the German Navy's total effort on D-Day. Fire gripped the destroyer now, as she slipped lower in the water. The blaze became a belch of black, acrid smoke. And slowly she sank.

The assault was soon to start, and back aboard the midget subs the vital hour neared. X-20 marked the spot for Force J, as the coast outline of Juno beach was indistinct. And X-23 stood guard on the surface off the Orne so that Force S should not go too far east.

Not a sound or sign on the air till Honour heard the first faint throbbing through the water. A dull, droning, soulless sound, but with the recognizably regular beat of engines. Ships' motors bringing the armada in right on time. Then, heaving low over the horizon, they advanced. L.C.A.'s, L.C.I.'s, L.C.T.'s, L.C.F.'s, L.C.S.'s, L.C.G.'s. Landing-ships and headquarters-ships. D.U.K.W.'s and "Rhino" craft. Twenty, thirty, forty ships in a column, and the lines reaching right away to port and starboard. But mainly on the port side, as the X-craft was more or less the limit of the eastern assault line. Closer, closer, till after all the solitude of the submarine over the last three days this seemed like a miracle. Men crouched low just above the outline of their landing-craft. A host of heads bent on a purpose as proud as any in history.

Hundreds of men—like Corporal George Tandy, Royal Marines, coxswain of L.C.A. 786, and aged nineteen. Seven miles out in the still-swirling sea his assault landing-craft lost its steering-wheel while being lowered from the parent ship. The crew's duty was to get the thirty-two soldiers in that craft ashore, and in such a sea only one way existed to do it. Tandy slipped over the stern and stood with one foot on the rudder-guard, and guided the rudder with the other. With fearful frequency the sea hoisted him high in the air and then plunged him back into its pounding waters. For four and a half long hours Tandy stuck it, through mines and everything else. Numbed, bruised, bewildered—but alive.

As L.C.A. 786 and all the others crept closer to the coast the battleships braced themselves for the attack. Terrific tension, as the angles of their guns slowly widened to the exact elevation. Thin fingers poised, pointing to land—and the day of reckoning. D-Day.

IO

First Blood to the Skymen

THE CHANNEL STOPPED YOU, BUT NOT US was chalked in foot-high letters on an airborne glider during the evening of D–1. The blackened faces of troops contrasted with the white chalk. And they did not seem to mind that the glider was numbered 13. Camouflage sprouted through the netting over their tin helmets. In smaller letters beside the main message, one of them had written carefully, "Remember Coventry, Plymouth, Bristol, London. Now it's our turn.

Over at another airfield, preparing for a flight on D-Day, troops sweated and heaved as they shoved a jeep up a ramp into a glider. Anti-aircraft guns were also loaded, together with a mass of equipment needed to ward off German counter-attacks.

Earlier Eisenhower had talked to American airborne forces as they quit their canvas tents to get ready for the flight. And Air Chief Marshal Leigh-Mallory went round to every airfield from which Allied airborne forces would be taking off later that night of June 5.

At 2230 that night sixty men of the 22nd Independent Parachute Company were drinking tea out of mugs from a mobile canteen, and smoking beside half a dozen Albemarle aircraft on the runway of Harwell. These men were to be the pathfinders for the 6th Airborne Division, commanded by Major-General Richard Gale. Not only black but brown and green paint darkened their faces, and among as much as 100 lb. of gear they carried Stens, ammunition, knives, and grenades, plus a bag of Radar beacons and lights strapped to one leg of each man for marking the dropping-zones.

Another twenty minutes, and the paratroops filed into their planes. Darkness now, as at 2303 the first Albemarle taxied down the runway, cleared the hedges at the perimeter, and droned south. The other five followed rapidly. Seventy-seven minutes later, at 0020 on D-Day, they were over the three dropping-zones. Despite the advantage of moonlight, and that half the aircraft ran in twice or more, only one stick of paratroops landed correctly on the three zones. All the visual beacons for one zone were lost or damaged in the drop.

The pathfinders parachuting down near Ranville were scattered—principally by the high wind, which carried them east of the intended zone. Since the main force they were to guide would be due in under half an hour they had no time to attempt a recovery. Instead, they lit their beacons where they landed.

Due to drop at the same time as the pathfinders was a *coup de main* force (six platoons of the 2nd Battalion of the Oxford and Buckinghamshire Light Infantry) under the command of Major R. J. Howard. Their task was to capture intact two vital bridges: the one on the only through-road over the Orne river, the other over the canal between Caen and the sea. Theirs was an airborne assault by gliders. Like the later main force, towed by Halifax bombers acting as tugs. At exactly 0015 the bombers slipped their tows and then went on to attack Caen, while the gliders circled silently down. Their audacious assault plan was to crash-land on their actual objectives. Howard was in the leading glider headed for the canal bridge, and its wheels gripped into the ground only 47 yards (who measured that?) from the eastern end of the bridge. It grasshoppered the rest of the way, ending in barbed-wire, with its nose broken. Howard and his men had to grope their way out via the cockpit instead of through the door. The two other gliders aimed at the canal bridge crash-landed close behind them. The enemy was sheltering from the sudden crescendo on Caen by the Halifaxes, so Howard's men raced on to take the bridge. A spatter of machine-gun fire from the far side killed the commander of the first platoon. They ousted the defenders from a pill-box and a near-by network of trenches, and ensured that the bridge would not be blown up by the enemy.

Eight hundred yards to the east, at about the same time, the other gliders landed less accurately. But two of the three platoons got to their bridge over the Orne within minutes, and found it undefended.

Consolidating the captures, the pathfinders found that, although the enemy had prepared both bridges for blowing, no alarm of invasion had reached them, and so the charges were not in position.

So the bridgeheads had been won. Now the pathfinders must hold them until the main forces reinforced and relieved them.

Half an hour after the pathfinder-drops, and at just about the moment the two bridges fell, the 5th Parachute Brigade joined the invasion. Their story started at 2000 hours on the evening of June 5 when the 7th Parachute Battalion was called from a pre-battle rest. Few of them could sleep. All identification by letters or other evidence was surrendered, and 620 men went out to the airfield in thirty-three lorries, one lorryful for each Stirling plane. An occasional quiet song floated across the stilled airfield. Then they went through the routine of sipping mugs of tea and smearing dark camouflage on their faces so that no sniper should pick them out against the night sky. Even collapsible dinghies were crammed into some of their kitbags, since they would be operating near two rivers and might need to get across.

The briefing over now, watches were synchronized as they stood near propellers waiting to turn. Then they stepped off English earth, and the Stirlings climbed into the sky of that immortal night and flew high over the Channel. People still awake in coastal homes murmured to themselves, "Another raid over there." But this time they were wrong.

At a quarter to one low cloud blew over the dropping-zone. This obscured some of the beacons and made accurate air navigation impossible. The Stirlings circled, trying to find the exact spot. Suddenly the anti-aircraft defences sprang to life, spitting shells and tracer upward. Flak hit two of the thirty-three planes. The night wind fanned the fires, and a deadly drone presaged the start of two spirals down, down into the French fields they sought to liberate. Two Stirlings, their crews, and forty precious paratroops.

Promptly at 0050 the other thirty-one aircraft came in low over the zone and dropped their human loads. The descent took only about ten seconds, but to the paratroops, exposed to a tracery of fire from below, it seemed something out of time altogether.

Lieutenant-Colonel Pine-Coffin was commanding this drop, but, due to the pathfinders' problems and the low cloud, the battalion landed badly scattered. As they neared the ground the scene grew dangerously lighter each moment. With a succession of bumps they were down, but, although they landed quite near the dropping-zone, many were unable to find it. Luckily, Pine-Coffin managed to get his bearings when a flare from one of the aircraft silhouetted the old church at Ranville, which had stood serenely in the village for six centuries. Now he knew which way to go.

Pine-Coffin found Lieutenant Rogers, and together they assembled some men. This was a slow business, but expedited by Rogers' Aldis lamp, which blinked out as a pre-arranged signal to the troops. For Rogers himself, however, it could have been fatal if it had attracted enemy fire towards him. In the confusion he had little time to dwell on this.

They were not exactly keeping their arrival secret, as another means of attracting men to the commander was by their regimental call blown on a bugle! This combination of blinking and bugling mustered about one-third of the 620 men dropped from the thirty-one aircraft. By 0215 the number rose to some 250. They dared not delay any longer, as firing from the canal bridge suggested that they were already needed there. When they reached the bridge, however, they found with relief that the firing had been no more than ammunition exploding in a German tank; and soon Major R. J. Howard's radio code signals of "Ham and Jam" told them that both bridges were in fact safely in British hands. With real relief they ditched their dinghies, and by 0300 were in the planned positions near the bridges. Many of the men were without their special weapons, lost somewhere in the French fields as a result of the unlucky air drop.

Two hundred and fifty men with a few pistols and Stens, but no 3-inch mortars or medium machine-guns. No wonder Pine-Coffin was not too happy about their ability to hold the bridges. But before long A Company settled into the village of Benouville, and B Company in the hamlet of Le Port, keeping one platoon actually on the bridge over the Orne. Pine-Coffin had C Company in reserve.

"The hour before the dawn" will always mean to A Company the moment at Benouville when the enemy suddenly attacked them on three sides simultaneously. Carrying across the air to the other companies came sounds suggesting that the attack was in some strength, so Lieutenant MacDonald led twenty men from the reserve C Company, ill armed for such a task, to get through to Benouville. This they did, fighting all the way till they found A Company still warding off attacks on all three sides.

Two platoons of B Company, meanwhile, dug—not literally —into the escarpment of Le Port, while the third platoon wrapped itself around the canal bridge. One platoon for a vital canal bridge was scarcely what the planners had intended; sporadic fire kept the men alert for their lives every second, and made them wish for those paratroops who had been dropped far from the right zone. One of their two particular aircraft discharged its troops no less than 13 miles from the centre of the zone. They might just as well have been 1200 miles away at this precise moment.

At 2330 on June 5 the first of the Stirlings to carry the 12th Parachute Battalion gave a mechanical cough as its engines spluttered into life. The battalion's objective was the village of Le Bas de Ranville, and, like the rest of the brigade, they had a quiet flight across the Channel.

As the first aircraft approached the coast one of the aircrew removed the hatches, and they could see dimly the white waves breaking on the beach, lines like those identity stripes painted around the body of their aircraft. Then from sea, beach, and cliffs to strange silhouettes of woods, and the patterns made by fields and hedges. A red light, then a green one. Go. The parachutes fluttered out and floated down. Only the sign of the wind through the struts. Then the ground interrupted this idyll.

It took until about 0200 for the 12th Battalion to muster enough of their number to make a start towards their goal of Le Bas de Ranville.

Lieutenant-Colonel A. P. Johnson, commanding them, collected more men who had landed outside the dropping-zone, and together they all advanced on the village.

Then came their first brush with the enemy. Just on the outskirts they were stalking along the edge of the road when they suddenly saw two vehicles bearing down on them.

"Fire!" called an officer.

And an enemy motor-cyclist lurched off his machine before it careered madly on and into a ditch. The other vehicle turned out to be an armoured car, and burst through before being stopped at the approaches to the bridge. A focus of fire sent it streaming off the road, and from it staggered the German officer responsible for the defences of the bridges—a belated arrival. Further investigation into the car revealed the remains of a meal and some rouge and face-powder. Evidently these were intended for a destination other than British paratroops about to enter their first French village.

Meanwhile the 13th Parachute Battalion began their particular piece of the jigsaw—clearing the adjacent village of Ranville and its vital bridges over the Orne. Vital, too, was the task of getting rid of the anti-airborne poles which dotted the ground earmarked for glider landings later in this eventful night.

Those of the 13th who came to earth in the specified area fared well, but many of the rest—nearly half of the battalion strength—came to grief amid the surrounding trees. Desperately, they tried to free themselves in the gloom of the woodlands, but a number were located and killed by enemy fire before they had a chance.

But the majority were able to respond to the brigade's hunting horns, which blared out into the night as if attached to some phantom pack. The enemy garrison in Ranville heard this blood-curdling call with terror, and by 0230 they had all been overrun and Ranville had fallen: the first French village to be liberated.

While this historic, if small, action went on the company detailed to clear the landing-fields for the gliders were going about their job thoroughly, and the main glider force of seventy-two machines, with guns, transport, and equipment, prepared to take-off over in England. Their time of landing had been worked out for 0330, to allow them two hours before daybreak in which to complete their mission.

Shortly before 0200 the air armada began. The tug planes roared down the runway, their engines racing to take the strain of guiding a glider. Then the tow was taut, the rope quivered into a straight line. Plane and glider gradually moved. The ground slid beneath them; the wheels left it and went on revolving; there was no turning back.

All the troops could see as they crouched in their gliders was rain outside the cockpit, and now and again a glimpse of light from their particular towing aircraft. Guiding them where? Unseen below them, the sea
armada sailed on south—some ships 10 miles, others 50 miles, from the D-
Day coast. Then as the cloud cleared they caught a momentary glimpse of
the ships edging nearer. But back in the cloud again the gliders' wings
wobbled in the gusty gale—a wind which sent a shiver through their
wooden framework.

0300, and the enemy coast below. Denser cloud now, and no sign of
even the tug's rear light. Just as they really needed good visibility the clouds
closed in on them. Then the inevitable flak started; a kaleidoscope of
colour flashing all around. Seventy-two gliders and as many tugs seemed
silhouetted at once. As if they were frozen still in the sky. Sitting targets at
2500 feet.

One glider was hit just enough to throw it off balance. The trouble was
that neither the towing aircraft nor the gliders themselves could manoeuvre
much while they were still linked. It was an unpleasant position, to put it
mildly. Over on one side another glider got a direct flash of flak, and twenty-
six men plus the pilot perished. Then another glider went down.

Over the Channel songs had been sung. Not now.

Beneath them they saw the weaving, watery lines of the Orne and the
Canal de Caen threaded through the land. Over the target area now, but
they were the targets. Below, the beacons and the flak all became inter-
mingled in colourful confusion.

Then, one by one, the tows parted. The gliders wavered in the wind
before their noses angled down through the flak. One last magic moment
of quiet after they had got out of the flak and before scraping the ground.
A last dive in the dark, with beacons, lights, roads and churches, and other
unidentifiable shapes lurching on each side of them. Any second now. This
was how the first assault troops would be feeling a few hours later on the
beaches. For airborne troops the moment of truth had already come.
Obstacle posts were torn and ripped right out of the ground. The splitting
and splintering gliders groaned to a halt, some upright, others upturned,
others actually on end with their tails pointing high to heaven. The men
clambered into the cornfield which was their airfield, leaving a litter of
gliders facing in every direction of the compass, crazily up against hedges
or actually touching one another. But however the airborne men had
arrived, they were here, that was the important thing: in the proper place
at the right time.

While enemy guns still fired into a sky so lately filled with the slow,
vulnerable gliders, the men moved quickly through the ripening corn,

rustling it as they went. And then came the less soft sounds of equipment being shifted into action stations.

On the perimeter of the field a sentry challenged some one, and the code name response came at once. None of them could take chances.

On the field an alarming panorama presented itself. The whole zone seemed to be full of hopelessly wrecked gliders— each minus a wing or a wheel. And even as the early arrivals glanced at the apparent desolation a late-comer bumped in low over the corn and smashed straight into a house on the perimeter. In fact, however, two out of every three gliders landed safely and accurately. Most of the men and their weapons came to no harm, and ten of the eighteen anti-tank guns were left in working order.

So, as quickly as they could, they moved off towards Ranville church. The only opposition to be seen took the form of a rapidly retreating German military car, and then soon afterwards the British took their first prisoner— a chestnut-brown horse which had been minding its own business on the landing zone! The animal came under the care of Major-General Richard Gale's aide-de-camp, and accompanied them to their temporary headquarters at Ranville. Perhaps he would prove a lucky mascot.

Gale himself, ignoring the occasional punctuation marks of snipers' bullets, took a jeep to survey the state of affairs at the bridges which the British held.

The airborne operation as a whole proved to be far from plain sailing, or flying. One Albemarle tried seven times to find the dropping-zone, but before it could do so it was hit by flak, and had to turn round to head for home. At the actual moment the shell exploded the Brigade Major of the 3rd Parachute Brigade—Major W. A. C. Collingwood—was waiting to jump. The blast blew him through the opening, and his line wound round one of his legs. As the aircraft aimed sadly north once more he actually hung there beneath it for half an hour, with a 60-lb. kitbag weighting his other leg. Eventually the concerted strength of those safely inside the plane succeeded in hoisting him aboard the Albemarle again. The postscript was that the plane got back to England, and Collingwood insisted on joining his brigade, which he did later on D-Day.

The brigade's mission was far-flung, and not made easier by the wild night and inevitably inaccurate dropping. Their task was to destroy the bridges in the Dives valley and seize a ridge between the Dives and the Orne. In fact, the two rivers looked indistinguishable from the air, which constituted another difficulty. Coming into this chaos, the aircraft encountered ack-ack fire, forcing them to undertake urgent evasive manoeuvres, with the result that Brigadier S. J. L. Hill and his men jumped while the planes were travelling too fast, and were consequently carried beyond their goal.

The 1st Canadian Parachute Battalion dropped between 0100 and 0130 into an area forty times as large as planned. One aircraft had no choice but to return home to Down Ampney without dropping any of its number of troops, because, as it shuddered at the impact of enemy flak on its fuselage, a parachutist fell into—instead of through—the exit, and wedged it tight till they were minutes and miles past the dropping-zone!

As another aircraft crossed the mouth of the Canal de Caen it was met by a stream of tracer which cracked past only 15 feet to starboard. The plane at once swung violently left, and when the men had sorted themselves out they found that they had altered course so severely that following pilots probably confused the Orne and Dives rivers. Many of the eighty-six Canadians taken prisoner by the enemy as a result of the scattered drop rejoined their units soon afterwards—a testimony to their ingenuity in any circumstances, foreseen or otherwise.

Several sticks of the 9th and 1st Canadian Parachute Battalions fell into the river Dives or in the flooded, desolate wastelands beside it. Some men were drowned in these swamps—just one tragic way of dying on this day of days.

The 8th Canadian Parachute Battalion, under the renowned and experienced Lieutenant-Colonel Alastair Pearson,[1] dropped in a much more scattered pattern than had ever been intended, and as a result some paratroops were trapped in the tree-tops of the Bois de Bavent. Pearson dropped safely, but he had scarcely shaken himself free of his harness when a bullet hit him in the hand. Despite losing blood steadily, he went on with his duty, and rounded up enough men for their job of destroying two bridges.

Four of the five bridges over the Dives were blown up as rehearsed, but the fifth only succumbed due to a daring improvisation. Pearson's men met a group of sappers who had landed north of the Bois de Bavent. They explained that they had not enough explosive left, and so the sappers drove their jeep, laden with the necessary charges, straight through the enemy-held town of Troarn. Miraculously, they survived machine-gun fire aimed right down the road at them, and they managed to blow a gaping gap in the bridge.

Like so many other airborne units, the 1st Canadian Battalion suffered a severely scattered drop, and some were cut off from the rest by woods or marshes and taken prisoner. The Germans lined up five of these Canadians and summarily shot them. Four died, but the fifth was only wounded in the leg; somehow he slipped away to make contact with the

---

[1] Afterwards Colonel Alastair Pearson, O.B.E., D.S.O., M.C.

Resistance, and was soon hobbling off to rejoin his unit. The Canadians, needless to say, succeeded in blowing their bridges over the Dives and at Robehomme.

Captain R. M. E. Kerr of the British 13th Battalion landed right in the river Dives, but managed to struggle free from his harness, stagger ashore, soaked and shivering, and find a farm which four other parachutists had also reached. The French family were pleased to see them, even though it was the middle of the night, and a young French boy offered to take them to their objective of Varaville.

With his help they found the place at about 0330, but violent enemy action warned them not to enter it. They recognized every sort of weapon, and so skirted the village and entered a wood. Quite suddenly a German patrol appeared from nowhere, and through the night air one of them came close enough to hurl a stick grenade, which burst on the boy's head. This was war now....

So we come to the main mission of the 3rd Parachute Brigade: to destroy the dangerous enemy battery by the coast near Merville.

Major-General Gale said, "The Hun thinks that only a bloody fool will go there. That's why we're going!"

To Lieutenant-Colonel T. H. B. Otway, Royal Ulster Rifles, and the 9th Battalion, 3rd Parachute Brigade, fell the duty of destroying the battery: a strong-point with four 150-mm. guns (it was thought), housed in thick concrete, ten machine-guns, mines, and other elaborate defences. He had to be sure to silence the battery by half an hour before first light, so that the invasion fleet could begin the bombardment in the knowledge that the beaches west of the Orne estuary were safe from the fire of the Merville guns, which could conceivably knock out enough of the British invasion forces to endanger the entire operation. The enemy garrison was thought to number about 180 men.

The involved plan included eleven separate parties, each with a specific job. Added to these were to be three troop-carrying gliders, which would crash their way right into the midst of the battery just as the paratroops were due to start their assault.

The glider force and two other parties took off from Brize Norton and Harwell at about 2330, the rest earlier, at 2310. The first to drop were the reconnaissance party, to mark the dropping-zone and find a route to the battery through the defences. Wearing jumping-socks with the alarming decoration of skull and crossbones marked in luminous paint on the left breast, they dropped quite close to their intended spot.

The next part of the plan, timed for 0030 and 0040, went into operation as a hundred Lancaster bombers flew in over the battery to saturate it before the start of the main airborne assault. Unluckily the weather was again against the Allies, and not at all good for highlevel night bombing. A great weight of 4,000 lb. bombs screamed down through the clouds, but exploded half a mile from their target, which, in an attack of this precision, meant that they were virtually wasted. One or two of them actually fell near the airborne reconnaissance group as they groped their way towards the battery; these men were understandably shattered to suffer this extra hazard of bombs from their own air force.

Next came the main drop. Four minutes away from the zone, and already confusing the mouths of the Orne and the Dives in the darkness, the pilots also had to contend with intense flak. Veering violently to evade it, they gave the paratroops a nasty few minutes. Men with 80-lb. loads plus parachutes were flung all over the aircraft as they reeled to escape the searchlights. There was nothing for it but to go ahead with the drop— despite the conditions. The sticks of paratroops groped their way out of lurching aircraft in an order as different from their normal disciplined descents as it was possible to imagine.

Instead of being concentrated into an area roughly a mile long by half a mile wide, the paratroops were spread over 50 square miles. The stick earning the doubtful distinction of landing farthest from the target came down 30 miles away! So much for the weeks of rigorous rehearsal.

This was bad enough, but worse followed, with the loss of the five equipment gliders. The strong squall over the Channel strained and finally snapped the towropes, and the quintet glided helplessly down into the sea, taking their anti-tank guns, jeeps, and much more with them: equipment Otway and his men would need before many more minutes had elapsed.

Meanwhile Otway himself was flung fiercely from his Dakota, which was banking steeply away from the ground fire. It was nasty enough to jump by parachute in the middle of the night from a steady aircraft, but this was the worst way possible of launching the War's most vital operation.

And then, of all places to land, he and two others drifted down into a garden beside the H.Q. of a German unit, some way from Merville. The enemy at once fired on them with Luger pistols, but none were hit. Then one of the other two paratroops, Otway's batman, clambered on to the roof of the greenhouse attached to the house and heaved a brick through the window. The Germans apparently assumed that this must be a grenade, and while they were recovering the trio of British paratroops rushed out of the garden and were gone.

They moved as fast as they could towards the rendezvous, and when they reached it found that practically everything had gone not according to plan. The five-day briefing was discarded at one stroke as soon as Otway realized at 0250 that the total strength of the battalion had grown to only 150 men, with twenty lengths of Bangalore torpedo. No 3-inch mortars; no 6-pounder guns; no jeeps; no trailers; no glider stores; no sappers; no field ambulance; no mine detectors. On the credit side: some signals; a machine-gun; half of one sniping party; six medical orderlies, who would be needed before much longer. In one way this simplified the situation. Yet, looked at soberly, it seemed mad to go on.

Otway decided to advance at once.

They could not waste more time looking for guns which might have dropped almost anywhere in Normandy. For they were still a mile and a half from Merville. So they set out—decimated but determined. Walking through high-banked lanes within a mile of Merville seemed unreal, yet here they were.

One part of the plan that happened more or less as anticipated was their meeting with Major G. Smith and the reconnaissance party, already in the environs of the battery. Smith told Otway that he and his men had cut one fence, negotiated a minefield inside it, and spent some time in those early hours trying to place the exact sites of the sentry posts from the sounds of the Germans on guard. One patrol passed precisely two feet from where they were waiting.

Otway and the main force advanced farther and reached the party actually charged with the task of penetrating the minefield. Despite trip-wires and other obstacles, doubly dangerous in the dark, these men had forged a route through the mines and marked it with their heels. And not a single casualty had been caused. This took the main force to the inner wire.

0424: only a few minutes to zero hour, as two of the three gliders bearing the special, almost suicidal, assault teams arrived overhead as planned. The tow-rope of the third parted early on, and the glider had to land in England, instead of right in the teeth of the murderous Merville fortifications.

But two were present and correct, even if everything on the ground was not. Both tugs and gliders received hit after hit as tracer from the ground tore towards them. Despite this inferno, one of the planes circled the battery four times before releasing its glider. But as no star shells could be fired by the paratroops—they had been lost in the drop—the pilot of one glider understandably became confused between the battery and the village of Merville. Just in time he swung the glider clear of the village, but it came down some 4 miles away.

So then there was one. Anti-aircraft fire had hit four of the special troops on this last glider, and, with the machine itself starting to smoulder, the pilot decided to get down without delay. He saw a large field a short way from the battery, but suddenly spotted a *Minen* sign too. By now the wheels were on the grass, yet somehow he managed to hoist the glider clear of what could have been a fatal field, over a hedge and road, and bring it down again in a safer spot. Safer from mines, at any rate. The glider was wingless and burning now, and as the men—whether wounded or fit— plunged out of it they took on the Germans in a useful diversionary action which helped to leave Otway free for the main task.

As the glider came to its halt six enemy machine-guns opened fire on Otway's base from outside the perimeter. Four more inside it brought the total to ten. The lone Vickers gun with the assault force silenced three of its opposing number, while a diversion group did the same over on the right flank.

Now the die was cast. At about 0435 Otway ordered the starting-signal—and the first of the twenty lengths of wire-blowing torpedo shot forward over the uneven ground. These Bangalores did their job well, and left the vital gaps in the wire defences.

Working through mines and through craters made by shells and bombs, the assault force (divided into two parties) forced themselves forward in the face of frightening machine-gun fire. The plan was now far simpler than originally. One party went for the gunners themselves and closed them in combat, until the sight of the parachutists' skull sign provoked a German to screech out in terror, whereupon that particular group gave in.

The other assault party raced straight for the big guns. They fought their way across the bomb-scarred ground until they saw that two of the doors of the main emplacements were open. Fingers forced hard on to triggers, the party fired everything they had through those doors—and the Germans inside surrendered out of a panic-stricken desire for self-preservation.

Within minutes the paratroops destroyed three of the main German guns by Gammon bombs. Another one they put out of action successfully by the expedient of exploding two of its own shells simultaneously through the barrel. (The four guns proved to be 75-mm.'s—not 150-mm.'s, as expected.) Lieutenant M. Dowling was fatally hit during the action, but as his job was to check that the guns had definitely been neutralized he struggled on, somehow, to do this before he collapsed and died.

Only twelve minutes or so since Otway had given his signal to start the final offensive, he was ordering another signal, this time to the naval force assembled off shore, telling them that the Merville mission had been accomplished with time to spare. All through the preceding hours the signals officer had carried a companion in his battledress blouse. Now he tenderly took it out, and a slightly startled pigeon blinked at the scene all around. With a confirmatory message of their victory, the bird was flung high into the smoky air above the battery, and later on D-Day it landed safe and sound at its destination in England!

Then Otway took stock, and found that out of his tiny force of 150 men (far smaller than was originally planned) nearly half were casualties. Eighty still stood on their feet; the rest were killed, wounded, or missing. So a handful of men with one Vickers machine-gun had stormed one of the most fiercely fortified strong-points on the French coast, and captured and destroyed it within fifteen minutes of launching the assault.

Half an hour after it was over H.M.S. *Arethusa* was due to begin the naval bombardment—the starting-signal of the invasion by sea.

But the stage was not yet set from both wings for the final, withering onslaught. While the British paratroops stormed Merville and the bridges around the vital Caen area to the east, away on the west the Americans aimed to do the same sort of thing at Ste Mere-Eglise, behind Utah beach.

In the fiery afterglow of a storm-streaked sunset Eisenhower hurried around seven airfields in southern England to talk to his paratroops—their helmets dotted with camouflage, faces daubed dark. Before he was back at Southwick House the planes were airborne. Briefly, the tasks of these two airborne divisions were as follows:

The 101st U.S. Airborne Division was to ensure safe exits from Utah beach by occupying the causeways inland over the swampy ground. (One regiment had to follow the same pattern as the British followed at the Orne, and blow up the bridges along the Douve.) The 82nd U.S. Airborne Division, dropping near Ste Mere-Eglise, was to see that the seaborne forces would not be hemmed in behind the series of inland inundations.

So much for the theory.

Ahead of the waves of carriers fighters created cover and a clear route for the first paratroops—the pathfinders. These twenty pathfinder aircraft preceded the main force of 432 carriers bearing 6600 paratroops of the 101st Division. The main force took off at 2215. Despite having to fly in low, and thus render themselves vulnerable to flak, these first planes reached the six dropping-zones, for both divisions, aided by a thick, enveloping cloudbank. But these same clouds made accuracy very difficult for the following aircraft. Formations flew tight until they reached the French coast, but then the flak flew into them. One plane lurched to a hit, its port engines afire. Wheeling round desperately to head for home, it left a sheet of fire—a searing semicircle in the sky as it spiralled downward. Then the seconds passed and a sudden mushroom of flame burst from the ground.

Other aircraft veered violently to escape the flak, so that they were flying too fast and high for accurate jumps. But the men piled out, black shapes slipping from the belly of the planes. Operation Albany was on. Actually the flak fire did comparatively little damage, owing to the cloud conditions, but the human element—so often overlooked—produced an effect not envisaged. For most of the pilots, this was their baptism of battle, and the anti-aircraft fire unleashed against them caused excessive evasive action.

The 101st Division dropped from aircraft desperately trying to shake off the shattering effect of flak bursts as experienced by men for the first time. This evasive action was natural, and, in fact, coupled with the weather, accounted for the few losses in the air. But it also meant that the men were strewn over a 25-mile length of landscape. They were literally pitchforked from wildly weaving aircraft without any idea as to where they would come down. As the sound of shells and engines throbbed away above, the single, scattered parachutes billowed out unseen, their grey-green khaki colourings invisible in the 0130 darkness of D-Day just begun.

Some of the men fell even farther afield, miles from their objectives during the middle of the night, in a foreign land, where the scenery seemed indistinguishable one field from the next. Some one, however, had thought of this, and so the whole division carried clicking snappers, which they sounded to try and find each other.

Typical of the confusion was the case of Lieutenant-Colonel Robert Cole. He landed actually near Ste Mere-Eglise, where he collected thirty men of his own division and a few from the 82nd Division. Backtracking north, they all headed for the two northern exits of the beach, and the group snowballed to 75 men. On the way they met and killed some members of an enemy convoy, and then moved on towards the coast.

The battalions aiming to capture the southern-beach exits also had bad drops; in one instance eighty-one planes were scheduled to drop their troops in Zone C, and actually only ten aircraft found their mark.

The enemy had evidently anticipated a drop in Zone D, for the aircraft ran into concentrated ack-ack fire over this area. An oilsoaked building near the drop-field was set on fire as they actually floated down towards it, and then was heard the familiar deadly chatter of machine-guns and the clonk of mortars. Silhouetted, with all their 'chutes and supports, many of the Americans were riddled in the air before they had a chance to reply.

It was too soon then to count the cost, but, in fact, only about 1000 of the 6600 men in the division reached their rendezvous by dawn. And, far more serious, some 1500 were killed or captured, while more than half of their equipment dropped was lost as the bundles fell futilely into the surrounding swamps or into fields covered by enemy fire.

They needed that lost equipment and ammunition desperately. Captain Charles Shettle came down, and actually walked towards the nearest town, looking for his men. He found fourteen of them, and by the time he had managed to reach a bridge over the river, at about 0430, the number had risen to thirty-three.

Despite fire from the opposite bank, they forced a crossing and occupied the east side. This scratch bridgehead force accounted for a few of the enemy and their machine-guns, but by dawn the fight became unequal as the Americans ran short of ammunition—so much had been dropped in the swamps—and had no hope of friendly forces to reinforce them. They withdrew to the west bank soon afterwards, and held it.

Another objective of the American 101st Division was the lock on the Douve at La Barquette. Again, inaccurate dropping nearly caused the complete failure of this mission right at the outset. Some of the sticks of paratroops bumped down deep in enemy territory, others in swampy bottom lands to the west, and one command's personnel was particularly hard hit. The commanding officer was killed almost at once, and his executive officer captured. All the other company commanders and staff were missing initially.

In the light of this an accident which partly saved the day could be called doubly providential. As the jump signal flashed in Colonel Johnson's plane a bundle of equipment became tightly wedged in the drop door! There were a furious few seconds while they fought to free it. Then it sailed out. But if Johnson and his men had jumped on the signal they would have found that they had unloaded prematurely and were short of their zone.

Moving south, Johnson collected 150 miscellaneous men and advanced to a junction north of the lock. A force of fifty men reached the lock in a single dramatic dash, and dug in on the soft ground before the enemy could bring it under shellfire.

Then, just in time, fifty-one gliders soared out of the early sky to reinforce the 101st Division. The bodies of the great gliders churned up the French earth as they scraped in to land accurately beside the main rendezvous. Welcome white-painted stars near their tails cheered up the scattered Americans, who saw them from their various vantage-points.

These fifty-one Waco gliders, carrying command personnel and anti-tank weapons, as well as 150 troops, landed just before dawn. This type of landing had never been attempted before without full daylight, and, although they came in accurately, many of them were wrecked as they hit the small Normandy fields. Men and materials both suffered, and Brigadier-General Don Pratt, assistant commander of the 101st, was killed in landing. The losses remained reasonable, however, and with the extra troops Major-General Taylor, commanding the 101st, secured all the vital exits from the western causeway leading off Utah beach, including the village of Pouppeville. They could not blow the bridges, but succeeded in their main task.

An hour after the main 101st sticks were dropped the 82nd Division followed. The regiment earmarked to take Ste Mere-Eglise fell within two or three miles of the dropping-zone, but this was, in the words of the official account, "far from good." Many men found themselves nearer the 101st, and actually fought with elements of the other division for days. But about half the force of 2200 men landed in the dropping-zone, and most of the others assembled quite quickly. They were fortunate to find themselves in an area almost free of Germans, and they took advantage of their luck. They landed at 0230. By 0330 Ste Mere-Eglise was in their hands, and the main road from Carentan to Cherbourg successfully cut.

The planes carrying this regiment ran into fog and—a flak change from cloud—and the chances of a tight drop seemed slim. But some of the planes which had moved out to prevent possible collisions circled back before flashing the green light. The result: the good drop already described.

Colonel Krause learned from a Frenchman that the Germans had recently established themselves along the roads outside the town, so he planned to take the town and erect road blocks before daylight.

"Go directly into the town, without searching buildings," he told the paratroops, "and while it's dark use only knives, bayonets, and grenades." This was so that enemy small-arms fire could be spotted by sight and sound.

The paratroops streamed silently down the straight main road running right through the town; at the same time other paratroops outlined the town's perimeter. Across the fields, the churchyard, and the compact orchards they moved, till they entirely surrounded the town. Then they raised the very same American flag which they had flown over Naples when the Italian city was entered, and within two hours of their arrival they made Ste Mere-Eglise the first town to be taken by the Americans in the invasion.

The success at Ste Mere-Eglise assumed added point as a critical situation developed along the line of the Merderet river, where the well-laid plans of the other two regiments went astray as soon as the sticks started to fall in a pattern very different from that planned.

The regiments flew in on time, between 0230 and 0300, only to see that the preceding pathfinders had not been able to mark the dropping-zones, because the enemy were actually among them. Puzzled by the absence of marker-lights, many pilots overshot the zones, and whole groups of para-troops splashed down in the watery marshes along the Merderet.

Aerial photos showed only a grassy swampland, but in fact the area was one of wide floods, owing to the closure of the La Barquette lock. The grass growing out of this lakeland had sprouted so thickly that from above it looked like a prairie, instead of treacherous water several feet deep. Into this water dozens of heavily laden troops were plunged, and, far from it being an offensive operation, the first task was to rescue as many as possible.

Only one man in twenty-five of these two regiments came to earth near his intended zone, and the whole force had to fight for its life, almost with-out worrying about destroying bridges over the Douve or the Merderet. Nevertheless, they did fulfil a useful role in occupying the 91st German Infantry Division, a reserve earmarked to tackle any invasion army on the beaches.

With enemy fire building up in one particular place, counter-measures were held up while the Americans tried to retrieve a jeep and an anti-tank gun from the marshes, where they had fallen from heaven.

Men of another battalion, under Colonel Timmes, established a bold bridgehead at one place, but within an hour it was lost. The German artillery countered quickly. Small-arms fire came from the south, and tanks rumbled from the west. So the main force pulled out, leaving the bridge-head in the hands of four officers and eight men. This dozen Americans, with grenades, rifles, and one machine-gun, fought off the enemy—seen now as well as heard—and Gammon grenades shattered two of the lead-ing tanks trundling towards the bridge. But they were not equal to armour, and had to withdraw.

Dawn brought Operation Detroit and fifty-two gliders with weapons and transport intended to equip and reinforce the 82nd Division. But once again inaccuracy proved the stumbling block, and only twenty-two of them got to the landing-zone. Meanwhile swampland and other hazards had multiplied the difficulties and the engagements of the airborne troops. Instead of two or three neat operations, they fought fifteen to twenty separ-ate little battles, often only a few hundred yards away from each other, yet unable to link up or get a clear idea of what was happening or where their services would be needed most. The two American airborne divisions did pave the way for their colleagues landing later, though not as planned.

Through this night, too, the air was alive in a dozen different ways. Aircraft of Bomber Command, 1136 of them, thundered through the night to drop 5853 tons on picked positions, such as coastal batteries. Again the silent ships heard the reassuring roar of their engines, both before and after the operations, which finished at dawn.

There were smaller, secret sorties, too, such as Operation Sunflower, covering the drop of Special Air Service reconnaissance parties in six areas.

Already the enemy's Radar stations had been rocked with rockets streaming into unlikely woods, so Leigh-Mallory could report that in the vital period between 0100 and 0400 hours, when the assault armada was nearing the lowering-positions, only nine enemy Radar stations were in operation. And during the whole night the number of stations active in the Neptune area (the entire invasion coastline) only amounted to eighteen out of a normal ninety-two. No station was heard operating at all between Le Havre and Barfleur, the two cape extremities covering the D-Day goal.

The enemy received no Radar warning at all either of the sea forces or the airborne operations. While the first paratroops floated down easily, wondering what awaited them, the Luftwaffe's night fighter force was flying furiously around the Amiens area, where electronics had created for the Allies "ghost squadrons" of bombers requiring interception. Another scientific miracle that further confused the badly bewildered Germans on that night was our dummy parachutists, complete with special delay devices to emit cracking sounds like rifle fire! These were duly reported between Le Havre and Rouen, east of the actual invasion front, after aircraft crews had bundled the dummies out of their planes, chuckling at the thought of the Germans' reactions when they discovered their mistake! Even at 0400 the precise places of the main attack could not be anticipated by the harassed von Rundstedt. This was a strategic triumph—real paratroops, dummies, diversions, tinfoil dropped to simulate ships, and the rest of the ingenious ideas, and all in the middle of the night! Where was the mass attack going to take place? The answer was not long in coming.

II

The Yanks Ashore

OUT of the morning mist broke a barrage mightier than sound itself, the concerted crescendo of almost 1000 guns in shattering sequence, violent volley. Across the sea the shells whistled and whined to the Normandy shores, and the decks of the ships shuddered with the quivering recoil.

The starter's gun. Here was history about to be born—being made, as cloudy columns of suffocating, smudgy smoke rose in a grey-black blot along the fringe of France. D for Deliverance, and men's hearts really in their mouths, or their throats—or their stomachs. A glance at a watch; muted mutterings; a prayer; parched tongues.

And above it all the bombardment: an electrifying explosion erupting first from the ships, then flashing across the sullen summer sky before sunrise, and ending ashore; next the attack by air—fighter-bombers yelling in at sea-level to assault artillery positions inland, and the highlevel, aloof drone from one-and-a-third thousand American heavy bombers. Not a single enemy aircraft took off to interfere. Here, at last, was the reward of the long years of struggling for superiority in the air.

Compressed into thirty mutilating minutes, the U.S. 8th Air Force raid rained down a devastating tonnage right up till the minute of H-Hour, the time scheduled for the first assault troops to hit each particular beach.

So under an umbrella of pummelling, pounding fire, unequalled in history, the landing-craft crawled in—helmeted heads keeping as low as possible above the sides of the craft.

First blood to the Yanks. At H–40 minutes, or 0550, battleships, cruisers, and a dozen destroyers of Task Force 125 sent shells streaming into the batteries of Utah beach. And, as the clock crept round to 0600, 276 Marauder medium bombers doubled the dose with over 4000 bombs on seven beach objectives.

Next, while the assault craft came to the last lap before the beaches, the thirty-three vessels of the Utah beach fire support group added their quota. Seventeen of these craft mounted rocket launchers, and discharged their weapons when the first waves of troops were 600–700 yards off shore.

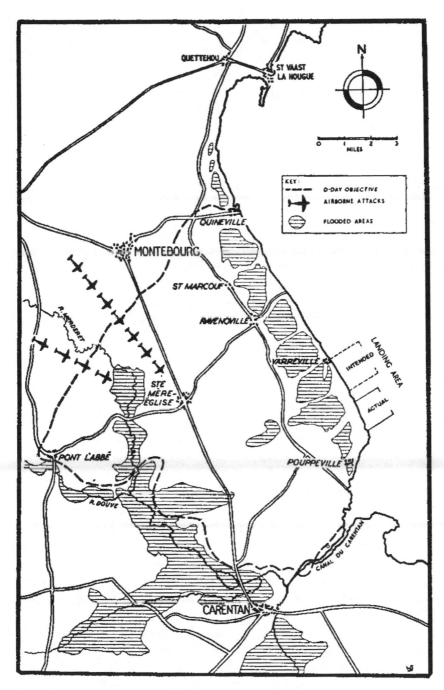

THE UTAH BEACH SECTOR

Although the coast defences were not in general as effectively elimi-
nated as had been hoped, those short, shattering sessions of sheer hell did
neutralize them for the vital assault minutes. Entanglements and minefields
were destroyed in some cases, the beach mines exploding added to the
eruptions all around. The very volume of the fire shook the defenders and
paralysed their communications. Drenched by the double bombardment
by sea and air, the defence remained dazed. Almost complete surprise
appeared to have been achieved by the Allies.

Even as the telltale wake of the 4th U.S. Infantry Division neared the
shore the Germans seemed mesmerized by the fantastic ferocity of the
onslaught, coming at them from all angles, so that the actual invasion
troops on Utah beach met only slight and spasmodic opposition. The
weather was worse than the fire from the shore.

One of the earliest mishaps occurred when two control vessels were put
out of action. As they left the transport area to head for the beach one
fouled her screw on a chain buoy and could not go on. The second control vessel continued, but amid the cataclysmic cascade of an exploding
mine she was suddenly swamped and sunk. Another eruption, and an
L.C.T. dipped dramatically into the surf.

While this was in progress the tank-carrying L.C.T.'s delayed landing
their thirty-two amphibious tanks until they were only 2 miles out,
because of the bad weather. This cut down the risk of being swamped by
an angry sea 3–4 miles off shore.

Meanwhile the haze from the bombardment, coupled with the strong
tidal conditions and the loss of the control ships, threw the whole operation almost a mile off course. Unaware of this, as the initial assault craft
ploughed towards their landfall, the smaller ships still covered them with
the bursting barrage from their rocket guns. Some of these support craft
fired machine-guns over the heads of the first assault wave, in the hope
that the bullets bouncing on the beach might explode mines.

Passing minutes and mounting tension. The twenty craft in the first
wave arrived at the line of departure on time, and advanced abreast. Then,
when they were 300–400 yards from the beach, special smoke projectors
signalled the lifting of naval support-craft fire. These were uncanny
moments as H-Hour arrived—0630.

Exactly on time, the twenty assault craft lowered their ramps, and 600
men—thirty to each craft—strode into waist-deep water to wade the final
hundred yards to the beach.

Enemy artillery loosed a few air-bursts above the craft, but otherwise
opposition was light—luckily. Chewing gum, the Yanks waved their rifles
as they reached the dry sand.

"Goddam, we're on French soil," some one shouted.

The eight L.C.T.'s, each with four of the D.D. amphibious tanks, would be in about the same time, while second and third assault waves were due within fifteen minutes.

The one-mile error in position proved an asset, for beach obstacles here were fewer than in the sector planned farther north, and also less formidable shore defences existed than those opposite the intended beaches. But with the tide still slightly lower than anticipated, the Yanks faced an expanse of open beach to be crossed before they could scramble to the sand dunes lying low, yet inviting, at the top of the beach.

This entire side-slip could have had serious results, of course, but immediate measures prevented confusion. Brigadier-General Theodore Roosevelt rushed to the rear of the beach to check the causeways to be used for the advance. With his aides he hurried back to the landing points to improvise plans.

Seconds counted, but there was still only a slight pepper of bullets instead of the heavy fire feared.

The casualties came at sea. Enemy guns got direct hits on two L.C.T.'s and sank them. Men struggled in the sea. Weapons sank to the bottom.

The demolition teams were the men who mattered now. The plan was that eight naval teams should clear 50-yard gaps in the first band of obstacles. The teams were due ashore at H + 5 minutes. Yes, it was in the water that the danger to the invaders lay. One of the eight craft carrying demolition men slithered to a stop in the sand at 0635. Just as its ramp thudded down to the water's edge an enemy shell shattered the whole bow. Death struck six Americans. One clutched wildly at his head. Another folded up, almost in half.

Other obstacle men jumped into 3 feet of water, each with 60 lb. of explosives. Within minutes they blew the first gap at the junction of the beaches.

As the Americans threaded their way up and off the beach other craft brought in the next waves, and then, about a quarter of an hour later, the first eight D.D. tanks bobbed inshore, and, once aground, trundled out of the sea to cover the infantry from close range. Their value in support and surprise could not be overestimated, and the already reeling German defenders inland fell back before this new element, which was actually rolling in from the sea and firing heavy weapons from the shallows.

Now bulldozers and all manner of vehicles were throbbing urgently up the beach. Major Tabb's vehicle did not stand up to the buffeting water as it left the landing-craft, and sank. Tabb acted promptly; he managed to save his crew plus a radio, and made for the beach, where he contacted Brigadier-General Roosevelt.

But, apart from these isolated losses, the expected opposition was missing. Meanwhile more specialists sailed in to tackle the beach obstacles. They placed charges by hand against most of them, the rest being pushed on to the beach by tank dozers. Periodic bangs marked the end of these obstacles, only a few of which had mines attached to them. In an hour the whole beach had been cleared, and of this force of 400 men, six had been killed and thirty-nine wounded. So far, then, casualties remained remarkably low. Could this rate be maintained on all the beaches?

After the engineers forced their way through the mines and all the other paraphernalia the next obstacle calling for their explosives was the sea-wall at the top of the beach. Until it was breached neither tanks nor other vehicles could drive off the quiet but dangerous beach zone. For already the enemy guns inland had got the range of the beach and started shelling. So they blew holes in the wall by the causeway exits and unravelled the coils of barbed-wire, as well as piercing paths through the sand-dunes. Bangalore torpedoes, mine detectors, explosives, and other tools of the trade all opened exits off Utah beach.

Meanwhile the sun rose, and for a moment pierced the continuous cloud, throwing sickening shadows beside the few crumpled corpses dotting the water-line. And the infantry commenced clearing out houses and enemy garrisons. Some of the Germans had been so staggered by the bombardment that they did not open fire at all. As this proceeded more battalions landed, so that by 0800 four had landed, and by 1000 two more. An orderly advance began along the various exits, though alarming setbacks were suffered by the infantry wading south through the inundated interiors. The water in this flooded region was normally waist-deep, but because of ditches and odd holes many of the men found themselves completely submerged.

And after Utah—the Omaha onslaught.

The morning of D-Day. Aircraft tow gliders carrying troops to
reinforce the airborne landings.

Paratroops smear their faces with black grease while waiting to embark.

The flotsam of invasion lies all along the coast, from Utah to Sword.

In the storm which struck a fortnight after D-Day the Mulberry harbours were severely damaged.

12

Hell on Omaha

OVER at Omaha the morning made the Utah landings seem like a peace-time party on the beach. Here hell was the only word with which to describe the time from 0300 onward; indeed, from 0251, when the headquarters-ship *Ancon* anchored in the transport area 13 miles off shore.

The assault was to be delivered by the 1st U.S. Infantry Division, with the 116th Regiment attached from the 29th U.S. Infantry Division. The 29th Division was to follow up and take over the western sector of the area.

The wind force of 10–18 knots caused waves here to be up to 6 feet high, while on the beach the breakers measured 3–4 feet. At this time, 0300, the assault infantry units began loading into their small craft, lowered from parent ships. Some were immediately swamped, and so the pattern was set: a double battle against elements and enemy.

Then came the tragedy of the first twenty-nine amphibious tanks on the left flank, floundering, foundering, sinking, in the watery wilderness before dawn. Launched at H–50 minutes, 6000 yards out, they began within minutes to suffer the crippling damage of broken struts, torn canvas, and engine trouble from water flooding the engine compartment. The remaining three tanks of this battalion could not be launched because the ramp of their L.C.T. was damaged. As landing-craft came within a few miles of the shore they passed men from the sunken tanks struggling in life-preservers and on rafts—those who were not already drowned. Over on the right flank the D.D. tanks could not be launched ahead of the assault at all, owing to the sea and the fate of the first thirty-two, so the landing-craft carrying the infantry had to plod and toss towards the shore without this vital vanguard support.

Right from the line of departure spray drenched the assault craft. Most of them started to ship enough water to necessitate the use of pumps, which were incapable of carrying the load. There was nothing for it but for the troops to bale out with their helmets, which at least occupied not only their hands but their minds.

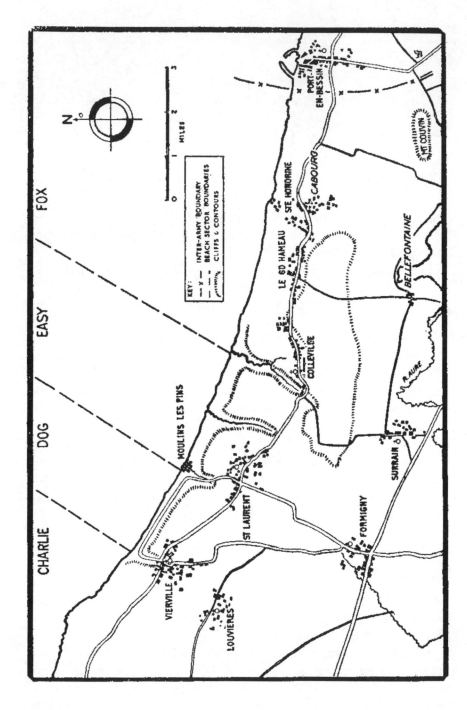

THE OMAHA BEACH SECTOR

Ten out of the 180–200 landing-craft used in the early waves were definitely swamped—some almost as soon as they were lowered, others nearer the beach—but nearly all the men were saved by naval craft or passing ships.

So, from the outset, the troops were drenched again and again, and in addition soon became cramped, seasick, scared, and weakened: practically the worst possible way of starting strenuous action on an enemy shore.

But at least they had been through this sort of training before, and many remembered the recent full-dress rehearsal at Slapton Sands, near Dartmouth. One officer thought the whole thing still seemed like another big tactical scheme, and could not get the feeling out of his head that it was going to be a miserable two-day job with a hot shower at the end. But he could scarcely have been more mistaken.

Despite all the scientific aids concerning winds and current conditions, panoramic photographs, and actual visual beachmarks, the entire navigation of the Omaha assault gradually became more chaotic, so that by 0600 craft were coming in anything from a few hundred yards to a mile off-course. The unnaturally wild weather made navigation over 13 miles inevitably inaccurate. And, what was more, the strong onshore wind whipped the tide higher than it would have been normally, so the underwater obstacles were awash sooner than anticipated, and hidden deeper every minute. By this time many men had been seaborne in their little landing-craft for three hours and had reached a low ebb of efficiency.

This was the position as H–35 minutes brought the bombers on to the scene. From 0555 to 0614 this force of Liberators added another dramatic disappointment to the already hard-tried troops. In their anxiety not to hit any advance craft coming in near the coast the bombers missed the beach defences and obstacles altogether. Operating in overcast conditions with a low cloud base, they released their patterns inland instead of in the immediate beach area. This mass attack achieved the net result of 13,000 fragmentation bombs falling from a quarter of a mile to 3 miles beyond the beaches. Dust drenched the beaches, but that was about all. Although the attack may have smashed much of the German communications, it left the landing-craft to face murderous mortar and shell fire during the final few minutes of their run in.

The concentrated naval barrage broke five minutes earlier, at 0550, and continued until H–3 minutes. The battleships *Texas* and *Arkansas* poured some 600 rounds of heavy shells ashore, and then came the cruisers, destroyers, and support fire. The aim was to neutralize not only the beach defences but positions which could lay flanking-fire on the invasion points. But, as with the air assault, the cloud prevented accurate range-finding, and the ships had to err on the side of overshooting. It was to prove a costly margin of safety.

The Liberators droned into the distance. Sixteen more minutes to go. The naval shells were bursting well behind the beaches still as the time ticked by on thousands of watches. More mortars from the shore. And any minute they had to get out of the craft to face the next stage. All along the line the navigational side-slip went on—from the westerly Dog Green[1] beach, past Dog White and Dog Red, to Easy Green, Easy Red, Fox Green, and Fox Red at the extreme east.

There was no point in relying on anyone now. Some of the tank-landing-craft—specially strengthened to allow their self-propelled artillery to fire while still embarked, and so boost the close support fire—failed to keep their position in such intensely difficult conditions.

Nearer, nearer now, advanced the first assault forces on Omaha. Then 0627. The overpowering pounding from the ships reached a crescendo of stupendous sound, then suddenly stopped, dead on schedule. There was one thought in the mind of every man: Just three more minutes, just a few hundred yards of water.

Four hundred and forty yards out the leading craft came under heavy fire from automatic weapons and artillery ashore. The beaches were unscarred by the air bombardment.

0629: men crouched down in their landing-craft, clenched their teeth and hands, and waited as that last sixty seconds circled away.

Right away on the west flank, on Dog Green, directly in front of an opening at Vierville, the tank landing-craft came in. At once the L.C.T. carrying one company commander was sunk just off shore. Five officers were either killed or wounded in an instant.

Eight of one company's sixteen tanks landed, and started to fire from the water's edge.

An amphibious tank hit an underwater obstacle in the murky morning and exploded. This was due to the fast-flooding tide. Near by a landing-craft suffered the same fate from a direct hit before its occupants had begun the battle.

One of the six assault landing-craft carrying the leading company in the assault on the western sector (the 116th Regiment) foundered and started to sink. Well out of their depth, the men had to jump, and Rangers passing

[1] The invasion planners had divided the French coast between the rivers Vire and Orne into sections, labelled alphabetically eastward. The three sectors of Omaha, D, E, and F (Dog, Easy, and Fox), were in turn divided into sub-sectors; Dog Green, Dog White, Dog Red; Easy Green, Easy Red; Fox Green (reading eastward).

in another craft saw them leaping hopelessly from the L.C.A. and being dragged down by their loads.

The assault waves were coming in late—four to six minutes.

0635 on Dog Green. A 970-yard strip of hell. The remaining five craft had stopped short of the beach, grounding 100 yards out on sand-barriers. The enemy's automatic weapons had got their range, and their fire was actually beating on the ramps before they were lowered, or else bullets whipped into the surf just ahead of the ramps—where the men would be stepping any second.

Ramps down; and ramps meant sixteen steps to who knew what? Some of the Yanks clattered down and fell waist-deep into water. Others found themselves up to their necks, their heads targets for the fire from shore. From two particular points the enemy hit with diabolical results.

As the range of the ramps attracted a convergence of fire, some of the men dived over the sides or kept actually under the water for as long as they could. Stiff, weak, seasick, and loaded, they trudged in through the water, the uneven footing making their progress all the more hellishly slow.

As if this were the signal for which the enemy had waited, all boats came under criss-cross machine-gun fire.... As the first men jumped, they crumpled and flopped into the water. Then order was lost. It seemed to the men that the only way to get ashore was to dive head first in and swim clear of the fire that was striking the boats. But, as they hit the water, their heavy equipment dragged them down and soon they were struggling to keep afloat. Some were hit in the water and wounded; some drowned then and there.... But some moved safely through the bullet-fire to the sand and then, finding they could not hold there, went back into the water and used it as cover, only their heads sticking out. Those who survived kept moving forward with the tide, sheltering at times behind underwater obstacles, and in this way they finally made their landings.

Within ten minutes of the ramps being lowered, A Company had become inert, leaderless and almost incapable of action. Every officer and sergeant had been killed or wounded.... It had become a struggle for survival and rescue. The men in the water pushed wounded men ashore ahead of them, and those who had reached the sands crawled back into the water pulling others to land to save them from drowning, in many cases only to see the rescued men wounded again or to be hit themselves. Within 20 minutes of striking the beach A Company had ceased to be an assault company and had become a forlorn little rescue party bent upon survival and the saving of lives.

Meanwhile mortar fire scored four direct hits on one of the L.C.A.'s, which literally disintegrated. A Company—or what was left of it—

exhausted when they reached the shore, then faced 200 yards of open beach before they could hope for cover from a sea-wall or shingle bank.

Darting desultorily from one beach obstacle to another, the men tried to get away from enemy fire. The remnants of one boat-team attempted to help, forming a small firing-line on the first yards of sand, in full view of the enemy, but despite this heroism, many of the company became casualties—as much as two-thirds of the total strength.

H + 15, or 0645. Two L.C.A.'s carried a small U.S. Ranger company of sixty-four men in to the right of the Vierville opening. (The Rangers were the equivalent of the British Commandos.) An anti-tank gun got one of the craft, killing a dozen men. The other L.C.A. headed on—only to be strafed by a machine-gun as the Rangers were half-way down the ramps. Without waiting to organize, the survivors set out across the 250 yards of open sand to the base of a cliff. The time it took to get there: three or four minutes. Mortars and machine-guns hit more men as they advanced. The wounded crawled behind. A few got there. Under the shelter of the cliff, the Rangers took a breath and a count—thirty-five men lost, twenty-nine left.

The Rangers faced the fiercest onslaught of all on this right flank. Storming ashore in face of one of the few exits from Omaha—actually opposite Vierville—another company met the fatal fury of at least two German strong-points, which were covering the road through the place.

Gripping their guns in both hands as they jumped off the ramps, one or two men were hit in mid-air and never reached dry land. Others crouched, crawled, or chased their way towards the only shelter—the sea-wall. All of them met the murderous inferno of fire from land. This was it: the moment of truth, life, death. The toss of a coin. Am I going to get it? Am I? Am I? Luck, chance.

And their only chance—the wall. Some staggered through the shallows, others struggled towards it diagonally. And all the time the hail of hell went on.

Someone fell hit. There was no one to help him. He might live, or he might not. A wrecked craft drifted crazily broadside on to the shore, its job done. A Ranger lay face down in a pool of water, stained red.

One hundred and thirty Rangers landed there. Sixty-two survived to reach the sea-wall. Less than half their number. Men had been mown down.

Why was the defence so strong? Unluckily the enemy troops in the area had just been augmented by a field formation, which happened to be holding a stand-to exercise on the coast, manning the defences, as the Allied assault began.

The rest of the regiment came in past poles and spikes sticking

alarmingly out of the water, but luck was on their side. G Company landed more than half a mile east of their intended Dog White beach, on Dog
Red, where the earlier barrage had started grass fires. Smoke from these
created a complete screen between the beach and the defences, shrouding
their vulnerable position from the bluffs. Not stopping to query their fortune, they scampered across the tidal flat, relieved that the smoke was still
sufficiently dense to stop the almost continuous line of enemy emplacements from attacking them. If the barrage had not knocked out many of
the defences at least it had laid an unintentional smokescreen. They were
half way up the flat before any firing at all reached them, and then it was
inaccurate, causing only a few casualties.

Much heavier fire met the other sections of this company, which lost
fourteen men on Easy Green beach.

F Company hit Easy Green right in front of the fortified Moulins Les
Pins. Three sections of another company were shattered by concentrated
fire from various weapons, and it was not until three-quarters of an hour
later that they got across the exposed expanse of sand. By then half were
dead or wounded, and the rest in no state for assault action.

At the same time as A and F Companies were plunging into the pain
and eternity of Dog Green and Easy Green the rest of the regiment hit
beaches farther east, earmarked for the 16th Regiment, to a similar blaze
of fire from almost point-blank range.

Men of E Company were put out in waist-deep water, but hit a deep
runnel as they waded in, and had to swim through surf and strong currents, which wrenched them east. Flame-throwers, mortars, bazookas, and
small arms were all dropped in the struggle for survival. Yet when E
Company finally dripped breathlessly ashore they dragged themselves up
to the sheltering shingle having lost only two men from enemy fire.

A little to the left a drifting section of F Company unloaded in neck-
deep water, and seventeen men out of thirty-one died on the way to the
shingle.

On to the Fox beaches and the other American assault regiment—the
16th. Craft scattered badly over a front of 800 yards, thus weakening their
power-through-concentration. Although the final run-in did not incur
many losses, crossfire caught the craft exactly as the ramps went splashing
down. Bullets seared into men as they jumped. And as others stopped to
drag the wounded ashore they were hit in the water. Soaked uniforms
hung heavily on them; soaked, wounded men weighed still heavier; and
by the time they staggered up the sand—still 300 yards from the shingle
bank—all they could do was crawl in ahead of the tide. Most of one company's 105 casualties for the day came between 0630 and 0700.

Stray sections of E Company, 116th Regiment, bobbed in on the same shore. Their commander, Captain Laurence Madill, lurched across the beach, already wounded. Weaker each second, he returned to the water's edge to salvage mortar ammunition. Machine-gun bullets hit him twice more. As he reeled and fell his last words were, "Senior non-com, take the men off the beach."

Mortars and machine-guns combined to take a toll of one in every three men as F Company, 116th Regiment, landed in front of enemy strong-points.

Just as the right and centre assaults aimed at Vierville and St Laurent, the left struck for Colleville. This was the Americans' strategy of head-down, head-on battering attack, at the precise points where the enemy were likely to be strongest. The morning would decide on the wisdom of such strategy, but it looked as if it might be a lesson learned dearly, in terms of human life.

So at Easy Red and Fox Green, on either side of the Colleville exit, the stark scenes of Dog Green were partly re-enacted.

Over on the east men swept in by the surf landed soaking and swearing under the very guns flanking the exit. Some of the craft sank before they even faced Fox Green. Others were hit by shells on the run-in. One shell exploded right in the middle of the men in a crowded craft.

But, somehow, despite the surf and the shells, they came in, late and out of place, but still at Omaha on that memorable morning. None of them living to-day would have missed it. Fortunately the general drag eastward pulled many of them just far enough away from the perils of Fox Green. Seeing the battering bursts of fire from this area, they modified the original head-on dash, and struck out east towards Port-en-Bessin, adjacent to Arromanches, where they were due to meet the British.

The cliffs rising east of Fox Green helped to shield this movement, and so the full fury of Dog Green was not repeated. Nevertheless, it was bad enough, although the supporting destroyers and rocket craft stood close inshore, in vulnerable waters, to try and cover the movement off the beach.

Suddenly a salvo of sheer sheets of flame spat at an angle into the air, announcing the opening fire from rocket craft: a volley equal to the firing-power of 200 destroyers! A breath taking, breath-holding barrage. And these craft could come in closer than destroyers.

I Company, 16th Regiment, had a couple of craft swamped, and ended up far east of the Fox beaches. L Company, 16th Regiment, were luckiest of all. Artillery hit a landing-craft a few seconds after the last man left it, and one of the company's sections showed that success was possible by spreading out widely to move up the beach—thereby losing not a single man. In fact, L Company was the only one of the eight in the first assault to be ready to operate as a unit after crossing the lethal lower beaches.

With these first moves went a special engineer task force to tackle beach obstacles. Delays in loading and the wholesale mishandlings meant that half of the sixteen teams reached shore ten minutes or more late. At least three teams landed where there were neither infantry nor tanks to cover them with protective fire. And men loaded with equipment and explosives staggering through several feet of water presented sitting targets.

Only six of the thirteen bulldozers beached in working order, and enemy artillery at once hit three of these six.

As eight naval engineers dragged the pre-loaded rubber boat off their landing-craft a shell burst just above this load of explosives. One of the eight lived....

A mortar was responsible for hitting another rubber boat full of explosives as the men pulled it through the surf. Amazingly, only four were wounded.

Over on a landing-craft a shell hit the deck to the accompaniment of a multiple detonation, which killed every one on board.

Finally, as one craft came towards the shallows a shell struck the ramp, hurling three men into the water. The craft drifted, dazed, out of control, and another shell caught her bang on the bow. Fifteen men died.

Yet despite these disasters, the engineers went on—and actually got to work on those deadly beaches. One of the three bulldozers left had to postpone its manoeuvres to stop and give shelter to the hard-pressed infantry. Every clang of a bullet against the bulldozer meant, possibly, a life saved.

Yes, the engineers were working under impossible difficulties. One team was all ready to blow a lane through the beach obstacles when a landing-craft came hurtling up to the foreshore on a wave, crashed into the obstacles, and detonated seven mines.

Another team laid their charges for a 30-yard gap and were just skipping back to take cover when a mortar shell struck the primer cord. The premature explosion killed or wounded nineteen engineers.

But in their allotted time they blew six gaps all along the Omaha front— though, owing to loss of equipment, only one could be marked.

Most of the high proportion of 41 per cent. casualties to engineers were sustained in that first half-hour, trying to clear a way for the second waves.

13

Death on Dog Green

IT was 0700 and the death on Dog Green was repeated as the second waves touched down in a series of landings lasting forty minutes. The remnants of A Company, 116th Regiment, were still staggering under the shock of those first twenty-five minutes as B Company bottomed. By this hour, too, the tide had flowed right into the obstacle belt—and through it by 0800 but the beach obstacles were not yet gapped in many places. No one had advanced beyond the shingle; tanks were unable to give much covering fire; and the tide would have risen eight feet in the next hour. Not a bright prospect.

By luck, only a small part of the three companies actually landed on Dog Green, where the same shattering, clattering crossfire reduced their strength in minutes of massacre. Everything was happening in minutes—seconds, even; yet seconds could seem eternities. A machine-gun burst stabbed the line of the tide, and its bullets broke the surface, throwing up spurts of spray before reaching and riddling a wounded G.I. as he hung on to an underwater obstacle. His grip gave way.

The same destructive fire pinned B Company to the water's edge.

Some of the craft were saved by the tide as the wind whipped them a little to the left. Behind the cover of a providential pall of smoke the men got across the open beach to the blind side of a sea-wall, and overcame all obstacles, wire, and mines to penetrate inland.

Following ten minutes behind B Company, C came in at 0710 at the west end of Dog White. One of its six craft got off to a bad, if not fatal, start by running right into a mined obstacle. For twenty frantic minutes they manoeuvred in the surf to get free without detonating the mines! Only one other craft suffered a setback: the sea threw it against a ramp, and it capsized, spilling the men into five feet of water, and losing all its precious flame-throwers and charges.

Still almost as many died in the water as ashore. Three of D Company's six craft shipped water seriously, and one had to be abandoned before the invasion began.

Four hundred yards out another one suddenly sank in a stream of surf, and the men were flung into the water, where they struggled to swim for shore. Desperate over-arm strokes threshed the waves, as the men swam under a blinding barrage of mortars and bullets. About half of them reached the damp sands.

A section of D Company disembarked a long way out, and saw rifle-men lying full-length in the shallows, sheltering behind the steel obstacles. Those who eventually got ashore had, for their total arms, one mortar—without ammunition.

So it went on. Death and glory. Battalion headquarters and Headquarters Company of one battalion came in on time, but when the ramps went down the fire was so intense that many men took refuge behind some tanks, only to find these the targets of large-scale artillery fire.

Later Major Sidney Bingham, Junior, battalion commander, tried to organize an assault on Moulins Les Pins, but so many of the fifty men he gathered had rifles clogged with sand that they could not really build up any volume of fire!

Then the reinforcements arrived thick and fast. Tired and cramped, they were glad that the enemy fire had lessened a little, for as one of them put it, "The burdens we ordinarily carried, we had to drag."

Still machine-gun bullets kicked up the sand, but the men took shelter, and worked out that the machine-guns were delivering fixed fire, so advanced along routes away from the bullet-marks.

Yet some fire was inevitable. Losses were low here, for, in the words of a survivor, "It's surprising how much small-arms fire a man can run through without getting hit."

Lighter losses were the general rule for later assault waves. Some were shielded by burning grass, but the decreases in losses was probably due more to the fact that as the landings increased the enemy had to divide their attention between more formations. As the main command group beached at about 0730 one craft knocked a Teller mine off its perch without any explosion! The enemy's fire from the bluffs was masked by the smoke of burning grass.

Meanwhile, back on Dog Green, the enemy was disturbed by fire from Allied destroyers and smaller craft who had seen the reception given to A Company, 116th Regiment. Defying opposition and the risk of running aground, these ships swung towards Dog Green beach, to bring their guns on to the two strong-points still dangerous to the Americans. The bombardment had the desired effect, and enabled the troops to regroup on the beach behind any available cover. They were even able to get a line out to a couple of wounded colleagues wading ashore. Their landing-craft had been wrecked, and lay low in the shallows as the waves broke over it.

Gratefully they grabbed the rope, and were hauled up to the beach by men up to the knees in water. Then, quickly, they all dispersed, and only the landing-craft remained.

Fierce fighting went on along all parts of the beach. The 4-mile stretch of Omaha was well covered at either end by sheer 100-foot cliffs. The main crossfire came from the bluff overlooking the western sector and from the central exit point at which the American landings had been aimed. Hence the fatal fire-power mustered against them.

Engineers were still working furiously as the second assault waves of the 16th Regiment bumped over the sand-barriers and through the thick obstacles off Easy Red. More losses now, as the cramped, heavily laden troops could only advance at walking-pace: physically, they could not run. Enemy snipers picked off many as they made the uphill trek from the lower beach. Nevertheless, they got supporting weapons working within a quarter of an hour.

Bullets, swamping, fire, mines, artillery hits—so the sound and fury maintained its cacophony. One craft got hung up on an obstacle, and an enemy machine-gun fired on it steadily, mercilessly, until its occupants were dead.

The smokescreen of burning grass in the centre sector was proving an obstacle to the Americans, as well as protecting them. They could scarcely see any landmarks or a way through the minefields. Added to their being well east of the appointed place, this made early movements erratic. Inevitably, the beaches became more crowded, with no exits yet available. Enemy guns managed to penetrate through gaps in the smoke, and soon their shells started exploding around the later landing-craft and vehicles. Plenty of forces were coming ashore, but they could do little that was constructive without exits.

The first hour was over. Then came one of the worst disasters of the day. L.C.I. 91 was approaching Dog White at 0740, carrying the alternative headquarters of the 116th Regiment. Artillery fire hit it on its first attempt to get through the obstacles. Backing out, the vessel came in for a second try, but the tide had flooded high, and Element C obstacles were scarcely showing. The L.C.I. could not get through, so the ramps were dropped in water six or seven feet deep. As the officers led the way down, an artillery shell fell right on the crowded forward deck, sending up a sheet of flame. Burning, screaming men jumped or fell into the sea, struggling to swim ashore under continued artillery fire.

As if this tragedy were not enough, L.C.I. 92 came into the same sector a few minutes later, and suffered almost as severely. It struck a mine; the fuel tanks exploded and burst into scorching fire, which burned for hours after the last man had jumped for his life to escape roasting.

Conditions for landing the vehicles now arriving could not have been worse. If the jeeps, trucks, and the rest managed to get close enough in to avoid deep water, and unloading in surf under fire, they found that they were on strips of sand narrowing hourly, and without any exits. The traffic jam began. One battalion lost twenty-eight of its thirty-six machine-guns, while water and sand made guns unusable. Colonel Canham reported three-quarters of 116th's radios useless. Meanwhile the rising tide was drowning wounded men stranded on the edge of the water.

Stunned and shaken by that first hour, the men were glad of the apparent safe cover of the sea-wall and shingle bank. They had no wish to go on at present. But some officers at once saw the danger of this. Morale was low. If they were not careful they would be open to counter-attack before they had got off the beaches.

Even at Easy Red, where the resistance was lighter, the Germans were preventing the 16th from leaving the beach. They got across the firm sand, grey-brown under the ominous scudding clouds, but then the beach banked up steeply into a shingle ridge. Beyond this were wire obstacles. A steady fire forced them to keep their heads down.

The decisive factor proved to be—leadership. Where did they go from there? No one could see how to advance straight over the top. Then a young lieutenant and a sergeant, already wounded, suddenly stood up, disregarded the frequent firing, and calmly walked over to look at the wire beyond the embankment. Somehow they were not hit. The lieutenant returned and, hands on hips, looked down at the men lying behind the shingle.

"Are you going to lay there and get killed, or get up and do something about it?" he called across to them.

None of them moved, so, with the sergeant, he got the explosives, walked back to the obstacles, and blasted a way through the wire. At last the men stirred, and the lieutenant led the way in single file under continuous fire up a path prickling with mines. So, slowly, they got to grips with the enemy defences which covered the beach.

Another company landed and followed the same route. But they were exposed to the double danger of shelling and the mines. Shells burst near by, yet they dare not stop nor lie down. The mine menace on land was only a few inches under the surface all the way. One moment a man was trudging up the path. The next, a blinding burst, and his pal in front lay heaped ahead of him. And all he could do was walk round what was left.

The remnants of an isolated section of B Company, 116th Regiment, were stopped early on by fire from a well-concealed emplacement. The lieutenant in charge went after it single-handed. But, tossing a grenade into the rifle-pit, he was hit by three bullets and eight grenade fragments, including some from his own grenade. He clutched himself, and fell, but not before turning his map and compass over to a sergeant and ordering the group to press on inland.

While the second waves were being bundled ashore from a fierce sea on to a fiercer shore three companies of the U.S. Rangers had to assault the sheer cliff face of Pointe du Hoe, three miles west of Dog Green. And to do it they had the Wheezers and Dodgers' cliff-scaling gear they had tried out in the Isle of Wight. The aim was to try and neutralize a battery believed to be located on top of the cliff, which could fire on either of the two American assault areas—O and U. The battery was understood to consist of six 155-mm. howitzers.

As the cliff rose sheer to a height of 85–100 feet, the ten assault landing-craft carried three rocket guns apiece, firing grapnels which pulled up plain ropes, toggle ropes, and rope ladders. Each craft also carried tubular-steel extension ladders, while four D.U.K.W.'s mounted a 100-foot extension ladder.

Companies E and F were scheduled to scale the east side of the point, and D Company the west; the landings were to take place at H-Hour, 0630. Unluckily, the general drift eastward also affected the Rangers' craft. One of their ten L.C.A.'s was swamped soon after leaving the transport area, while further trouble came from the supply boats: one sank, and the second had to jettison all packs to stay afloat. A small gun situated on the cliff-top sank one of the D.U.K.W.'s, but the nine surviving L.C.A.'s sailed in under covering fire from two destroyers, whose armament fired shells all over the area beyond the battery. At H-Hour the barrage was lifted, and the craft had to go on alone, but the destroyer *Satterlee* spotted the enemy recovering to man cliff-top trenches, and so swept the place for a final time with her guns.

Despite this, as the craft beached over half an hour late—and all on the east side—scattered fire killed fifteen Rangers on the heavily cratered shore.

Immediately on touch-down they fired their rockets over the cliff, but some failed to carry as the ropes attached were soaked with water. The D.U.K.W.'s could not get across the cratered beach, so their ladders were not much use.

Germans appeared, peering down over the cliff, and started to harass the Rangers with occasional rifle fire and some grenades, which merely had to be lobbed down. But the Rangers picked off these snipers as soon as they exposed themselves on the skyline, and *Satterlee* swung in at close range to strafe the cliff-top a second time with all her guns.

One or two ropes were cut by the enemy at the top, or slipped from their anchorage, but within less than five minutes of touch-down the first Rangers bobbed to the top. Others followed, walking up the cliff almost horizontally. They scrambled up the sheer Pointe du Hoe in any way they could, and plunged their faces flat on the ground as they came over the top. Below, the beach and rocks looked miniature. Ahead, the enemy might appear any minute. Not a pleasant place in which to linger.

Up there on the top they found a No Man's Land of destruction, with all landmarks gone, and the ground so cratered by naval shells that if they got even five yards apart they were out of contact. The few Germans they saw quickly went to ground in a network of mined dugouts. Operating according to rehearsals, the Rangers split up to head for the gun positions, only to find them wrecked and the guns removed.

Patrols fanned out at once, in pairs of Rangers, to search for the secret spot hiding the battery, when they came under heavy fire from the south. They pushed on, nevertheless, and wiped out the two nests of resistance, though not before losing fifteen men, killed or wounded. Then they regrouped and took up a defensive position, while preparing to look again for the battery.

Meanwhile down at the foot of the cliff things were happening. By 0730 all the Ranger boat-teams were ashore, and by 0740 all were up the cliff. Just west of the promontory an anti-aircraft site started sweeping the area with fire, so a dozen of the boat-teams were sent to attack the position. Suddenly the Germans who had been driven to ground by the first assault of Rangers emerged from their tunnels and trenches and overwhelmed eleven of the twelve men. The one man to escape stumbled through the craters to the command post to tell the news, and another assault was improvised against the site. The attackers had got just half-way to the strong-point when artillery fire pounded down on the party—killing or wounding practically every man there.

Back inland the Rangers set out on their patrols at once, and at about 0900 two of them came on the missing battery down a lane off the main road. Cleverly camouflaged, the five guns were sited for fire on either Omaha or Utah beaches, and were accompanied by plentiful stocks of ammunition. But no enemy!

So the patrol of two Rangers wasted no time in case the Germans appeared, and destroyed two of the guns with incendiary grenades. While they returned for more grenades they summoned a second patrol, who polished off the job of disabling the guns and firing the ammunition. Four Rangers had put out of action potentially the most deadly enemy emplacement facing the entire American sectors of the invasion.

In case the command post did not guess by the deafening explosions, word was sent back that the main mission had been accomplished. And meanwhile the small force at the Pointe du Hoe were in something like a state of siege. Gradually, they cleaned out the Germans in that incredible maze of craters and trenches, but it was a slow business. The only signal which the commander, Colonel Rudder, could send was:

"Located Pointe du Hoe—mission accomplished—need ammunition and reinforcement—many casualties."

Down on Dog White began the assault on the bluffs. The uphill struggle—uphill in every way. Colonel Canham had an injured wrist but went on with his work. General Cota walked up and down behind the sea-wall, urging men of the 116th to get moving. Private Ingram Lambert was one who responded. He jumped over the wall, crossed the road, and set a Bangalore torpedo to clear a track. But a bullet from a machine-gun killed him. The friction igniter on the torpedo failed to act, so Second-Lieutenant Stanley Schwartz went over and fixed it. The explosive blew a big gap in the double-apron barbed-wire entanglement. The first man of the platoon to advance through the gap fell shot; others followed and got through. Captain Berthier Hawks, who had suffered a crushed foot in landing, got to the top of the bluff with his men of C Company.

A Ranger formation joined C Company. In the smoke, though, they scarcely realized that anyone else was in that area. As they advanced they had to wear gas-masks against the smoke. When they reached the top, too, they thanked the rapid retreat of the Germans, which had caused the enemy to leave their *Minen* sign as warning of a minefield—a field from which engineers later lifted 150 mines.

By 0830 the last groups were leaving Dog White, though now fire from enemy mortars began to straddle the slope up. It killed two men near General Cota, and knocked the general off his feet.

Slightly east of Dog White a group of privates moved towards Moulins Les Pins, but the head-on chatter of a machine-gun stopped them. First-Lieutenant William Williams crawled in carefully and assaulted it single-handed with a grenade; he was wounded in the process.

Owing to the general confusion of the landings, nothing was going according to plan. And the advance off the beaches in the central Dog sectors became almost individual enterprises. Few of the men knew where they were or how to get to where they should be! Small units wanted the company of larger ones, and so joined them, regardless of regiment or battalion. Sporadic enemy fire caused casualties, and the way through the mines was hard.

Back to Easy Red now. Sections of E Companies of both the 16th and

116th gapped the wire in the 100-yard-deep shingle embankment at the top of the beach, and then got delayed by mines in marshy ground at the foot of the slopes off the beach. A treacherous area. And they were attacked by firing from higher ground. One man tried to clear a path with a Bangalore but was killed by an anti-personnel mine. These anti-personnel mines were set to detonate by trip-wires and made matters difficult for a time.

There were further mined areas—and some fake minefields. G Company of the 16th found a route through the mines by the grim method of going over the bodies of two men killed there a little earlier. While the company made its way through the mines Captain Joseph Dawson took one man on ahead. Half-way up the bluff a machine-gun at the head forced them into cover. Dawson sent the soldier back to bring up the company and then crawled through the bush. The enemy lost sight of him. The next time they saw him he had circled round to a crest beyond the post, and crouched 30 feet from them. As the Germans spotted him they shouted, "Achtung!" And the gun swung round towards Dawson, who hurled a fragmentation grenade at the same instant. The Germans never fired on him, for they were all dead within a second of its exploding.

Back at the beaches the Americans were still struggling—the day was still desperately in the balance. They had as yet scarcely a toehold in Europe. By nightfall it must be a foothold if they were to succeed. The strain of streaming enemy fire was beginning to tell on the young American army. Through no fault of their own they continued to lose men and equipment. And the quicker they came ashore, the harder it was for the enemy to miss.

The American engineers could not cope with the network of underwater obstacles at the speed required by the build-up of forces, nor were they adequately equipped in strength to create the vital safe passages through the minefields behind the beaches. So even when the vehicles and armour came ashore, they could not move more than a few yards. Confusion was nearly complete. Apart from one or two spearheads thrust through the lines, the Americans were still defending rather than attacking, and the depth of their defence amounted to an average of a mere hundred yards, with the tide still rising.

The first section of the 16th Regiment command group, coming in at 0720, lost the executive officer and thirty-five men on the tidal flat. Then Colonel George Taylor brought in the second section at 0815. He found both regiments disorganized, shell-shocked, hugging the embankment, and suffering casualties all the time. He looked at the litter of bodies on the beach, the broken vehicles, and the holes made by hundreds of shells. Then he said tersely, "Two kinds of people are staying on this beach, the dead and those who are going to die—now let's get the hell out of here."

He collected small groups under N.C.O.'s and sent them through the wire and on towards the bluff-top.

At just about the time that thousands of people were going to work all over Britain another group were threading a tortuous way through the mines. They cut the wire successfully and started their job. Every second this day there was the smell of smoke and sound of shells, mortars, or machine-guns, punctuating and almost numbing their thoughts. Now mines too. The leading platoon gingerly plodded forward. The dust of the dunes blew inland with the wind.

The first bang. Second. Third. On all sides, it seemed. No panic. There could be no way back to the beaches. They had to get through. The way barred behind, mines ahead and on each flank. A corporal clutched his face wildly as one mine blew itself to bits. A private stepped just beside one— and it ripped his leg apart. Fumes from the explosive stank. Everywhere it was the same, with thin lines of wounded men marking the way: men who dare not move a muscle for fear of firing another mine. But a gap had got to be made, blown by their own lives if necessary. And at last they were through.

Along on Fox Green, north of Colleville, the second assault lines had snaked ashore across the beach, and had been hit hard on the way. Yet by 0800 an assault had started up the rises—and also on Fox Red, where the bluff merged into a partial cliff. At this eastern end of Omaha tanks were rumbling up the sloping beach, and the commander of L Company, 16th Regiment, stood up to direct their fire on to enemy resistance points. He was at once shot dead.

Another section of L Company got to the top of the hill, but had to stop suddenly and telephone the beach because fire from one of their own destroyers was focused on an enemy strongpoint only a little way ahead— and they had no wish to be hit from behind, having survived the ordeal of the beaches. As soon as the naval fire ceased the Americans stormed the strongpoint. Half the thirty German prisoners taken were wounded.

Other small isolated assaults were going on all along the front, from the extreme west beach beyond Dog Green—designated Charlie. Rangers who survived the blaze of beach tracery and mortar found themselves stuck at the base of a 90-foot cliff which was impossible to climb. They moved carefully farther west still, and 300 yards away found a crevice in the slope. Using bayonets for successive hand-holds in the cliff, and by pulling each other up, they grasped and gasped their way towards the top, monkey-walking the last part with toggle ropes attached to stakes in an enemy minefield near the crest!

The penetrations made in the period up to 1000 hours could not be followed up properly because the engineers were still working under innumerable difficulties, so that at 0800 no gaps yet existed in the shingle. Vehicles started to arrive, and threatened to clog the beaches (which were still under artillery fire), so at about 0830 vehicle landings were suspended temporarily. The 16th Regiment got its half-track tanks ashore, but could not move them more than 50 yards through the litter of disabled vehicles. Its six howitzers loaded on D.U.K.W.'s never fired, for one by one the D.U.K.W.'s were swamped, and twenty men drowned. The artillery, too, were suffering. One group was immobilized as soon as it landed. The battalion commander, Colonel Mullins, soon saw that they could never operate guns in those conditions, so he decided to make the best of it. "To hell with our artillery mission. We've got to be infantrymen now."

Colonel Mullins lived up to his words, and, although wounded twice, went to work, organizing little groups of infantry. Next he led a tank forward to direct its fire on an emplacement. The point was hit. He ran across an open stretch towards another tank—but never reached it.

The D.U.K.W.'s seemed to be far from justifying their name, for five more were swamped, and a further four lost when circling the rendezvous area: one of them turned turtle as they started the run in; another stopped with engine trouble and became a "sitting duck"; and the last pair got close enough to see there was nowhere possible to land, stopped to talk it over, and were promptly set on fire. Eight men swam ashore safely.

The heartbreaking losses to vital vehicles continued, and three L.C.T.'s struck mines at high tide. One capsized into seven feet of water, while on another a howitzer had to be jettisoned, with a huge splash, to keep the craft afloat.

The tanks which did get ashore had a rough time, trapped between high water and the embankments—a good target from the bluffs. The commander of the 74th Tanks came aground at 0820, but saltwater got into his radio, so the command group had to run up and down the bullet-swept stretches contacting their tanks. Three of the five men were killed in the process. At the other end of Omaha the commander of the 743rd Tanks, Lieutenant-Colonel John Upham, was shot down as he walked over to a tank.

Nevertheless the tanks kept on firing. An infantry battalion-commander said soon afterwards, "The tanks saved the day. They shot the hell out of the Germans, and got the hell shot out of them."

Dozens of different actions went on every minute. Naval fire was beginning to help the troops now. And landing-ships were developing bolder techniques to tackle the now-nearly submerged obstacles. L.C.T. 30 drove at full speed through them, with all weapons firing, and continuing to fire on enemy points at once on touch-down. L.C.I.544 also rammed her way through the obstacles while actually accounting for an enemy machine-gun nest in a fortified house. A barrage-balloon, broken adrift, flew crazily, surveying this scene three hours after the first seaborne troops had hit land.

0935. To a waiting world which knew nothing, yet sensed something, communique No. 1 was issued by Supreme Headquarters, Allied Expeditionary Force, announcing the opening of the Second Front.

> Under the command of General Eisenhower, Allied naval forces, supported by strong air forces, began landing Allied armies this morning on the northern coast of France.

Within minutes Britain and Occupied Europe heard the news. Over the B.B.C. morning music was interrupted as John Snagge's clear voice read the communique.

Yet at that precise time the American commanders were actually having to consider diverting part of Force Omaha through the British Force Gold beaches, though eventually the emergency measure was not necessary.

This was a crucial moment: too many vehicles, too few combat troops. The earlier waves were dug-in on the sand, but the beaches were still subjected to the deafening fire which pinned and penned the entire assault there.

Too few troops—and too few exits. How had it happened that the Americans found themselves faced with such a crisis, which, if it did not jeopardize Operation Overlord as a whole, certainly left the success of the western half of the assault in doubt?

First, since the assault craft had been lowered some twelve miles out, on a night when an on-shore wind drove the sea streaming coastward, the dangers of swamping and difficulties of navigating were naturally increased.

As Admiral Ramsay records, "In the rough weather that obtained when the assault forces arrived in the lowering positions the longer passage inshore for the assault craft from the Western Task Force appeared to add appreciably to their difficulties."

Second, the Americans aimed to land right in front of the German strong-points, instead of between them, trying to take them by direct assault.

Third, the presence of the German 352nd Division on the coast at Omaha, unknown by the Allies until too late.

Fourth, the Americans rejected Montgomery's reliance on landing heavy armour accompanied by all the specially developed designs for over-coming obstacles. Not using flail tanks, flame-throwing tanks, and anti-obstacle armoured vehicles, the Americans were left with the flotation-gear D.D. tanks, and when these could not swim ashore as planned all the 1st Division had were bulldozers. Meanwhile the severely harassed American engineers were trying gamely to neutralize pill-boxes with pole-charges, and to smash their way through barbed wire and thick concrete with packets of explosives which they had to position actually by hand, while, through their very vulnerability, they were as often as not being fired on from beyond the obstacles.

They were the first to agree with Colonel Taylor to "get the hell out of here," but the question was still how—and where?

14

The British land—with Tanks

BETWEEN four and five in the morning the first landing-craft of
the Eastern Task Force—British and Canadian—were lowered
from their parent ships, or slipped tows, some eight miles off shore,
along a line between Arromanches in the west to Ouistreham in the east.
Allied airborne forces had already been fighting for several hours over on
the mainland, while the American craft off Utah and Omaha lowered farther out to sea, were having a rough time of it.

And here in the Gold, Juno, and Sword sectors the weather was just as
bad. Gone was the watery-blue sunset some one remembered in the
Solent a day or two before, and in its place were just the wind and the
waves. Above the wind at that unlikely hour men heard a bugler somewhere actually sounding the General Salute. Then they were on their
own—little crowded craft buffeted by four-foot waves. Some of the ships
making their way across under their own steam had been forced to return.
Others kept doggedly on their course. L.C.A. 712 had been damaged by
the sea soon after leaving the Isle of Wight area, but chugged on across the
Channel until the time came to slip her tow. This caused more trouble,
with the tug vessel and the L.C.A. rising and falling at different moments,
and generally being buffeted against each other. At last the job was done,
however, and then later they really began to learn how little their troubles
had been before.

All through that night crammed craft had been moving slowly in long
columns, shepherded by such ships as corvettes, who would dash up
alongside with loud-hailers. Now, in the night's gloom, the camouflage
colours were unseen. The final briefing was past, and last evening's games
of Housey-Housey were forgotten.

Lorries and armoured vehicles jolted about on the raft-like "Rhino"
ferries, and some of these snapped their tows to add to the confusion.
Rifles and Stens slung over the rest of their kit, the men sat and rested and
thought, or were sick into the special bags issued for the purpose.

0445 The Merville battery won. Nearer now to the shore.

Every one in the D.D. units was up early for final waterproofing and sealing of the tanks. Breakfast even, and radio sets to be warmed up. Launching-drill to be dress-rehearsed for the D.D. tanks.

Over in an infantry landing-craft the Warwickshires swung and tossed in the flat-bottomed boat. They were issued bundles of maps, and at last they learned the proper name of their destination: Lion-sur-Mer. They knew they would be aiming at first for a gabled house—if it were still standing. Few managed to eat breakfast.

0515. Bombardment time. This was the precise planned hour when the leading landing-craft would come within range of the enemy coastal defences—if they could be seen so far out at sea in such a misty dawn.

So, to the accompaniment of a supporting air attack, the British Navy opened fire forty minutes before sunrise—from H.M.S. *Arethusa*, off the Orne, to H.M.S. *Ajax*, facing the famous beaches of Arromanches. H.M.S. *Ajax* engaged the only one of the enemy's heavy coastal batteries which retaliated to the bombardment. This was at Longues, between the British and American sectors. Fire from other enemy batteries at La Riviere and Ouistreham ignored the advancing landing-craft to concentrate on the capital ships—too far out to be in much danger of direct hits. This fire was largely ineffective owing to the continuing air assault—inaccurate as it inevitably was in such conditions—and the Allied measures to prevent the Germans from ranging and spotting. Credit for successful spotting in connexion with our naval barrage went to the pilots of single seater fighter aircraft, who flew to and fro over that dawn invasion coastline reporting the range and effect of the ships' guns.

Just as on the American front, this murderous assault built up in intensity as H-Hour slowly approached, and certainly did its job of occupying the defences while the landing-craft gradually throbbed within range.

Exhilarating, electrifying, exciting, provided you were not on the receiving end of the shells.

Lancasters were the aircraft chosen for Bomber Command's last pre-invasion assault on coastal defences. In the grey half-light the planes flew over mountains of thick cloud, interspersed by clear patches which revealed the dim, zig-zag wakes of invisible ships far below. This was 0453; the ships were starting to take evasive action against possible fire from the shore.

On all sides of E, for Easy, were Lancasters, converging on the shoulders of land at the mouth of the Canal de Caen.

"Right, right, steady, steady," called the bomb-aimer, lying prone in the nose.

Then the 1000-pounders went away. Now the fields and houses were visible below, plus the pattern of bombs, but nothing else. Somewhere near there would be the airborne troops, struggling to consolidate, but no signs showed.

Then, recrossing the coast, came activity at last: the first fighters. But they proved to be an anticlimax. They were American, not the Luftwaffe! Little stabs of flame shot out to sea from small explosions along the coast, but the Lancasters could not see much, for the cloud was still tantalizingly thick. Flak ships were firing now; they picked off an unlucky Lancaster on its way home.

Down below, as the aircraft struck the sea, the barrage went on where the bombers left off. Lieutenant-Colonel Hastings, of the Rifle Brigade, 6th Battalion the Green Howards, had turned in with a whisky-and-soda, slept soundly, and now awoke to the sound of the Lancasters' bombs. Now they were to be lowered after only one practice into a heavy sea, so that every wave threw the small assault landing-craft against the side of the ship. Their Marines heaved, sweated, and swore! But for ten minutes the craft could not throw off the hook which held them. Finally, after several threatened swampings, they cast off and joined the hordes of landing-craft circling round in the water.

As it grew light they could make out the shore easily, which, remarkably enough, was very much like the aerial photos they held! The water-tower still stood, and it all fitted in. Six or seven miles to go now. They tried to tow a craft that had broken down, but the rope kept snapping, so they gave up.

Meanwhile those manning the imposing tank landing-craft could see shells bursting south of the Western Task Force. The wind had dropped—but no lower than Force Five, and the sea remained rough. This was still almost too much for the amphibious tanks, so as it became lighter, and the time for launching the D.D.'s drew nearer, the tank crews awaited with interest the signal from Brigadier Prior-Palmer, on the headquarters ship. It would tell them to "swim or not to swim" the tanks. Yet this was a moment of mixed feelings, for sickness still eclipsed the sense of expectancy which they felt.

"Floater 5000."

The signal came shortly before 0630 and meant that the distance for the tanks to be swum had been shortened to 5000 yards. The L.C.T.'s closed to this distance, less than 3 miles from Sword beach, opposite Lion-sur-Mer. The big craft came into line, anchored, and, in a strong wind blowing now from the west, started to launch the two squadrons of amphibious tanks—twenty D.D. Shermans to each squadron. All the L.C.T.'s except one launched their tanks well, despite the sea, and the naval supporting fire increased in strength.

Most of the forty tanks got off to a good start after the launching. In the one craft which was unlucky in launching— L.C.T. 467, carrying the leader of B Squadron—the first tank tore its canvas and could not launch, thus blocking the way for the others in the craft. Lieutenant-Colonel Rugge-Price wanted to jettison the tank but was overruled, and the L.C.T. was eventually beached late.

L.C.T. 465 launched four of its five D.D. tanks according to plan, but the fourth broke the chains of the ramp door as it descended—so the fifth tank had to be carried back to England.

One of the tanks in A Squadron suffered ill luck too, its propellers failing to engage the water. In the sweeping surf the tank could make no headway, was soon overcome by the waves, and sank. As it went down, however, the crew inflated their rubber dinghy and pitched into it, to be rescued.

Once the tanks were in the water things went well. The crews picked up their pilot boats, and the columns steered steadily for the beach in good formation. They had never experienced so rough a sea in training, yet the tanks stood up to it all. Now that it was full-light they could see the dramatic display of the barrage bursting among the houses on the sea-front, and the fighter-bombers racing up and down dangerously low over the beach. Some of the rockets from the ships were falling very short, and Lieutenant Burgess, in one D.D., was hit by a splinter, and later died from the wound.

With the assault landing-craft, reassuringly right beside these unarmed vessels came the formidable rocket craft. Here were the Wheezers and Dodgers in spirit. Moving in closer than destroyers, cruisers, and other support ships, the rocket craft loosed searing salvoes of drenching fire on every possible point ashore; one salvo was equal to the fire-power of the whole destroyer-strength of the Royal Navy—a sobering thought. The hiss of their banks of rockets fizzed far over the waters as the craft rounded rapidly to get in position again.

Through field-glasses the Warwickshires could see their gabled house— and the spouts of shooting water as shells from all sides fell into the sea. Black-and-white smoke on the beaches; one or two Messerschmitts now, and two landing-craft actually hit by bombs. Another struck a mine, but most of them got through. Funny, whining noises now. Their first enemy fire. Thumping chests and a deep, sinking feeling in their stomachs.

And with the Eastern Task Force sailed forty-five Hedgerows— Wheezers and Dodgers once more—those tows of mortars for countermining the beaches and breaching by sheer blast as many shore defences as they could.

Like the other assault landing-craft, the L.C.A.'s carrying the Hedgerows could barely battle with the sea conditions encountered on the run in; of one flotilla of nine, all except one L.C.A. sank. Most of the Hedgerow craft came through, however, including L.C.A. 712, whose tribulations had begun the previous day. Lined up on its assault station after the trouble with the tow, it was just being prepared for firing when a 6-inch shell shattered its armoured doors. Despite this and heavy small-arms fire, the commander continued with the attack, and saw his salvo of bombs explode half-way up the beach.

Ill-equipped for such seas, the L.C.A.'s often found themselves nearly flooded by the surf, and L.C.A. 1071 shipped a lot of water. Its tow also parted before the appointed time, but it aimed towards its target: a gap in the sea-wall filled with sandbags and overlooked by a green house. Holding on his course, the commanding officer suddenly swerved to avoid the top of an obstacle popping out of the tide, and fired his Hedgerow. As he turned he saw the bombs burst on and beyond the wall. At once heavy small-arms fire from the house holed their ensign, but as the wall was breached he headed towards the parent ship. The sea still threatened to capsize the craft, but he got it back, and was hoisted inboard.

L.C.A. 876 went so close that she almost ran aground as she fired her bombs, which blew a tremendous breach in the seawall. Other Hedgerow craft fired Teller mines beneath the beaches, and on the Gold sector, especially, these pre-assault salvoes helped the men to land later.

All along the line the craft were getting nearer, nearer, and the sea more and more filled with vessels of every kind.

0710. Sea mines too had to be avoided. Dead ahead of an L.C.A. a buoy and moored mine bobbed above the surf. The helmsman heaved the wheel with all his force. The craft swung just clear of the mine, but was rammed by a tank landing-craft only a few yards away from it. The L.C.A. was holed below the water-line, and the sea swamped in fast. The hole was too jagged to be bunged. The Royal Marine coxswain called for full speed ahead on both engines.

"Starboard engine burnt out," came the answer. At this precise moment another craft collided with the L.C.A., knocking it broadside on to the beach.

Still struggling with the wheel, the coxswain righted it, and drove it close into the shore.

"Come on, boys—OUT."

The troops leapt into three feet of water and waded ashore.

Then, lightened, the craft swung round and struck a mine. No one was killed—miraculously. But next came the bullets of snipers whining down from high points beyond the beach.

The British invasion was on. The aim of the attacking force (the Second British Army) was to take the ground contained between the cities of Bayeux and Caen and the sea that day.

In the Gold sector was the 30th British Corps. There it was too rough to launch the amphibious D.D. tanks, so the assault plan had been modified at the last moment. Consequently, exactly at 0725 the first groups of Monty's armour rolled ashore from their landing-craft, and at once started clearing a way for themselves—and for the infantry to follow—through the mines. First came the specialized armour of "Crabs" (flail tanks), "Crocodiles" (flame-throwing tanks), and A.V.R.E.'s (armoured vehicles, Royal Engineers). These last were the "demolition demons." Four minutes after H-Hour, at 0729, the infantry dashed, determined, down the ramps, and on to the beaches, bullet-swept from the snipers. Later would come the D.D.'s, beaching behind the infantry.

First ashore on the right flank of Gold were the 1st Hampshires—aptly, since the invasion had largely assembled around Portsmouth and other parts of that county. Coming ashore right by Le Hamel, they found that this stronghold had almost escaped the effects of the air and sea bombardment. As the men bore bravely up the beach they were pinned down in their tracks by accurate, sustained fire from mortars and machine-guns.

But although the Allied attack had not been able to pierce the strong concrete reinforcements of the Le Hamel guns on the seaward side, the Germans did not succeed in their hope of wiping out the troops advancing up this beach. They had made two false assumptions: first, that the invaders would land at high tide and so be nearer the defences than they were; second, that their own heavy guns were protected from aerial and naval bombardment, and attacking battalions would have no means of silencing them. As it turned out, the Allied troops were outside the arc of fire of the enemy guns on landing, and by the time they were within it the specialized armour had flailed ashore, and was straining everything to cover the infantry and clear the way.

The first sight which met the men's eyes as they dug in wherever they could, or tried to reach the sea-wall, were three Crab tanks, with their flails furiously beating the beach to explode a way through the murderous mines. Resisting fierce opposition, the Crabs continued up the sand, leaving their tracks as evidence of their dire determination to get through They did not last long, however, before they were hit by enemy fire, and stopped. Some of the crews staggered out and joined up with the infantry.

One Crab actually got off the beach area and engaged the main enemy strong-point in a sanatorium overlooking the shore. Finally this Crab too went the way of the others.

In the same brigade were the 1st Dorsets, who landed at a point east of the Hampshires. Here the A.V.R.E.'s and other armoured vehicles were much more than a match for a sketchy defence system. They levelled practically every obstruction in sight; made sure that the patches of clay on the beach were well covered, so that the D.D. tanks and others would not get stuck; filled in potholes caused by shells from Allied or enemy fire: and unwaveringly erupted routes through the widespread mines. The Crabs really took the offensive—perhaps this was the first time tanks had done so in an invasion from the sea. Within a couple of hours they were bursting to the west behind Arromanches.

In the Gold sector, as elsewhere throughout the British beachheads, thoroughly prepared plans were enforced to tackle the layer after layer of underwater and surface obstacles known to have multiplied during the spring. In fact, the Germans' Western Wall stretched right out to the line of low water in such a way that the obstacles were covered at high tide. One of the reasons why Montgomery landed at half-tide was to make the job of tackling these submerged snares a little less hazardous. But, in fact, the full advantage was not quite gained, since the tempestuous tide of that night and the next morning swept the sea in thirty minutes or more ahead of its scheduled time.

All along the beaches the frogmen went in with the first fighting troops. They were men of the Royal Navy and Royal Marines, like Lieutenant R. E. Billington, R.N.V.R., who commanded the courageous band of three other R.N.V.R. officers, a captain, and five other non-commissioned Marines. These ten men were with the first of the Landing-Craft Obstruction Clearance Units, and nearly all were "Hostilities Only" men, who, before the War, had been engineers, carpenters, and clerks.

As their landing-craft neared the shores from Arromanches to Ouistreham they prepared for this operation which would have so vital effect on later waves of craft. And they thought especially of Element C, which had been produced in considerable quantity, and formed a formidable network designed to destroy any craft that hit it.

Element C was a 2¼-ton mass of steel mesh, like a 10-foot-high and 10-foot-broad picket fence under the water. Each fence would have to be —scientifically destroyed as it could not be liquidated merely by a single explosion. Because the tide was running in early, Element C became more deeply submerged than had been intended, and the frogmen looked apprehensive as they watched the water rolling inshore ahead of the landing-craft. Then they had to contend with five-foot metal pyramids, completely hidden by the tide.

To all these vicious obstacles was attached some explosive mechanism—mine or shell—so that even if the landing-craft merely grazed its bottom against one of them, a concentrated charge right below it would detonate and wreck the craft. Even if there was no contact with a mine, the strength of the steel alone was liable to tear a fatal hole in the light landing-craft.

For five intensive months they had been preparing. And what a new world it was for them! Wearing the now familiar skin-thin diving-suits made of rubber, and flapping fins on their feet of the same material, they began the basic work of human self-propulsion beneath the sea. Fitted to their suits were protective helmets, and breathing gear to keep them alive. That was the first thing, to swim and breathe in their strange seaworld—but it marked only the beginning. Next they must be prepared to handle highly lethal hazards and horrors, all aimed at destroying any invasion craft—or themselves. Now all those months of training were about to be distilled and channelled into the first and most important part of their invasion work.

Coming in with the 6th Green Howards and 5th East Yorkshires on that east end of Gold beach, opposite La Riviere, Lieutenant H. Hargreaves tried to remember what he had learned. Yet somehow it all seemed utterly strange. Then fully four hundred yards out, the enemy opened up on them, and as the craft came closer the shells spluttered in the surrounding water.

With Hargreaves were eleven men in the unit. An L.S.I deposited them into their small craft at exactly 0700, and although many of them scarcely expected to survive the day, they never hesitated for an instant. Mustering maximum speed, the craft went for the beach, to find that the first obstructions were already more than awash and a long way out to sea—in fact, they were covered by half a fathom.

In view of the frequent firing, the sooner they could slip over the side the better for all concerned. So, without wasting time, they got to grips with a row of unpleasant-looking posts, sprouting with mines on top. There was nothing they could do about the firing. Somehow they had to try and forget it. So it was really just as well that the job in hand took all their energies. The double danger continued minute after minute that morning: the mines to be tackled on top of posts, and the chance of being hit while only half-hidden in the incoming tide.

After the posts, Hargreaves and his fellow-officer on the La Riviere sector had to face the next problem: wooden ramps and steel structures, both

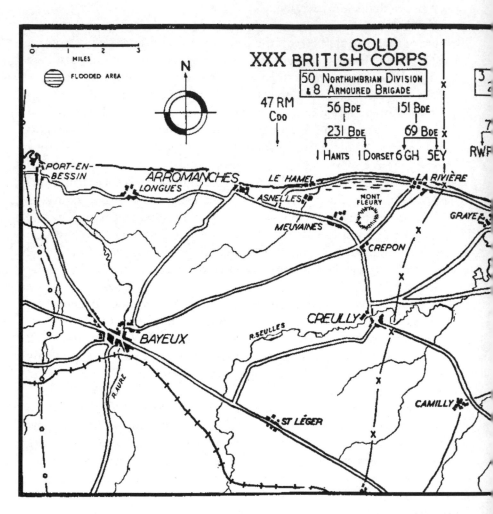

GOLD
XXX BRITISH CORPS

50 Northumbrian Division & 8 Armoured Brigade

47 RM Cdo

56 Bde

151 Bde

231 Bde

69 Bde

1 Hants   1 Dorset 6 GH 5 EY

RWF

THE BRITISH A

E Y = East Yorkshires; G H = Green Howards; N S R
Own Rifles; Regina R = Regina Rifles; R M Cdo = Ro
S L = South Lancashires;

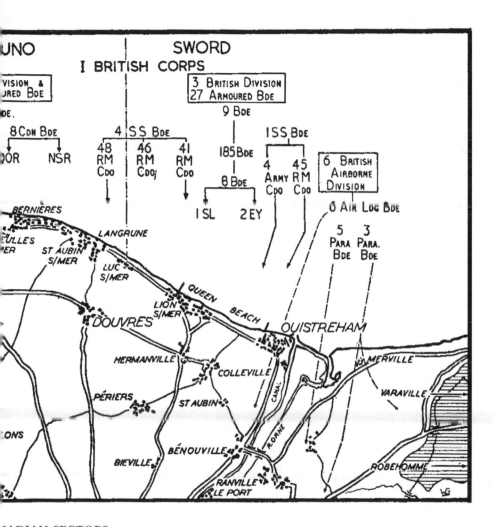

decked out with deadly mines or shells. As calmly as they could they worked towards the shore, while fire from the defences fell all around them. It proved a terribly tiring task, but soon they had cleared a minimum opening for the following landing-craft to use safely, and they widened it as quickly as they could.

The special kapok jerkin, tested so gallantly in Horsea Lake only a few weeks earlier, proved itself immediately, protecting them against the severe blast from mines and shells under water. In fact, a little farther along the coast the jerkin was instrumental in three men of Hargreaves's party surviving.

Operating just out of his depth, a naval petty officer frogman was suddenly stunned by a shell or mortar bomb, fired from land, which fell near by. The blast cannonaded through the intervening water, sending him reeling into unconsciousness. One of his colleagues managed to swim over to him and help him to the surface. The petty officer was shocked severely, but after a while recovered completely. Without the jerkin he would never have survived the initial blast, for another man, making for the shore and not so near to the scene, was killed.

Another frogman dived for his first live mine obstruction. Groping around the base of a steel pole, he found it. No sun shone through the murky water, and the mine was attached so close to the bottom that the mud churned up as he gripped it gently. This was the real thing. For a second he held his breath behind his breathing equipment, and then tried to relax. He could scarcely see the mechanism, but somehow his fingers closed round the right part, and in a few moments the mine was harmless. Half the job was done. Then he set the small explosive charge in order to get rid of the obstruction itself, and as he swam to a safe distance it cracked through the water, bringing the pole toppling towards him. One less hazard to tackle. Not as bad as it might have been, he thought, as he headed on to the next.

Meanwhile Hargreaves was finding the going hard, purely from the physical point of view. The heavy surf swept in powerfully towards the flat beach, and he had difficulty in keeping still enough to handle the innumerable mines and booby traps with which the obstacles were equipped.

Slowly, however, he and all the other frogmen forced their way inshore, until near the beach they began to sense the added danger of sniping as the concealed Germans, still within range of the shore, in houses or elsewhere, looked on them as sitting targets. Machine-guns raked the beach too. That must have been worst of all: to be handling death in the water every minute and at the same time to know that somewhere behind their backs were the snipers' guns, trained on them.

On and on they worked. There seemed no end to the nightmare of the obstacles, with the ingredients of sudden death concealed about them. Hargreaves and the others eventually cleared 1000 yards of beach throughout the depth of 400 yards. Altogether this party destroyed or disposed of 2500 obstacles— practically every one of them mined.

Hargreaves himself was wounded in the shoulder, but carried on with his job to win the D.S.C.

The landings which took place on that morning of unrelieved greyness and gunfire claimed two frogmen killed and ten wounded, some seriously. Ten per cent. casualties—lower than had been expected for such a risky job.

So the work went on, and landing-craft of every kind poured through the gaps. Of course, the frogmen could not clear more than an initial lane through the murderous mesh   there were far too few of them to do more. But most of the craft came in safely. Many had to risk uncleared approaches, because the time element was vital, and the safe channels were too narrow for them all to pass through.

Regularly after 0730 there came rending sounds, as the bottoms of the landing-craft scraped to a standstill against the obstacles, and the men had to pile out into the water and swim ashore with full loads. Or, if they were less lucky, the obstacles ripped the bottoms right out of the boats, which were left in anything from two to ten feet of water, and with gaping holes. A few sparked off mines, and the spray spurted over the craft as they cracked with the blast. One moment men crouched in an L.C.A.; the next they struggled in the water. Yet not many were lost.

And all the time the frogmen worked, disconnecting the mines in the gloom of the sea-bed, and then breaking up the obstructions of steel and concrete with their own explosives. Element C, in ten or more feet of water, was the worst nightmare. Totally submerged, the frogmen swam horizontally, their arms stretched straight at their sides and fins flapping, around strange, sinister-looking steelwork. They planted their thirty-six small charges one by one at strategic points on the structure, and then swam out of the way as it exploded. One more example of Element C went to pieces and fell to the seafloor—where it lay, only 18 inches high. It was now too deep to damage any craft.

The craft came in—through the gaps and grinding to a halt. The last yard or two; one of the big landing-craft pressed on the sand, and a Teller mine sprang into life. And death followed for many of the men. Other Tellers caught craft or men, but the assault did not waver.

Luckily the resistance was weaker at La Rivière than at Le Hamel, for the Allied bombardment had done its job better. Much of the tiny town looked a mere mass of jagged brickwork as the infantry stepped ashore. Since the D.D. tanks could not get in yet, support craft came close behind the men in an attempt to cover the hectic moments of landing. Firing only a few feet above the heads of their own men, these floating support weapons aimed at finishing off the defences which still survived after the barrage. Sergeants waved to their platoons to follow them as they splashed through the water and dashed for cover. But, by a fluke, the 5th East Yorkshires landed at a point which was untouched by the earlier holocaust. The men tore towards the sea-wall for their very lives as they met this mass of bullets and shells. One fell killed. A bullet stung into the leg of another as he ran. He stopped for a second, dropped flat, and crawled, blinded by pain, for the wall. Only a few yards. Dimly he saw it. Somehow it didn't seem to get nearer. Would he ever get there? Would he? Pain. Then he passed out. Perhaps he would be rescued later. Perhaps not. But the battle went on just the same.

An 88-mm. gun shelled the vehicles as they drove ashore. It got a couple of the vital A.V.R.E.'s. A flail-tank churned its way through the last yards of shallows. It was about to touch the shingle as an 88-mm. shell hit it. Thick smoke poured out of it. Troops behind took advantage of the cover to race diagonally ashore as the wind blew the smoke south east.

Then the shells began again.

"Get down and don't bunch," yelled a corporal. Less chance of casualties.

But the strong-point did not last long. Its guns had a limited angle of fire, so another flail tank sped in at a sharp angle, and smashed it for ever from under 100 yards.

Off the beach now, through the grassy dunes. The enemy fell back to fresh positions and machine-gunned the dunes. The thin grasses waved as the bullets flew overhead. The Tommies moved into extended order as they stepped cautiously over the rubble of a brick wall, then on towards the town, with close range fighting from shop to shop. A line of bullets kicked holes up a white wall.

On the beach west of La Rivière snipers had stopped the 6th Green Howards in their damp tracks. They dug in wherever they could, but until the A.V.R.E.'s drove ashore they were at a standstill. From behind the shelter of a wall the Germans mixed grenades with snipers' fire. Then the A.V.R.E.'s reached the upper beach, and, covered by two of them, the infantry stormed up to the wall and hit the enemy point-blank on the once-peaceful sea-road. After a brief period of resistance the sight of the demolition vehicles startled the Huns, who began to retreat. So the value of armour was beginning to be apparent all along the British line.

One company of the Green Howards negotiated a minefield, with only minor losses, and then found themselves confronted by stronger enemy resistance. They were on their way to take the important Mont Fleury battery, which had already been well pasted by both the R.A.F. and the Navy.

Despite resistance, they were making good headway towards the battery when the company commander noticed that two of the enemy pillboxes on the route had been bypassed by the leading platoons.

Thus started an action which earned the one Victoria Cross won on D-Day.

Taking Company-Sergeant-Major Stanley Hollis with him, the commander advanced to try and clear them. When they were only 20 yards from this live pill-box a machine-gun opened fire from the slit, and C.S.M. Hollis instantly rushed straight at it, firing his Sten gun through the grid. In a split second Hollis jumped on top of the actual pill-box as he recharged his magazine and forced it home. At the same time he wrenched out a grenade and threw it through the door of the pill-box, following it with Sten fire. Two Germans dropped dead, and Hollis rushed in and held up the rest as prisoners. As soon as they were safely taken he ran over to a neighbouring trench, and cleared several of the enemy out of it. By this action he certainly saved the rest of his company from being heavily fired on from the rear, and so enabled them to open the main beach exit from this end of Gold sector.

Taking the V.C. story to its end, later on D-Day, in the village of Crepon, the company encountered a field gun and crew armed with Spandaus, at 100 yards' range. Hollis was put in command of a party to cover an attack on the gun, but the movement was held up. Seeing this, he pushed right forward to engage the gun with a Piat from a house at 50 yards' range. He was observed by a sniper, who fired; the bullet grazed his cheek. At the same second the enemy gun swung round, and fired at point-blank range into the house. Masonry started to fall all around them, so Hollis moved his party to another position. Two of the enemy gun crew had by this time been killed, and the gun itself was destroyed soon afterwards.

But Hollis then learned that two of his men had stayed behind in the house. He at once went to try and get them out. In full view of the enemy, who continually fired at him, he went forward quite alone, using a Bren gun to distract their attention from the two other men. Under cover of this heroic diversion they were able to run back to the company—and Hollis too got back safely.

Wherever the fighting was heaviest throughout the day Hollis displayed daring and gallantry, and on both these occasions he alone prevented the enemy from holding up the advance of the Green Howards at critical stages.

As the citation ends: "It was largely through his heroism and resource that the company's objectives were gained and casualties were not heavier; by his own bravery he saved the lives of many of his men."

As C.S.M. Hollis was busy clearing the pill-box near the Mont Fleury battery the reserve companies of the Green Howards came in under mortar fire. The commander of C Company was killed at once.

As Lieutenant-Colonel Hastings's craft beached, their view was hidden by smoke. They passed the first obstacles—old rusty shells on poles sticking out of the water. An A.V.R.E. on the beach exploded in a searing sheet of flame.

Hastings pointed to the spot where he wanted to land, but the L.C.M. was not exactly responsive. They swung broadside on to the shore, missing the shells on poles by only a few feet, and then came to premature rest quite a long way from the beach. But the L.C.M. was definitely grounded. Hastings called out, "Lower ramps."

But nothing happened. The mechanism was jammed. There could be no worse place in which to delay. Then a huge ex-guardsman applied his square shoulder—the ramp opened. The beach looked far off and the water deep. Hastings walked to the edge of the ramp and then sat down and dangled his feet over the edge—"not a very inspiring performance," he recalled. The water was only up to his knees. Without any difficulty they waded ashore, and scrambled up the beach.

An occasional cry from within the wire of the minefield proved that it was not a dummy lay. As they got to the top of the incline the first flail tank came up to it, having cleared a gap from the beach for vehicles. The operation was proceeding exactly to plan. Hastings ordered his tanks to follow up through this gap; they had now completed the first phase of their task. As he toured the companies he saw the mass of shipping still nosing inshore, and mortaring on the beach. Despite the enemy opposition still to be encountered, the most serious moment of the day for the 6th Green Howards came when a friendly Frenchwoman plied them with cider so strong that their whole advance appeared to be endangered by drunkenness!

While the 30th British Corps hammered it out on Gold Beach the 1st British Corps had been allocated Juno and Sword beaches—the 3rd Canadian Division on Juno and the 3rd British on Sword. Away on the far left, beyond the Orne, was the 6th British Airborne Division. Due south of the line between Juno and Sword lay the key to the ultimate success of the bloody battle which was being fought to establish the beach-heads—the key of Caen.

Reefs and rocks were additional hazards in the central Juno sector, and because of these and the tide the landings here had to be timed later than on any other beach. The defences thus received the longest warning of the Allied approach. Even chugging in as carefully as possible, several craft fouled the rocks or went aground on the reefs, and so became perfect targets.

The divisions which were to land on these beaches had stiff tasks, since the enemy's mobile position was known to be much stronger here than behind the American sector of the coast. Once again the weather prevented the amphibious tanks swimming ashore as planned; as at Gold beach, they had to be disembarked directly on to the beach after the infantry had landed.

H-Hour was fixed for 0735–0745, but it became clear that it would have to be later, as the Canadians' craft rolled uneasily through seas heavier even than elsewhere. The air and sea barrage missed most of the shore strong-points, and the stage seemed tragically set for a repetition of what was already occurring on Omaha: raw, savage slaughter.

The tide was driving in violently now, washing over the middle of the underwater obstacles. The 0735 landing-plan accepted as inevitable that many obstacles would be submerged, but by now the situation was worse. And each passing minute meant that the defences had longer to revive, after the noisy, if inaccurate, bombardment.

Most of the landing-craft got through the maze of mined obstacles at the low-water mark. With the usual near-misses and occasional hits they hit the beaches at about 0800 astride Courseulles-sur-Mer. At this late hour the engineers had little time to tackle the obstructions before the tide made it a task for frogmen.

The troops of the 7th Canadian Brigade picked their way ashore actually through the beach booby traps, to be greeted with fire focused on them from both banks of the mouth of the Seulles.

They looked round for the A.V.R.E.'s, or for some other armour—but none was in sight. Because of the battle, the assault vehicles were well back and had to plough a path through the surf. Then, with a serious situation developing, the Canadian infantry whistled with relief as they glanced behind them to see the first batch of D.D. tanks. The tank landing-craft had come within half a mile of the high-water mark to tip the D.D.'s out among the mines. One or two at once had their floats, tracks, and everything blasted by mines, but the rest came roaring out of the shallows to support the men.

The troops rushed the beach with dramatic daring, streaming Sten gun fire at the pill-boxes and foxholes. The D.D.'s loosed their heavy armament at the biggest sources of opposition. Buoyed by this success, the infantry pushed inland at the rate of a mile an hour, but the inevitable crowding of vehicles and armour on the beach slowed up the second waves of assault. Nevertheless, by 1000 all beach objectives had been gained, only two hours after touch-down: great credit to these tough Canadians, who had been training all spring in the heathland around Witley, Surrey.

While they stormed the beach the tide rose still farther, and the empty landing-craft returning to sea ran into trouble with the outer rows of obstacles. Of one battalion's twenty-four landing-craft all except four failed to get back to their parent ships, either being sunk by mines or ripped and rent against the steelwork.

The 8th Canadian Brigade attacked opposite Bernières, quite alone. This was a narrow front, and the sea swirled around the rocks. An attempt to launch the tanks through these breakers would be bound to fail. So it was up to the Canadian and French-Canadian troops.

The early craft came reeling in on top of the surf, and were deposited higher than expected up the beach. As the troops suddenly found themselves there, with the waves receding, they saw a stretch of only 100 yards from the ramps to the sea-wall at the back of the beach. But every yard of it was covered and cross-covered by the Bernières defenders.

One company sprinted straight for the wall. Half of them were shot on the spot and never reached it. Some only moved a few yards before being killed, and the incoming tide washed over them.

In less than a quarter of an hour, though, the leading Canadian troops took all the strong-points. The last one fell when a flak-ship ran the gauntlet of rocks and fire to run in opposite the enemy, and saturate them from a range of only the depth of the beach. The follow-up regiment landing soon after 0800 met only sniping. Then the armour came ashore, with the troops supporting it. And as the armour engaged any enemy remaining the infantry swept into Bernières: French-Canadians liberating the land of their forefathers.

Apart from the infantry, the worst losses here were to big landing-craft bringing in the armour. Beach obstacles and Teller mines took their toll of damage.

What was it really like? Here are the recollections of one Canadian, Cliff Bowering, who was there with them:

That dryness in your mouth, the tongue like cotton wool, the cold, unreasoning slab in your belly. The sense of anticipation that defies description.

Your heartbeat trying to outdo the sound of gunfire and bombs. The wondering of what it will be like on the beach.

All the old clichés running through your head. Your nervous smile—but the effort hurts your dried lips.

Somebody laughs, only it sounded more like a croak. And it was too loud. The one-in-every-crowd wiseguy.

"Home was never like this . . . not much like the old ferry back home . . . I wonder who's missing me now. . . it's Paris first chance I get . . . anyone for tennis . . . "

"Can the chatter back there, we're going in."

The exact minute had arrived.

The ramp crashes down. You see what looks like ten miles of water between you and the beach. For the first time you realize two things . . . somebody's shooting at you, and there are a hell of a lot of ships on either side. And you're shooting back with a barrage that stuns the imagination.

You're in the water now. In the breakers. You try to remember how to walk in the water and keep your rifle up and dry. Yard by yard you move in. Smoke up ahead and the noise . . . it's like nothing you've ever heard before, even in the blitz. What a difference between this and battle camp. Brother, this is for real!

Wade some more. Shells sloughing into the water near a barge. Chug-crunch. A barge hit. A man goes down, and you lunge forward in fear. But he's up again—only stumbled. Beach up ahead. Another man down. He doesn't get up. Tracer to the left. Machine-guns. Planes diving in—R.A.F. You lovely babies from hell!

In the background the steady rumble and swoosh of the navy guns. God bless 'em! Softening up, they called it. And all last night and this morning pounding, pounding, pounding the pride of the Third Reich.

Your head tucked into your shoulders like a boxer weaving towards his target. Smaller target that way? Crouching lower as you walk, pretending you can't be seen—maybe.

Your mouth drier still. Hoping you don't have to speak, because you couldn't. Rifle up higher. You're on the beach. Rifle at the port. Shells coming in on the right. Machine-guns. Men falling. Funny, no one around you has been hit. This isn't so bad after all.

You think pretty clearly after that. Now you know what all that training was for. This is the job and things are going well. Too easy . . . a dull smack, a groan. The man beside you goes down, doesn't move. Face in the water. You move on. Sniper? Sniper, hell! That's a machine-gun. Let's go. Up to the sea-wall and down, and wait for orders. Orders.

The tanks didn't get in ahead of you like they planned. One of those things. You move on. Town called Bernières. One company badly shot up. Not yours, thank God.

Soon he was in Courseulles, and the Canadian who had cracked about Paris could at least claim to have taken over the Hotel de Paris there, off causeway No. 6, which was henceforth "Interdit aux Civiles."

Next came the Commandos.

A Mulberry harbour in operation. Some of the blockships can be seen in the background.

Spud pierheads enabled the floating roadways to rise and fall with the tide.

After the assault the dead lay where they fell.

The French commandos hurry ashore, complete with bicycles.

15

The Commandos storm in

SALUTE the Marines. Ten thousand took part in the D-Day operation. Two-thirds of the assault landing-craft delivering the infantry on the beaches were manned by Marines. Through the stormy seas they brought the fleet safely to landfall, and even then their job was not always done. Take the case of Sergeant Hunter.

Just before reaching one of the Juno beaches his L.C.A. received a damaging hit. The troops piled out, but the crew of Royal Marines could not return as planned. Sergeant Cecil Hunter and his crew had to take to the beach, and he at once looked round to see what he could do to help the assault. Near by the Canadians were exchanging a furore of fire with German mortars and snipers, but they wanted to keep in contact with the captain of a tank beached 30 yards away.

Hunter immediately decided to act as liaison between the Canadian sergeant-major and the tank captain. The two men had to pass messages if some sort of plan were to be made to get off that beach. Only thirty yards intervened—but the beach was constantly soaked with fire from rifles, mortars, and now other guns. Right through this concentration he crawled to take the first message. He waited for an answer, and then returned to deliver it. Snipers saw him, and adjusted their sights. He had some close shaves before getting back to comparative cover. Twice, that was. Then the fight flared more fiercely, and once more he had to get across those open yards. Every move with his arms or legs could have been his last Then another answer, making four journeys. Somehow he survived to win the C.G.M.

So to the Royal Marine Commandos. Four formations went into action on D-Day itself, Nos. 48 and 41 linking the Juno and Sword sectors. No. 48 Commando was to land next to the Canadians and swing left, and No. 41 was to land beside the British on Sword and swing right. Both these Commandos, together with Nos. 46 and 47, were part of the 4th Special Service Brigade, whose task was to land in the vicinity of Lion-sur-mer, take certain coastal villages (including Luc-sur-Mer, Langrune, and St Aubin-sur-Mer), push inland, and capture a strong-point at Douvres.

As at other points along the coast, the well-intentioned but ill-directed bombardment before the actual assault had not hit its targets, so that strong defence remained at St Aubin-sur-Mer, while the six little landing-craft of No. 48 Commando jogged and jolted shoreward. It was not only the sea that disturbed two of them, however, as they suddenly struck underwater obstructions in quick succession. Still a good way from shore, the Commandos felt the craft sinking lower in the water each second, and they could only just jump clear before both of them shipped so much water that they sank. The sea swept many Commandos out on the backlash of the tide, to be drowned beneath the weight of water and equipment. Some swam into their depths, though, behind the other craft, furiously flailing the water in their efforts to support sodden clothes, and even boots.

The moment they beached, the Commandos were met by a murderous hail of machine-gun, mortar, and shell fire. A mortar bomb burst near Lieutenant-Colonel Moulton, the commanding officer. Dazed, he dashed on. Captain M. B. Reynolds ran right into the deadly dots from a machine gun, which broke both his arms. He did not stop till he reached the Commandos' assembly area.

Wounded were soon scattered up and down the sand and shingle, and the padre, the Rev. John Armstrong, R.N., stayed exposed there, tending and comforting them as best he could. But, moving from one to another, he was hit and badly wounded himself. This was the Church Militant.

The survivors of the two wrecked landing-craft came ashore into this same inferno, and one was killed at once. But before long the Commandos assembled at their pre-arranged point, where a quick count showed a strength of 70 per cent. Captain Reynolds was losing blood fast, but insisted that he was all right, refusing to leave until actually ordered to do so later.

Despite the absence of every third man of the force, the Commandos grouped themselves ready for their task of taking the German strong-point at Langrune, just over half a mile from the beach: a fortification complete with pill-boxes and other devices for easy defence.

Meanwhile, 4 miles farther east, just into the Sword Sector, No. 41 Commando, under Lieutenant-Colonel Gray, found the reception even hotter than that of No. 48. Their targets were a strong-point at Lion-sur-Mer and another one believed to exist in an inland château.

Accordingly the Commando was to be divided into two separate assault units on landing. The plan was fated not to work out in practice. Although an advance message had stated that their particular beach was not being strongly defended by the enemy, the troops met fierce fire as they touched down. An immediate casualty was Major Barclay, killed before he could begin to lead Force No. 2 towards the château.

Captains Stratford and Morris were wounded, so the officer strength suffered a cut at the outset. Gray had to act fast; he took over Force No. 2 himself, but at once had to halve it to send help to Force No. I, facing the German strong-point in Lion-sur-Mer. The two mobile radio transmitters had been additional casualties in the water or on the beach, and so they could not summon any naval guns to assist them as arranged. Plans had a habit of not working, like the two damaged transmitters.

All morning the Commandos fought in face of overwhelming opposition. One troop succeeded in scrambling to some battered brick houses almost adjoining their objective, but then came the reaction of a counter-attack. After the inevitable withdrawal, again they assaulted the Lion strong-point, with some raw hand-to-hand combat, and eventually occupied it. This was a vital success for the 3rd British Division advancing off Sword, the division whose task was the most important of all to Operation Overlord.

By afternoon the depleted force found that its situation had become brighter. The Commandos scrounged a transmitter from somewhere—no one will ever know how!—so that then they could call up the destroyers for fire. But they had to be reinforced by battalions of Lincolnshires and Royal Ulster Rifles before they could ultimately take both the strong-point and the château the next day.

H.M.S. *Arethusa* and the rest of the warships in Naval Force S laid down by far the most effective and concentrated bombardment of any along the coast that morning of D-Day. On to the Sword strip between Lion-sur-Mer and Ouistreham, a mere 3 miles, they aimed an accurate and sustained barrage. First, the smoke and flashes from heavy guns against the lead-grey horizon; then the flashes ashore as the shells straddled the 800-yard depth of shore under attack. From 0515 to 0715 the attack continued, and in the middle of it Fortresses and Liberators—the latter well named for D-Day—released a rain of bombs that made the ground shake and shudder as each stick exploded. Once more the fighter-bombers flew almost at sea-level, just high enough to keep above the naval guns. And a heartening sight: a French squadron with the Cross of Lorraine painted poignantly on the sides of their planes. Their pilots saw their beloved France through the mists and dust below. From their hard-won positions on the Orne the airborne men listened to the bombing and looked over the few intervening miles as each fresh eruption lit up the dawn. Roaring rockets, the shiver of shells, and bombs bursting.

0715. The deafening crescendo—and then sudden silence as the craft sailed the last few minutes.

Unheard above the bombardment, however, a drama was taking place at sea. Despite a fairly heavy sea, two squadrons of D.D. tanks (of the 13th/18th Hussars) started to swim ashore from 4500 yards. These were overtaken by L.C.T.'s with A.V.R.E.'s. All went well for a mile or so, and enemy opposition was restricted to shell fire at craft from light batteries ashore. Bad visibility made accurate fire at the craft impossible, and losses were negligible. But this same lack of visibility caused a flotilla of large L.C.T.'s to head in right before the bows of the amphibious tanks. In a moment two of the tanks—at the best of times scarcely suited for navigating in a sea like this— had been hit by the tank landing-craft, and sank. Luckily a group of enemy rockets spluttering in the sea all around the L.C.T.'s forced them to adjust their course promptly. No more tanks were rammed, and, by a skill in navigation which rose to the emergency, the crews of the amphibians managed to avoid further accidents.

Captain Denny's tank was 700 yards from the beach when it sank after this collision. He was thrown clear, and picked up half an hour later, but although the rest of the crew had Mae Wests and escape apparatus, they never appeared again. All the crew of the other tank which had been sunk were saved.

0725. About half of the tanks reached the Queen beach,[1] in the Sword sector, abreast of the infantry. They touched down well to seaward of the beach obstacles, and were then converted, so that they could run on land. And there and then, hulls down in the water, they began to neutralize enemy fire from houses and emplacements. Some tanks were inevitably knocked out by shell fire, while others were swamped in the shallows by breakers. Despite flooded turrets, these tanks kept on firing until the guns were awash and the crew had to bale out. The rest of the 200–300 yards to the beach they covered in their rubber dinghies, dangerously exposed to the enemy.

Other armour arrived actually just ahead of the first waves of D.D. tanks, so that as the L.C.A.'s beached between 0725 (H-Hour on Queen White) and 0730 they already had the planned support of tanks and clearance vehicles.

As the assault started, so the job of the midget submarines ended. X-20 off Arromanches, and X-23 just a little way out off the Orne, headed north again. Soon the crews would be back in Blockhouse, sleeping soundly.

But not the 1st South Lancashires or 2nd East Yorkshires, of the 8th British Brigade. Exactly at 0730, as the armour opened fire from the water's edge, the South Lancashires slid ashore at Queen White to get clear

---

[1] Between Lion-sur-Mer and the western outskirts of Ouistreham, and divided into three sectors: Green, White, Red (reading eastward).

of their craft safely and swiftly. The defence seemed slightly less strong here than at other points, perhaps because of the supporting armour.

But, even so, the troops walked into a stutter of Spandaus and through the inevitable haze of smoke. Mortars against men; but then the D.D.'s cracked into action again, and the enemy fire slackened.

The amphibious Sherman tanks of C Squadron, 13th/18th Hussars, followed ashore at 0810, which was just as well, for the first two squadrons were depleted badly by that time. Out of the twenty in A Squadron only six survived, yet their job was done well. And when the leading tank of B Squadron first moved up the beach only one other tank of this twenty was in sight. These two joined forces and reached the sand-dunes. Unable to cross these, Captain Neave brought up a bulldozer to force a gap through; soon the shore was more or less clear, with the South Lancashires prodding forward fast into the dunelands.

By 0830 the infantry and the A.V.R.E.'s flailing away up the beach had cleared two or three exits for the remaining tanks, and then they swung rapidly right to take Hermanville within the next hour.

C Squadron blew off its special waterproofing and moved towards the newly made beach exits, leaving the beach still congested with men and vehicles. Through the sand were left the crazy trails of lorry wheels and tank tracks.

Meanwhile our little group of Warwickshires had stumbled ashore towards their gabled-end house, which by now seemed like the residence of an old relation. Guiding them safely ashore, it beckoned them up the beach and under cover. No one seemed hurt, thanks to their mascot—the house. Now it had played its part, and they hastened on to their real objective, which was, ironically—the cemetery!

Then they met their first Frenchman, complete with shabby beret and prominent spectacles. He wore an armband bearing the initials F.F.I. "Mine, Mine!" he shouted, pointing to their intended route across the fields. They ploughed on—almost literally—with mine detectors to the fore, but no mine revealed itself, and soon they reached the cemetery. There they dug in.

Peace for ten minutes, before snipers and machine-guns broke out.

"We're in the right spot," some one whispered grimly.

Their sniper team stalked silently through the near-by corn to track the enemy snipers, and soon one of these fell from a tree. One of the Warwickshires was hit in the knee and had to limp back to base. Then they cleared out of the cemetery—leaving about a dozen men there....

Farther east, at Ouistreham, the 2nd East Yorkshires had their landing-craft driven relentlessly through barricades of beach obstacles to get ashore.

There, on Queen Red beach, the opposition was stronger than on adjacent beaches, and they fought from one position to the next.

Once more the Commandos came to the rescue. The No. 45 Commando under Lieutenant-Colonel Ries formed part of Brigadier Lord Lovat's 1st Special Service Brigade, whose task was to clear Ouistreham, push southward, and link up with the 6th Airborne Division, who had been holding their positions on the Orne since the early hours of the morning. They beached on the western outskirts of Ouistreham and helped to rid the east end of the beach of small-arms fire, and cover it for the East Yorkshires.

After this little sideshow they proceeded to their main task of crossing the Caen Canal and river Orne, and then seizing the bridgehead on the far side of the river, thus holding the left flank of the whole Allied perimeter. They brought rubber dinghies and collapsible bicycles with them, but the dinghies were not needed, since the 6th Airborne Division had timed its attack from the east of the Orne so well that the Germans had been sufficiently surprised to neglect the blowing up of the bridges.

Ries led his men across the intact bridges, but an enemy sniper got the colonel in his sights, and he had to retire wounded. Major Gray took over from him, and No. 45 Commando moved steadily north towards Merville, which they knew to be already in the hands of the Allied airborne troops.

So the Allied beachhead began to take shape, but at 1000 on D-Day it was still too early to claim complete success.

16

"Get the Hell out of Here"

YOU could call it a beachhead—just. As the second wave of assault troops trod ashore on beaches from Utah to Sword the battle began in ruthless reality: the fight for a foothold. Craft carrying the initial assault troops returned north and passed the next wave; with these came jeeps, tanks, guns.

Still the sea proved an extra enemy. The tide rose higher now, and many of the landing-craft could not get far enough inshore. As they lowered their ramps the waves tilted them to an impossible angle for use, or else they snapped off altogether as if broken by some angry giant. So the men were left to jump for it, into three, four or five feet of water, or slide desperately down the buckled ramps. And ashore it was the same story as before on many of the beaches: shells, bombs, bodies, savage shooting.

Utah was neither worse nor better than most. The special squads were still struggling with the mines and obstacles, using inadequate equipment, and they now came under steady shelling. Too often the way through the mines was marked only by a wounded engineer waiting to be evacuated. But by 1000 hours they had made minimum gaps for the reinforcement regiment to land. Scorning the shells, the fresh troops moved north-west towards the area intended for the first landings.

Jeeps, tanks, and guns all arrived for unloading, marking the signal for the infantry to strike out across the causeways over the flooded regions just behind the beaches. The amphibious tanks took to these lagoons, leaving the causeways for the infantry. There was spasmodic shelling as the Germans dropped back before the armour. Then, at lunch-time, came the first link-up between forces from sea and air. At the far end of the causeways the Americans met their airborne men, who had been given the task of seizing the exits from the causeways. In places the American assault forces penetrated up to 10,000 yards inland. In view of what was happening over at Omaha, this was reassuring.

As shells still dropped on Omaha the one thing for the men to do was literally to dig into the soft sand, so that only a direct hit would get them. With jeeps or lorries for cover, they dug themselves in, while the engineers struggled to get to grips with the hidden yet ever-present enemy: the mines.

0930. The Americans had lost men and materials, they were disorganized, and pinned down along the beach by intense enemy fire.

At 0950. "There are too many vehicles on the beach; send combat troops. 30 L.C.T.'s waiting off shore; cannot come in because of shelling. Troops dug in on beaches, still under heavy fire."

As soon as the commander of the 1st U.S. Division received this signal from the troops ashore he dispatched the next assault waves and moved destroyers in almost to the beach to blast the Omaha opposition. As their bows cut through the waves they left a wide watery arc. Although the Americans were entrenched perilously near the enemy posts, the ships sent salvo after salvo whistling just over them at the Germans, and this helped to alleviate the situation. To the men who were still on the beach it had seemed a long six hours since 0630. All that went before D-Day was like another age. It seemed as if their lives had only begun at dawn, and already some had ended. Crouched in a foxhole waiting for the engineers to clear a way out, a G.I. stopped for a second to think what day it was. Tuesday. Last Tuesday he had walked over Portsdown Hill with a girl from Portsmouth. Looking down at the landing-craft crowded in the back of the harbour, he had felt then that this could not be far off. Now he knew.

The destroyers stopped engines now, a mere half-mile off shore, and as they swopped fire with the coastal strong-points the American assault troops landed in water which was only at gaiter-depth. More engineers came too, with their tools strapped to their backs. Covering the second landings came the rest of the amphibious tanks, taken right in by ship.

The troops needed every vehicle and weapon that could be mustered, but still the vital thing was to expand the narrow paths through the mines. Tanks could not pass yet, and vehicles were still accumulating. All through that long, endless morning the Yanks battled to "get the hell out of" that beach.

High tide came and crowded the vehicles still closer. M.P.'s tried to achieve order from this chaos. And, despite the destroyers, shells steadily fell on to Omaha as the second waves beached. Right in the thick of it they emerged, into a flashing furnace of smoke, death, destruction—and the guts of men.

Now they were about to burst out of those shell-swept and hell-swept shores.

So the order was to get off the beaches and up the bluffs—heading from west to east for Vierville, St Laurent, Colleville. Gradually 600 men struggled off Dog White, just east of Vierville. Bunching near the edge of the bluffs did not contribute to their progress. Still, scattered formations did reach the village during mid-morning, despite a certain amount of hindrance from machine-guns in the hedgerows.

Vierville fell at about 1100, and detachments of Rangers and of the 116th Regiment passed through it before noon, but were again halted by fire from hedgerows running at right angles to the highway. Each time they tried to advance enemy rifles and automatic weapons spat fire a few inches above the grass at a range of only two or three hundred yards. They decided to call off the advance along the coastal road and concentrate elsewhere.

Sniped at all the way, the command group of the 116th also reached Vierville by noon, and small skirmishes went on the whole time around the area, in which fifteen Germans were killed. Much later Colonel Canham found out for the first time what had happened on the beaches in front of Vierville. This flank remained the weakest throughout the day, with beach exits only beginning to be found by dark.

Back on these beaches, at 1300, heavy naval guns, including the main batteries of the *Texas*, directed their attention to guarding the Dog beach areas. The destroyer *McCook* radioed a message ashore to say that through binoculars—bringing the beach battle into sudden close-up from the bridge, pinpointing actual men, friend and foe—they could see Germans leaving emplacements to surrender. Thirty prisoners were quickly grabbed.

As soon as the barrage stopped General Cota returned down the exit road to the beach to see why no traffic was getting through inland. With only four men he sneaked all the way down, past the strong-points and the anti-tank wall, and out once more on to the flat, fearful beach—without drawing more than scattered small-arms fire. Five Germans, taken prisoner from holes in the cliff side, led them through a minefield on the way.

The 121st Engineer Combat Battalion, responsible for clearing the main exit from Dog beach, had lost three-quarters of its gear on landing, and suffered comparable casualties too. Precious time ticked away in collecting men and salvaging equipment. This they did to the accompaniment of snipers' fire from a dozen strong-points; cleaning out the enemy became difficult in the Hamel-au-Prêtre region, where their fortifications were linked by long tunnels.

1430. Lieutenant Charles Parker and his men left the château they had taken south of Vierville to head for the 5th Rangers' assembly area, by Pointe du Hoe. Preceded by a dozen prisoners, they got as far as an enemy prepared position before being stopped. They tried to "bull through," but found themselves outflanked and almost surrounded; to extricate themselves, they left the roads and struck out across country.

Over to the Easy beaches and the St Laurent zone. Anything less aptly named than Easy could scarcely be conceived. This was the position at 1000: M Company, 16th Regiment, was still pinned to the beach, while the 3rd Battalion of the 116th staggered up the high ground. The total depth gained around St Laurent during the day amounted to only half a mile: a mere 800-odd yards. The story from 1000 till noon was again of skirmishes, with resistance stiffening. A company of Germans controlling the approaches to the main crossroad, and with good fields of fire, caught a small American group by surprise machine-gun fire.

The 115th Regiment landing on Easy Red at high noon took most of the afternoon to clear the beach, and St Laurent held them up further. As their transport was not due in on D-Day, the men had to carry heavy loads as well as keep their wits well about them.

After Vierville and St Laurent had been reached by noon the slowdown assumed an air of inevitability. The one vital battalion of artillery which got ashore during the whole day on those deadly Dog beaches met systematic shelling and mortar fire.

This battalion set out for shore with a dozen guns. Some it lost on the rough run in or on landing. "Rugged," said a sergeant as he saw one of them have its barrel blown right off and lodge in the sand. By afternoon the battalion had only one gun left.

By 0900 parts of the 16th Regiment got past the bluff, and forced a thin wedge inland towards Colleville, piercing 1000 yards south in an hour. Then followed a heavy house-to-house engagement on the outskirts of the town, in which they were joined by small groups of the 116th. By a misunderstanding, these sections then withdrew to a specified bivouac area, leaving the enemy to filter through the gaps thus left. Since a pillbox overlooking Fox Green beach had swivelled its fire round inland to the south, the 16th found that they were cut off on three sides—if not completely encircled. For several hectic hours they fought on in a desperate action which was the only one to provoke an enemy counter-attack.

With the situation becoming more serious each hour, a battalion of the 18th Regiment swept up to relieve them and drive the Germans back in bitter fighting. Here, at the western entrance to Colleville, the 16th struggled against a dramatic backcloth of scudding clouds, tall trees, ripped roofs, and the strangely stark silhouette of a wrecked church, with its windows smashed and gaping.

The reinforcing 18th landed on Easy Red from 1100 to 1400, and General Wyman diverted one battalion after another from their original missions to take over those of the 16th. As they advanced the enemy fire continued to be ideally sited for covering strategic spots like gates and hedgerow openings. Typical of the fluid state of things was the experience of G Company of the 16th, which found itself with little resistance ahead, but fired upon from behind.

At the extreme east the 3rd Battalion of the 16th, on its own since dawn, went south towards Cabourg, but a three-man patrol ran right into the enemy and was captured.

Afternoon on the beaches, from Dog Green to Fox Red—three miles and more of confusion. Spasmodic shelling from the naval forces reduced strong-points, while enemy artillery inland returned the fire to the beaches. Easy Green got the worst of this, and even later in the day hits sunk or fired landing-craft. Vehicles trying to escape the artillery began to move laterally along the beach, looking for exits healthier than Moulins Les Pins. Despite the steady stream of artillery fire, the American engineers furiously forced their way through the obstacles. By now they were used to the flurry as bullets broke the surface of the sand around them. As the tide ebbed the task eased a little, and thirteen gaps were eventually marked by evening.

Meanwhile the landings went on according to plan as far as time was concerned, but not always in the right place. A signal said, "Fox Beach ready for development." So the 336th Engineer Combat Battalion scheduled to land there, headed for shore—but beached at the other end of Omaha, 4000 yards away!

At 1500 hours an engineer unit had to cross Fox Green in face of severe shelling. The men moved silently in pairs. Half had made the journey successfully when a bulldozer, working near the shingle, received a direct hit and burned into a molten mass. The only consolation was that the smoke covered the rest of the movement.

Over at Fox Red the 336th lost six men, but a trailer, loaded with explosives and towed by a tractor, negotiated the nerve-racking trip completely unscathed. Vehicles moved inland under the cover of fire from the sea. Between 1200 and 1300 bulldozers cut a road up the western slope towards St Laurent, although they were under sniper fire. Preloaded D.U.K.W.'s grounded on Easy Red and Easy Green an hour later, the enemy lacking artillery observation on the vital exits. But by 1500 enemy resistance around St Laurent caused another short stop, vehicles jamming bumper to bumper all along the road, and once more the engineers came to the rescue by clearing a branch road.

Both the over-tired 16th and the comparatively fresh 18th awaited armour. They had to hang on well into the afternoon, as it was 1400 before the first tanks and other armoured vehicles rumbled ashore and through the one available exit. And even then the concentration of targets attracted sustained shelling. One shell exploded right on a jeep, tearing its metal, and occupants, to pieces.

These first few tanks gave the infantry a chance to hold the position they had won. Right round the clock they had been facing odds. Now they steeled themselves to stand fast—thin columns of men on foot, beating off the German pockets of resistance while the build-up on the beach proceeded painstakingly. The naval barrage had stopped altogether, since the ships did not know exactly where the Americans were advancing. Nor could aircraft hope to probe the confused lines—even if they had not had to contend with the screen of smoke which hung suspended over most of Omaha.

The shells went on falling. Support troops landed, and then the artillery finally rolled ashore. Gun-carriers towing anti-tank guns splashed through the ebbing tide. This was what the troops were waiting for. Yet the ill luck brought by the elements made matters little better. The seas swamped six howitzers being borne ashore on D.U.K.W.'s. The other half-dozen of the battalion were tied in together, and fired their first salvo at 1615—a warm tea-time for the machine-gun nest near Colleville which was the target.

More heavy howitzers now, from 1500 to 1830, and more losses. Five were rendered useless as their L.C.T.'s met mishaps in the shallow waters, and several barrels were left staring blankly out of the sea. Losses rose to twenty-six guns, twenty-five vehicles, and other gear. With the beachhead so slender, medical units had been unable to set up stations, and treatment was given in temporary areas.

The sun was going down to the accompaniment of sniper fire and occasional heavier thuds. A maze of debris littered the shingle on Dog beach, with discarded life-preservers to the fore. Tangled barbed-wire, the wreckage of L.C.A. 1063, the tops of Element C, a stray barrage-balloon, and broken boxes of demolition materials. Some G.I.'s were established in a pillbox which was being used as a temporary H.Q. on Easy Red.

No, it had not been easy. And the armour arrived only just in time to meet the threat of a Panzer counter-attack. If the Germans had known it an attack in force against Omaha that evening might have had far-reaching effects. But, to their own cost, they allowed the Americans gradually to land vital armour, and thus gave them the chance to exploit their flair for mechanized warfare.

So the Yanks were a mile inland at Colleville. A few stray civilians, standing before the walls of what had been their homes, waved encouragement to the advance units. Side walls rising to roof height—only there was no roof, nor any rooms. Others, who had homes, looked out from behind scarred shutters.

By evening the balance had definitely swung in favour of the liberators. The American infantry, who had forced footholds in North Africa and, during the previous summer, in Sicily, were not going to be beaten now. Still outgunned, they cut the Colleville-St Laurent road and broadened their front to the 4-mile width of the original landings. Colonel Taylor had led them off the beach, but even he had not expected to see such a swing of the pendulum after those first three hours of hell.

At dusk Omaha was still under heavy enemy fire from mortars and longer-range artillery. What had been achieved there during that day? Most of the five regiments were ashore, but as for equipment of every sort, only 100 of the 2400 tons planned reached the beaches by the end of D-Day—an amazingly low proportion. Luckily most of the 110 pre-loaded D.U.K.W.'s landed, or else the ammunition would have run out entirely.

Casualties ran into several thousands. Over fifty tanks were lost, as well as much more armament and equipment. Fifty landing-craft and ten larger vessels never reached the Normandy shore at Omaha.

Even so, the situation might have been immeasurably worsened by the presence of enemy aircraft. If fighters or fighter-bombers could have intervened over Omaha in the critical early-morning stage anything might have happened. As it was, Allied air supremacy proved absolute. Only three Focke-Wulf 190's appeared, to be rudely chased off by air patrols sweeping over the beaches. Not until nightfall did the Luftwaffe get anywhere near Omaha, when twenty-two planes attacked shipping but without causing serious damage. One bomb did drop only 35 yards from the battleship *Arkansas*. Three aircraft were shot down during this attempted attack.

Over in England Eisenhower and Montgomery heard the reports coming in from the airborne troops, and later from the American and British beaches. As soon as they saw that the landings were fairly successful Montgomery hurried off in a launch to board a destroyer on its way from Portsmouth to Normandy. Not only did he want to visit the beaches at the very earliest possible opportunity, but he had to decide on the best place to set up his advance headquarters. Now that the Allies were ashore the time for Southwick House, or even Portsmouth, seemed past. He wanted to be on the spot. Eisenhower promised to visit him on the following day, and naturally chose Omaha for his first call.

So the second waves were ashore along Omaha, and the tanks too. For the 5000 ships and craft used in the whole operation the next duty was to get back to base for further work, or just to safety—those which were not being broken up by the tide or resting on the bottom and showing perhaps a few feet above water level. Soon they would all have to be cleared for the following supply craft.

During the afternoon one L.C.T. disgorged its tanks on Omaha and then headed north. Half-way across the Channel a torpedo from an *E*-boat traced a choppy course towards her. The L.C.T. shuddered as she was hit amidships. Nearly severed in two by the explosion, she had her hull held together by only a few rivets and strips of torn metal. These groaned and creaked with each roll caused by the waves. But the sub-lieutenant commanding her refused to abandon hope. The Isle of Wight was almost in sight now. Slowing down to avoid as much strain as he could, he nursed her home into the Solent with the great rent in her hull gaping wider and the craft settling lower.

Another craft weakened by enemy fire was given a blow below the belt—and below the water-line—by the weather, which broke her clean in two. Undismayed, and behaving as if this were a normal experience in the English Channel, the crew made both halves watertight, and steamed in the after-end, containing the engines, ahead of the severed fore-end. Getting ropes across the water to the fore-end, they then proceeded to tow that half for home, which they reached safely—back to front!

1000. Gold beach. The frogmen and engineers, fighting against time, the enemy, and the elements, were desperately clearing sea-lanes through the mesh and the maze of underwater obstacles, as the second group of assault forces of the 30th British Corps were due to land. These follow-up brigades actually touched down an hour later to give every one ashore extra time. As the obstacles yielded to expert demolition, and half a dozen exits from the beaches were established, the Beach Control Groups worked miracles of organization, so that there were hardly any traffic blocks.

And all the time men and munitions poured ashore. Men weighed down with 90 lb. of kit waded off landing-ships into water five feet deep. One group, clutching their ammunition boxes shoulder-high, turned their backs on their battered ship, with its White Ensign holed but hanging proudly. Still a blazing bedlam, the beach presented a picture of chaos, despite traffic control. A wounded man just lay on his stomach and waited, hoping for the best as the flash of a shell reflected gold in the studs of his soles and horse-shoes of his heels. Near him men still dug in while they waited beside Churchill tanks for their turn to advance. "Cheetah" and other names were painted gaily on the tanks' sides; their gun-barrels were pointed grimly inland; radio aerials were ready for orders to move those thick treads.

But the worst of the initial beach battle was over—here, at least. After landing from 1100 onward, both reinforcement brigades (the 56th and 151st) had passed through the beaches in an hour or so, and the depth of the advance measured 2 miles.

It was afternoon now, and the enemy were falling back before the methodical Montgomery strategy of infantry plus armour. Striking south-west, the two brigades pushed 6 miles from Gold, cutting the Bayeux road and reaching the main Bayeux-Caen road. So they made really spectacular ground, but the 6th Green Howards and 5th East Yorkshires (who had attacked at La Rivière twelve hours earlier) were just as far from the beaches—a tremendous effort. By sunset the 30th British Corps covered—aptly—some 30 square miles; their patrols were in the north-eastern out-skirts of Bayeux, and the perimeter also included Creully.

Only on the extreme right did resistance continue throughout the after-noon—from the German garrison at Le Hamel. It was this stubbornly-held strong-point which nearly wrecked at the outset the most outstanding operation of the Royal Marine Commandos during the entire invasion.

Between the British and American sectors stood Port-en-Bessin, a sleepy little fishing village which, if it could not be called a major port, would still be useful to the liberating armies as they advanced. Its harbour was deep enough to allow small craft inside, although not to be compared with the Mulberries which were yet to be assembled.

No. 47 Commando, led by Lieutenant-Colonel C. F. Phillips, had to take the little port, which had been well fortified to resist any such attempt. Here it was hoped that Gold and Omaha would be linked into one Anglo-American beachhead.

Because the enemy were known to have made the most of the village's natural defensive position in a gap between tall cliffs, the attack had to come from the land, and not from the sea. So the Commandos planned to land with the 30th British Corps at the right-hand side of Gold beach. From there they would march fully ten miles in a slight arc, sweeping through the Normandy countryside and back to the coast behind Port-en-Bessin. Everything they needed they had to carry—including explosives for demolition and automatic weapons—so that six stones in weight had to be borne by each man throughout those ten long miles.

The fourteen landing-craft of No. 47 Commando headed for the beach where the 1st Hampshires had just landed. The strong-point of Le Hamel seemed almost untouched by the dawn barrage, and the closer the craft drew to the shore the closer to them fell the enemy shells. To land where they were supposed to land would mean death and disaster for a force whose first aim was to break out of the beach at once and traverse enemy-held territory far and fast. Nor could they count on any armoured support. So they had no alternative but to divert their course east, which would involve an even longer journey to the port.

Now the next setback literally hit them. Between the twin assaults of the 1st Hampshires and the 1st Dorsets, the fourteen craft crept in towards the shore. One after another, four of them ran right into under-water obstructions only a few inches below the surface. The Teller mines attached to the obstacles were touched off—and the instantaneous explosions hurled the craft into the air in a grotesque fashion before they heeled over and sank in the swirling foam all around. The Commandos fought to free themselves from their kit, which could drag them to the bottom. Several succumbed to the overpowering burden and were drawn down before they could get rid of it. The surf did the rest. But most of them managed to wrench it off and strike out desperately for the beach.

So, as the ten craft came ashore, the survivors of the other four followed, some swimming, others wading neck-deep. It was all they could do to force themselves forward through the water, especially since it lashed back after each wave. But one by one they came, crouching or crawling. One in three of the total force had lost their arms and equipment; until they could capture some weapons they were without any means of defending themselves, as vicious mortar-fire clonked among them. They could only dash for the assembly area and wait there for whatever might come next.

Swelling the losses from the four destroyed landing-craft, the stubborn strong-point at Le Hamel and other pill-boxes found the sodden Commandos good targets for the cross-fire defence system. Without wait-ing a minute, therefore, the British got off the beach and covered some distance towards their first goal, La Rosière.

Nothing could surprise them now, and the mere fact that the Germans held La Rosière, instead of the British, did not daunt them in the least. They ran right into the village, firing at all the defended houses. Panes of glass were shattered by the sharp shots, and Germans rushed out to sur-render—hands behind helmets, terror-stricken. The war cries of the Green Berets died down as they collected up the enemy weapons. Then they moved on and reached Hill 72, two miles south of Port-en-Bessin. This hill was to be the base for the Commando's attack.

By now they were tiring. They had travelled ten miles already, but there would still be two miles to go. Here they were, under the shadow of Hill 72, but they were sadly behind schedule. True, a good proportion of the original force had fought through, and the survivors from the four wrecked craft were ready to attack the enemy with captured German guns.

But now it was nearly night, and they could not hope to take the port without the assistance of fire from the navy.

So they came to the core of the problem. A radio was needed to ask for and co-ordinate this barrage, and the only one of the Commando's four sets which had not been lost in the assault turned out to be "u/s" (unserviceable). Whether its failure would prove temporary or permanent, Lieutenant-Colonel Phillips could not know. But he did know that without it nothing could be gained. For the moment, as the sun set, they had to rest and try to repair their only link with the Allies at sea. Tired out after their fantastic day, they slept, not knowing what the next day might bring.

The fanatical defence at Le Hamel was not broken until a combined onslaught was aimed at it from land and sea. Under cover of a barrage from the sea, the 1st Hampshires and follow-up regiments then flanked Le Hamel and went on west to Arromanches. First the destroyers shelled the area, then the smaller support craft crept in closer and subdued individual strong-points which were still stubbornly firing. Ashore, armoured vehicles reached the Arromanches beaches—an important gain, as these would soon be the location of one of the two prefabricated Mulberry harbours which were already taking strange shape in various parts of the Channel.

Between the two British assaults on Gold and Sword beaches the Canadians lost a little of their wonderful initial impetus, for two reasons. First—machine-gun and heavier fire halted their sweep south out of Bernières. This jarring noise seemed strangely out of place on a road flanked by early corn and neat orchards. Second—at about 1130 the follow-up 9th Canadian Brigade plunged ashore before the armour which was already choking the little streets of Bernières could be cleared.

The time was noon, and a Bren-gun carrier of this 9th Canadian Brigade was driving down the ramp of L.C.T. N. 22.885. Another one was a couple of lengths farther inshore, in a foot of water, and the tracks of a third scudded through the muddy sand. Like all other vehicles used, these had wisely been waterproofed, so that at no matter what depth they were driven into the sea—within reason—they could still run. These armoured reinforcements cluttered up the beaches more and more, and even when they slowly moved into Bernières the vehicles were all still bumper to tail. Luckily nothing disastrous occurred through this hold-up, except that time was extremely precious on D-Day, and, if wasted, it could never be reclaimed. No fault lay with the Canadians, however. It was mainly the wreckage on the beach which slowed up progress.

By 1500 the way was comparatively clear again, and the Canadian tanks thundered right through to their end-of-day target—the Bayeux-Caen road. But because the infantry could not keep pace, they actually had to retreat a little!

At evening they met the British near Creully, and the Gold-Juno beach-head now measured a width of a dozen miles. Neither on the beach nor inland was this achieved without desolation, destruction, death.

But even with Nos. 48 and 41 Commandos assaulting between Juno and Sword, these beachheads could not be joined on D-Day itself. The Commandos did their duty well, however, with the help of the remarkable Royal Marine Armoured Support Group, which went into action on several beaches, including those earmarked for Nos. 48 and 41 Commandos. They were the first Marines ever to fight in tanks. Landing in Shermans and other tanks, they were instructed to operate for only a week, to break the crust of the coast defences, but so successfully did they manoeuvre that they ultimately advanced 10 miles instead of the 1 mile originally ordered.

Throughout the morning of D-Day No. 48 Commando had fought on the bloody beach of St Aubin-sur-Mer. Now they had to take Langrune, a fortified strong-point—a task which would need desperate courage. With the aid of their own tanks, they did reach part of the strong-point, by a clever alternation of storming and stealth. Despite their precarious position, practically on the doorstep of Langrune, the Commandos went straight at the face of these redoubtable defences, prickling with deadly devices and weapons.

Not even the Commandos could hope to take the strong-point unaided, but they could and did seize their chance when, the next day, armoured support shattered a thick wall which had been barring their way. It was, in fact, a wall intended to stop not men, but tanks. With the wall breached, the Commandos careered into Langrune in full cry. The Germans could not face this terrifying sight and surrendered with indecent speed. So the most powerful of the German strong-points fell—but again, not without loss. From the moment of landing on that shell-scarred strip of beach to the time of the fall of Langrune, No. 48 Commando lost almost half its number. This was the price they paid.

The adjacent Commando—No. 41—had ended the morning minus the radio transmitter which they needed so badly; then, as if by magic, they had acquired one soon afterwards, and so could call up the supporting ships for a softening-up barrage prior to their attack on the strong-point at Lion-sur-Mer and on the château.

The next day they were poised for the final assault when three Heinkels hared across the sky. Dropping down steeply, with the terrifying screech of the dive-bomber, they aimed an accurate bombing attack on the

Commando headquarters, killing three men outright and wounding nine more. Lieutenant-Colonel Gray was one of the injured. But the Commandos were used to sudden adversity by now. So, incensed by this reverse, they went on, reinforced by two infantry battalions (the Lincolnshires and the Royal Ulster Rifles), and took both strong-point and château. The survivors of No. 41 Commando, having succeeded in their double task, went on to Luc-sur-Mer and joined up with No. 48 Commando.

Sword beach stretched from Luc-sur-Mer to Ouistreham. What was happening on this crucial area north of Caen?

Four tin-hatted Tommies of the British 3rd Division sat on a gun-carrier speeding off its landing-craft and towing an anti-tank gun. On the side of the carrier was chalked the dashing name "Seadog." The Panzers had better beware.

At noon the tide still ran high, and as the Ulster Rifles poured out of L.C.I. L.299 they were faced with two immediate problems. The first was how to carry a folding bicycle through fifty feet of sea, holding on with one hand to a rope line attached to the shore. The second was—where was the beach? Here it consisted of only a yard or two of crowded sand, so they were soon on the promenade using their bicycles. Bombs fell around them as they wobbled along, past seaside houses with holes blown in their roofs—or else with no roofs.

"Talk about a blessed day trip." There was always the wag, even now.

Another L.C.I. came in: S.530. French Commandos lined up eagerly as the craft stopped. Then, with their berets tilted to one side, they slid down the sides of buckled ramps, and in a moment stood on the shore of their own country again, after an absence of four long years. But there was no time for sentiment. Machine-gun tracery reminded them that though the first attack was over, the battle had barely begun.

Meanwhile, at 0820, No. 4 Army Commando (the spearhead of the 1st Special Service Brigade) had landed a mile west of Ouistreham and stormed the western end of the town, to clear out the enemy there, who were still firing rifles on to the beach where the 2nd East Yorkshires had landed.

The 2nd East Yorkshires continued to be restricted all the morning. Meanwhile, with the tide tearing to its flood, the second waves of the assault struggled over submerged obstacles which were prickling with Teller mines. The sappers and frogmen were doing their best, but threading through the obstacles, the abandoned assault craft, and other debris was worse, if anything, than the lot of the first troops who had landed. And not only did they have to contend with the enemy—Allied self-propelled guns were by now keeping up a steady stream of firing from the very water's edge! To get ashore, the second waves had to sneak in low, so as to be sure of avoiding the shells aimed over their heads at inland positions.

For about an hour—a period which seemed longer to the men than any sixty minutes they had ever experienced before—the enemy artillery laid down an uncannily accurate barrage on Sword beach, blasting the British reinforcements at every step. Broadside on to the beach L.C.A. S.22 swayed crazily with the tide, while the body of a British soldier lay near by, flat on his back, his knuckles bent, his tin hat blown off.

Then some one looked up, and realized that the silver-grey barrage-balloons, which were intended to prevent the troops being dive-bombed, were actually responsible for the ranging of this barrage. At once their lines were cut, and they drifted along the line of the coast, blown by the stiff w.n.w. wind.

This did not mean that balloons failed to give their unique protection against low-flying air attacks, or their well-known morale value to troops operating beneath them. In fact, the question of where and when to fly the barrage-balloons was just one more important detail in the planning of the operation as a whole.

The Services agreed that ships would benefit by balloons, but that they must not give away positions (by Radar or by their visible presence) too soon. The ultimate decision was that balloons should be flown at 100 feet, and not less than 7 miles behind the early assault. But this height is the worst possible at which they can fly, for a balloon is inclined to react to air currents by diving down when kept at such a low altitude. Despite this, they were successfully flown at the required 100 feet. To fly the required total of 285 balloons for the beach areas a method had to be devised of flying two balloons from each L.S.T. Trials continued for some time before the necessary technique was perfected, but at last, on D-Day, quite an impressive force took the balloons across, and then sustained them, with the necessary hydrogen and replacements.

Historians have already recorded the strange facts that follow concerning the advance from Sword beach during the day. Since so much stress had been laid on the initial assault, the men inevitably tended to be unable to think beyond the beaches. And according to some informed commentators, like Chester Wilmot, the defensive mentality was unduly prevalent among some of the senior commanders. Wilmot has pointed out that the commander of the 8th Brigade in particular was "ill-cast for the rôle of pursuit."

The 1st South Lancashires, for instance, had taken Hermanville by 0930, but then dug in there instead of advancing farther, to their objective of

Périers Rise. The 1st Suffolks too seemed slow in capturing Colleville. Yet when their supporting artillery began to fire ranging shots on an enemy battery position which was scheduled to be taken, sixty-seven Germans hurried out with their hands up!

While the infantry were moving more slowly Commandos of the 1st Special Service Brigade had streaked straight through Colleville to the Orne, where, at 1330, they kept a late lunch-time appointment with the 6th Airborne. The sun had set before the infantry got to the same spot.

Meanwhile the three battalions of the 185th Brigade, which was to make the direct thrust at Caen, had gathered among the orchards of Hermanville by 1100. The plan was for them to ride on tanks down the main road from Hermanville to Caen, but at noon both the tanks and supporting artillery still stood on the beach in a frustrating traffic jam. Time passed quickly as the vehicles slowly got away, and then came the further complication of enemy interference on one flank of the infantry's assembly area. At last, even though the tanks were not yet available, the brigade commander could not risk any further delay. He decided that the 2nd Battalion of the King's Shropshire Light Infantry should advance on foot down the main road from Hermanville; the tanks should overtake them as soon as possible; and the 1st Norfolks should advance on a route parallel with the main road after the 1st Suffolks had captured a strong-point near Colleville.

Hopes of capturing Caen on D-Day were already fading fast, but there were some compensations: the opposition had not been as bad as had been expected. The only pity was that the British forces failed to extract the fullest advantage from this good fortune. In fact, Caen was not destined to fall for a long time yet.

So the beaches still formed the focus of the situation. Even though the gunfire was becoming less terrifyingly intense, the future fate of Europe was still being decided along those narrow stretches of sand and shingle. An early sign of success: a tank moving south up a beach, and two dusty Germans, hands raised and with a rifle barrel behind their backs, walking north in the tracks of the tank, smearing the sandy pattern.

Heavy Sherman tanks rolled in, carrying such unlikely things as a motor-cycle and rider. Gradually the beaches were becoming organized now; the tanks swung round, parallel to the land, and trundled off in single file: "Bunty," "H.M. Submarine," and others.

All along those beaches, as the crash and clamour subsided a little, the flotsam remained. Landing-craft and still more craft sunk, damaged, holed, mined, battered, blasted.

The sappers moved steadily with their detectors, searching for mines, then making them safe. Crab tanks helped too, their metallic flails pawing through the sand. Sometimes, in their haste, the Germans had helped by leaving the skull-and-crossbones sign *Minen* on posts! Salvage men decided which craft could be removed by sea, and which would have to be shifted ashore. Naval beachmasters of the Mediterranean campaigns prepared the way for the follow-up convoys to come.

And always the fantastic flotsam. Gas-masks, water-bottles, khaki in all shades. Behind barbed-wire a deserted German strong-point, with slits in the thick concrete. And right in front of it, on the soft upper sands, the remains of men. Men who died on D-Day: June 6, 1944. The aching aftermath.

"If I should die ..."

Many lay there who had never heard that line—had never even heard of Rupert Brooke. Yet there they were—inert, their duty done. A young naval officer by the shore swallowed as he saw them and knew that this was a moment he would remember all his life—fifteen years, fifty years.

A shell jerked him back to reality as it threw a load of damp sand across the shore. During the afternoon, with its air of activity and occasional firing, they began to bury the men.

A hundred different scenes. The special tracks being laid for the armoured vehicles to drive over the sand more easily; war correspondents interviewing troops, taking their first breather, to tell the world what had been happening; more German prisoners waiting in the water to be taken across the Channel; officers peering inland through field-glasses at the enemy position; men occupying trenches only left by the enemy an hour earlier; the Hindenburg bastion painted with the words, "Under New Management," and then the tenants, Sergeant Savage and his Chindits, with a Bofors gun; everywhere a five-minute smoke as a reward and celebration for still being alive and in one piece, a more practical expression of it as a beach clearance party found a full jar of naval rum bobbing about among the deadly steel obstacles. Up spirits! They gulped down a generous ration of it in a white tin mug, and then went back to business, which suddenly seemed less harrowing. Near by a naval officer was withdrawing the fangs from a Teller mine on top of an obstacle.

High and dry on an American beach three tank landing-ships stood stranded by the ebbing tide, their exit doors opened and cargo gone, leaving a void in their bows like some featureless face.

Wafting across every beach all the afternoon were the bitter tang of stale explosives and the strong smell of the burnt rafters of the roofs of hundreds of houses, which stood abandoned bleakly between the opposing forces.

Now the support men were taking over. Field telephones linked the hard-won beaches. And the wounded were being treated. Ever since the cataclysm of the barrage and the landings the medical corps had followed the men. Surgeons swiftly jabbed morphia into urgent cases, in tents which had sprung up under the shelter of trees (or anything else), to be used for operations which had to be performed immediately, or other urgent treatment. The surgeons, like the frogmen, faced the double difficulty of doing a delicate job while open to attack from enemy fire. Having to operate under tent conditions at all was bad enough, but for the surgeon to know all the time that the ground—and his hands—might shake in the middle of the operation made the work even tenser. One jolt to an instrument could mean a life lost.

So wherever possible the wounded were evacuated. D.U.K.W.'s, barely visible in the waves, chugged gamely inshore on a dual mission: to bring in fresh food and carry out the wounded to waiting ships. Medical corps men carried the serious cases on stretchers down the beaches to these R.A.S.C. D.U.K.W.'s, and soon they were safe aboard the hospital ships, heading for home.

V for Victory—and Valour.

And as the wounded lay on their stretchers, gazing up at the canvas covers of the D.U.K.W.'s rolling northwards, the convoys of support craft passed them on the way in. After the L.C.A.'s, L.C.I.'s and L.C.T.'s came the L.C.F.'s, L.C.S.'s, and L.C.G.'s, the landing-ships, headquarters ships, more D.U.K.W.'s, and then Rhino craft.

All the small support craft were manned by Marines. They presented an amazing array of floating design, including flat-bottomed, flat-nosed L.C.V.'s ("landing-craft vehicles"), under 37 feet long and among the smallest craft to steam across the Channel under their own power. L.C.M.'s ("mechanized landing-craft") were scarcely any larger. With the perilous voyage over, these L.C.M.'s and L.C.V.'s began weeks of work as sea-taxis in all kinds of conditions. Tanks, trucks, guns, ammunition, and food—all these had to be ferried across to wherever they were needed most, and they would always be exposed to possible attack by air or sea.

Vehicles were transferred from parent ships to Rhino barges to be brought to the beaches. During the afternoon of D-Day one of the few successes the enemy achieved was to set on fire a Rhino while it was actually alongside its parent vessel. The crew were in the middle of lowering the vehicles from the ship to the Rhino—so named for its likeness to the animal and the fire quickly spread throughout the length of the craft. It was already half loaded with petrol-filled vehicles and threatened to burn more and more furiously. Men lay about the Rhino, injured by the attack or overcome by the fire, which looked as if it would leap to the parent ship any moment and engulf the petrol and vehicles still due to be loaded. Then, like lightning, a group of Royal Marines clambered down into the flaming barge, with its lethal load of ready-fuelled vehicles, and somehow succeeded in transferring all the wounded to the parent ship, and then in forcing the blazing barge away from the vessel's side.

This was one of a thousand unsung incidents in the invasion. Incidents such as that of L.C.T.921. Her task of landing vehicles done, she turned to clear the way for others in those crowded waters. For an hour or two the return was as uneventful as the voyage south. A sense of anti-climax prevailed. Then, suddenly, a torpedo from nowhere erupted volcanically on her port side near the wheelhouse. Spray spurted over the deck. A man fell before the blast. The metal hull and casing crumpled as if they were cardboard, leaving a great gap where the sea splashed in. Frantically the crew bunged the leaks and sailed her on. The deck had really rolled up, exposing its metal supporting girders. Riding lower in the water, L.C.T.921 made slow speed north, and its crew sighted the Isle of Wight before dark. When she finally rounded the island and crept back to a berth in Southampton Water no one in the little semi-detached houses lining the coast noticed her obscure outline. She had returned damaged, but with honour.

Overhead 250 tugs and gliders droned across the sunset sky to take up the challenge; the name "Kitty" was painted on the nose of one. But while these airborne reinforcements were on their way to France the men of the 6th Airborne Division were still wearing the Red Beret bravely.

Eisenhower and Montgomery discuss points of planning at their headquarters.

As the battle moves inland the sappers and other troops clear the chaos on the beaches.

After the first assault the beaches are still under spasmodic fire.

17

The Paratroops hold firm

AT dawn, D-Day, the 7th battalion of the 5th Parachute Brigade, defending their bridge over the Canal de Caen, began to be harassed by locals who were listening apprehensively to the Allied air bombardment. Naturally they wanted to get away from the north of Normandy, which they rightly assumed would soon become a battleground. Not all the French wanted to move, however, and the matron of a maternity clinic at the Château de Bénouville remained there throughout the invasion, to see several babies born within the sounds of both Allied and German guns.

Wherever they were that early morning, the various battalions of the 5th Brigade felt alone in the midst of the enemy. Then the sound of the shells, as the Allies began the bombardment, cheered them. Soon they would no longer be on their own in this No Man's Land between two massive armies. They would be part of one—the liberators.

At 0715 the shelling suddenly stopped. This, they knew, meant that reinforcements would be nearing the beaches. But until these arrived the enemy were clearly going to keep the airborne vanguard dangerously occupied. Casualties mounted as snipers picked off paratroops from various vantage-points. Fire came from every conceivable place. None was considered too sacred—not even a certain church tower, which was obviously secreting several snipers, to judge from the intermittent whine which was emitted from it. Eventually the bomb from a paratroop's Piat scored a bull's eye on the tower, and a dozen of the enemy were killed. They were not troubled again from that particular source, but airborne casualties continued hour by hour; the wounded were dealt with in a cafe by the bridge of Le Port.

Three more hours passed, and at about 1000 guards spotted a couple of red berets striding towards the bridge. When challenged, they turned out to be none other than Major-General Gale himself, complete with military moustache and an air of efficiency to match, and Brigadier Kindersley. The latter's air-landing brigade was not due to land till the evening of D-Day, but in the meantime both generals were checking up on all the vital paratroop positions.

They had hardly arrived when two boats hove into view, clearly aiming for Caen. The paratroops did not wait for formalities but opened fire with a Bren gun and another precious Piat. Both hit their mark, the nearer boat, which moved aimlessly across the canal till it jolted against the bank, whereupon its German Army crew voluntarily forfeited their active interest in the rest of the War. Seeing the fate of the first boat, and exercising the female prerogative, the second changed her course and reversed rapidly towards the sea.

Nearly a complete cycle of the clock had passed now since the paratroops were inching down through the chill night air. The effect of those twelve hours began to be felt at about lunch-time. This was, therefore, the ideal hour, psychologically, for them to hear the skirl of bagpipes. Never before had these sounded so sweet to Sassenachs!

"They're coming!" a corporal called, voicing the feelings of all of those guarding the bridge. Then the first troops reached them and, despite snipers, quickly grabbed their hands. These were the Commandos, who had charged wildly through Colleville, their green berets bobbing triumphantly. Then at 1400 hours the piper of Lord Lovat's 1st Special Service Brigade marched over the bridge, drowning the sounds of mortars and bullets. This vital pivot point, seized and held safe for the main invaders, was later christened Pegasus Bridge, in honour of the paratroops who wear the insignia of the Flying Horse.

But the thrill of the link-up could not last for long. It was just one more incident in a day crowded with memories. In Bénouville itself A Company of the 7th Battalion had a bad time ever since being attacked on three sides before dawn. No reinforcements could get through to it until early evening, when word came back that, though all its officers had been wounded, the company was still holding its position. For seventeen hours the company fought on almost continuously, and at one point a German attack reached the regimental aid post before being repulsed. In the confusion of the moment, however, Chaplain George Parry was killed—a real grief to each man in the company.

All day it remained touch and go for A Company. Finally relief reached the men. Against a fitful sundown, with scattered cloud covering much of the sky, the great glider force scheduled for that evening flocked overhead on time, and in the right order and place. The graceful gliders lost height like giant birds of prey swooping earthward. Gradually they lowered their massive frames on to a wheatfield, which was one of the prepared landing-zones. A few missed the actual field, but all came to rest within yards of each other—so different from the drop of the previous night. For twenty hours the paratroops had held the bridges over the Orme and Canal de Caen. Now relief had come out of the skies.

Then, at about 2000 hours, the seaborne reinforcements broke through too, so that the paratroops' long vigil was really over, at least for the moment. But with the land link-up came a sudden sharp reminder that the War was still very much in progress. A lone Focke-Wulf 190 flew in, almost at ground-level, and dropped a big bomb on part of their precious bridge over the canal. But it failed to go off!

Lieutenant-Colonel Pine-Coffin counted all his men safely across the canal towards Ranville, staying at the bridge until the dial of his luminous watch showed 0100 on June 7. A whole day had passed since he had landed on French soil, and bridge was still safe in Allied hands. When the last man had gone he followed, and then had a few hours' sleep.

On D-Day a special officer, who had been dropped with the 12th Battalion, was contacting an Allied cruiser by radio, so that it could train its guns on targets north of the battalion, around Ouistreham.

With him were Captain J. A. N. Sim and some paratroops, 300 yards ahead of their main positions covering the village of Le Bas de Ranville. Lining a hedge as early light filtered between the branches, they glimpsed a group of unidentifiable men who might well have been British airborne troops. But they could not be sure.

Sim suddenly realized they were the enemy—and a great many of them too. They were getting nearer now. Here was exactly the kind of emergency that airborne soldiers had to be ready to meet when they found themselves in the van of an invasion. There was no time to ask for orders. Sim could actually hear the Germans. Waiting till they came as close as it seemed wise to permit, Sim whispered a command, and a Very light hissed into the air and across the intervening 50 yards. It fell right among the Germans, silhouetting their heads and shoulders in the lightening sky.

Instinctively, the enemy fell flat to the ground as the paratroops opened rapid fire from short range. Anything could happen. The British had the advantage of surprise, but it was soon lost, as two 88-mm. guns, advancing close behind the German infantry, came into play. The whole situation was fraught with danger, and the 88's started swivelling into action right in front of the paratroops. Sim, the special officer, and the dozen others carried on as best they could. They did not want to retreat, or the Germans might overrun the main positions. Two soldiers were killed outright. A bad bullet wound in the thigh of the special officer put him out of action. He would not be able to help his cruiser at present.

They held on for what seemed a long, long time. While the two 88's covered the Germans they tried to get round Sim's right flank, but the paratroops prevented this. The firing came in spasms, followed by periods of uncanny quiet. Then a German mortar bomb lobbed in their direction rent the air just at the top of their hedge. The situation deteriorated dramatically. Only four of the fourteen were alive and also without wounds: Sim, his batman, Sergeant Jones, and Sergeant Millburn. Still they returned the Germans' fire, but to stay there much longer could obviously mean the end of them all. The hedge could not be held.

Sim decided to withdraw. So the four fit men helped the injured to their feet, and they all set out back to the company's main position via a shallow ditch—too shallow for safety. All the time they were making this exposed withdrawal they offered targets for the Germans, only a hundred yards away at the start. Yet, despite it all, the remnants returned to the main position, through that 300 yards of hell, expecting every second to be their last. Sim was not beaten, however, and later returned with reinforcements to the very same hedge. C Company's anti-tank guns accounted for the Germans' 88-mm.'s, so things were easier now. and this time they held the hedge.

Sergeants Jones and Millburn were both awarded the D.C.M., but both were killed later. Sim received the M.C.

From the 12th Battalion to the 13th. Separated from the main strength of their unit, Captain Kerr and a party of about twenty men spent D-Day around the remote Bois de Bavent. To get there they had worn themselves out crossing several waterways, and were now among the swamps. Then, just as they felt that they would have to rest, they saw the gliders carrying their reinforcements dipping in to land with infinite elegance. This brought the first cheer of the day, to be followed soon after by another as a squadron of Spitfires, living up to their Battle of Britain reputation, shot down two enemy fighters, which crashed into the swamp quite near them. Two miles of this swamp-land took them six hours to traverse. Their destination was Le Mesnil, and the day ended as a Frenchman, who had apparently been celebrating the liberation prematurely, gave them somewhat incoherent directions for getting there.

South-east of Ranville the 8th Battalion of the 3rd Parachute Brigade was having an adventurous time. Some of them dropped a long way from their zone, and had brisk and brief encounters with the enemy. A few even found themselves floating down near the 5th Brigade at Ranville, and were taken prisoner by a local garrison—but only temporarily, for the Germans found it hard to hold paratroops for long. They caught Sergeant Jones, for instance, but with a supreme effort he grabbed hold of a gun, shot eight Germans dead, and escaped.

By this kind of extreme endeavour the 8th Battalion reached the outskirts of the Bois de Bavent. In all the circumstances Lieutenant-Colonel

Pearson was grateful to have over two hundred men with him, but he knew he must create an illusion of still greater forces. He at once organized a series of patrols. Pearson himself led the first of these, taking the opportunity to try and rescue any survivors they could find of a Dakota they heard had crashed near the woods. After they had crossed a river, Pearson left part of the patrol behind to guard the dinghy which they had used. They reached a small village, which was well behind enemy lines, but they were still not quite in the area where the Dakota had crashed. Pearson and a few others then advanced on a farm. Eventually Pearson reappeared, pulling a cart loaded with eight wounded men from the aircraft, whom they brought safely back.

Only the next day did Pearson have the bullet removed which had been lodging in his left hand during all the fighting of D-Day. He later received a third Bar to the D.S.O. which he already held.

Incidentally, the Dakotas had had a rough time altogether during the original drop. One had crossed most of the Channel when it ran into anti-aircraft fire from Allied shipping—not from the enemy. The pilot reasonably assumed that he must be over France already, and as he was carrying some bombs he let them go. The ships were now sure that the Dakota must be an enemy plane, and redoubled their fire. Violent evasive action became vital, and the laden paratroops were flung all over the floor of the aircraft. Then, for some reason, the green light signifying "Jump" went on. The first three men jumped, fell into the sea, and were never seen again.

But the various air-sea rescue services saved many of the airborne soldiers and pilots. Air-sea rescue squadrons were responsible, directly or indirectly, for saving the lives of no fewer than 117 paratroops during Operation Overlord—a staggering total.

The Americans, especially, benefited by the service. Two American aircraft were known to have gone into the sea just north of Cherbourg. The rescuing Walrus seaplanes arrived on the scene to find that the pilot had not been able to get into his dinghy, but was floating alive in his Mae West.

So far, so good. The snag was that his position was only 2 miles from the French coast. Yet, in spite of fire from enemy coastal batteries, the two Walruses landed on the water and picked him up. The batteries intensified their fire, and when the planes tried to take off they found that they had both been hit. So they set out to *taxi* across the Channel! Some way out they were taken in tow by an Allied ship. Both of them subsequently sank—but no one was lost.

Seventy miles out to sea the crew of an American aircraft was rescued successfully by two high-speed launches, when a group of Focke-Wulf

190's attacked one of the launches. Some of the boat's crew and some of the rescued aircrew received bad injuries from this air assault, and the boat radioed for medical aid. A faithful old Walrus took off with two American medical officers, made a rendezvous with the launches at sea, and so brought essential aid to the wounded men three hours sooner than would otherwise have been possible. The lives of at least two injured men were saved.

But back to the paratroops. Away to the north the 1st Canadian Parachute Battalion was remedying the bad dropping distribution. One stick had actually fallen west of the river Orne, several miles away. Despite these difficulties, they took Varaville as planned, and destroyed the bridge. Bringing their trusty Piats to bear, they exchanged fierce fire with the garrison of a pill-box until 1030, when the Germans gave in.

Farther north still the victorious 9th Battalion, flushed from their triumph in silencing the almost legendary Merville battery, advanced to their second task of taking a patch of high ground on which a small château was situated. However, it was not until the next day, when the Commandos came to their aid, that the position was captured.

Finally, over to the west the American paratroops fought for their lives throughout D-Day, and had to leave bridges unblown. But they did secure those vital exits to causeways across the notorious swamps. And as they struggled, often in ones or twos, the American glider pilots were gradually getting on with their unique and unenviable job of passing through the enemy—and Allied—lines to penetrate to the beaches, and so back to sea, and England, for reinforcements. Secure in the safety of a landing-craft, they smoked a cigarette, leant on their guns, and, unsmiling, swopped stories of how they had got back. Certainly they had done their full share. Now it was up to others for a while.

18

Beyond the Beachhead

S O the outer crust of Hitler's West Wall was crumbling. But as D-Day drew to an end the overpowering impetus of the initial assault began to be lost, and all along the coast thoughts turned to counter-attack. Some of it was just natural reaction: the recoil after surviving the fury of that first amazing morning. But the Germans were grouping to try and attack. Rommel himself moved up behind Caen as Montgomery landed to find his advance headquarters. So all the old enemies were facing each other again—and at pretty short range. German infantry were on the move towards the Americans in an attempt to cut them off from the rest of the beachhead, while the Panzers and S.S. were poised to strike at the British and Canadians.

Two dozen Panzer tanks tried to drive a wedge between the British and Canadians late on D-Day, but by this time our own D.D. and other tanks were inland, supported by mobile guns. After a slogging match of shells which rent the afternoon air the Panzers clumsily turned in their tracks and headed south, leaving five of their number smoking ruins. A second Panzer attack, due later in the evening, was forestalled to the hour by the landing of the large glider-borne reinforcement referred to in the last paragraph of Chapter 16.

Meanwhile the memories of the day were personal ones: each man's own fight multiplied a hundred thousand times—or, to be precise, by D-Day and D + I, 176,475 times. A major driving gaily in a captured 10 h.p. car; a captured lorry loaded with still-hot soup, coffee, and fresh bread for a phantom enemy unit; cigars by the box and wine by the barrel; dead cows in a field, their legs stuck strangely in the air; a fearful flash as a German mortar bomb hits an ammunition lorry, and one thinks of the driver inside; the first night, and in a tank harbour still helmeted men write home, or just fold their arms and fall asleep; four men carrying their wounded C.S.M. to a forward field dressing station; motor-cyclists resting beside their vehicles on the verge of the road; a mine-hunting Labrador dog, Jasper, has his head bandaged after a wound to his right ear; an old Frenchman unfurls a faded flag from his balcony as slates fall off the roof;

a Tommy carries a trophy, *Minen*, left by the Germans in their haste; another one has a sign ready to plant in a cleared path, "No Mines"; sappers sweeping for mines in the ruined square of Tilly-sur-Seulles; and four forlorn prisoners walk in front of a private with a Sten gun.

Night now, but no sleep. Often the enemy infantry were only two or three hundred yards ahead. And black-faced patrols crossed No Man's Land throughout the night. Stabs of light as guns fired or grenades burst, then quiet. With day came the big guns again, making the efforts of the individual infantryman seem pointless, almost; yet armour and men together would win or lose the Battle of Normandy.

In this confusion mistakes were made. Men of the Royal Ulster Rifles, bicycles abandoned now for the most part, were edging along a copse when, without warning, tracer tore at them fired from their own supporting tanks. It was not always easy to recognize uniforms from a moving tank, and across smoke-filled fields. Caught unawares, the Ulsters were in chaos for a few minutes, but few casualties were caused.

The next day the tanks fully made up for their mistake. They remained with the riflemen all the time they were advancing through a barrage which, it seemed, no man could survive. The Ulsters crouched behind, or on the flanks of, the tanks as they swung their guns towards the source of the barrage. And somehow they got through. While this was going on the Canadians threatened to outflank Caen, until halted by storm troopers.

D + 1, and back to the Commandos. The one Commando not to go into action until after D-Day was No. 46. They were originally going to land in the evening of D-Day, to attack two German batteries in their inimitable way. After getting as far as a mile or so off St Aubin-sur-Mer, where No. 48 Commando had had such a tough task earlier on, they learned at 2200 that the original raids had been cancelled.

Then, after a reasonable rest, they awoke at 0600 to learn of the new plan. A fluid situation existed still, despite the Allies' overall foothold. The Commandos were to take Petit-Enfer, yet another strong-point which was worrying the invaders. Three hours was not really long enough for them to alter their plans and equipment, but by 0900 Lieutenant-Colonel Campbell Hardy led them ashore. With the help of supporting fire from ships, and also tanks of a Royal Marine special unit, the Commando captured the strong-point at Petit-Enfer. Pushing on with the impetus of men fresh to the fight, they occupied La Délivrande, a couple of miles from the coast, where stunned villagers watched tanks roaring through their little street as they stood in front of a shop with its familiar, if faded, notice "Manufacture de Pâtisserie et Confiserie."

We must now move along the coast to follow the thrilling advance of No. 47 Commando on the fortified Port-en-Bessin.

As the starless night fell on D-Day they were trying to repair their one remaining radio transmitter. By morning the signallers had succeeded, having worked almost all through the night. Lieutenant-Colonel Phillips launched his plan at once and put the radio to use by calling up the Navy to ask for a bombardment at 1500 on D + 1 day. This was to be closely followed fifty minutes later by low-level attacks from R.A.F. Typhoons; then at exactly 1600 the Royal Artillery were to lay a smokescreen to cover the Commandos' advance on Port-en-Bessin.

Unlike some of the naval and air support tasks on D-Day, each of these was performed with absolute accuracy and to the second. The low-pitched rumble of H.M.S. *Emerald's* guns echoed across the intervening water and reached the ears of the Commandos near Hill 72. Next, the Typhoons screamed down, strafing the little port, with their rocket projectiles spurting from the wings. This was only the softening process.

At 1600 the smokescreen appeared, on cue, and the Commandos dived forward under its cover. They stormed into the southernmost strong-point. The next one resisted more fiercely. They took this too, though not without loss. A strange situation arose then. Two German flak ships, actually anchored in the harbour, turned their guns on the unexpected targets of British Commandos—rapidly moving men trying to storm their way through to the port. The ships' guns killed a tragically high number of Commandos before these could bring up their bigger weapons to put a stop to the slaughter.

Now another hazard confronted the Commandos. Phillips had left a few men to defend Hill 72, but an enemy force from nearby shelled and then scaled the hill, taking the British prisoners. So the main body of No. 47 Commando not only found itself dangerously delayed by mines ahead, where the main strong-point (on a hill east of the harbour) still remained to be attacked, but also jeopardized by the chance of an attack by the Germans who were now in possession of Hill 72.

While Phillips was considering what his next move should be, Captain T. F. Cousins scouted out a way up the hill to the strong-point. He reported his discovery to Phillips, and expressed his confidence that he could take the strong-point with twenty-five men. Phillips approved of the plan, and agreed that it should be put into operation that night. He gave Cousins fifty men and the precious mortar. Moving noiselessly up the hill path, Cousins and his faithful fifty completely surprised the Germans and grabbed their commander. Phillips sent up a second troop, and in a short time the Germans surrendered. Then it was no more than a matter of making sure of victory by clearing out the honeycomb of paths and passages that were all part of the point. Here some of the enemy still resisted fanatically, and Cousins, at the head of his men, was killed—after leading his men to victory in this amazing assault on the strong-point.

The night still held surprises, and the weary Commandos met Americans who had got off Omaha. The next day the British reached Port-en-Bessin in strength, so the link-up was complete. All that remained for the Commandos to do was to rush up Hill 72, overwhelm the dispirited enemy there, and free their companions who had been captured the previous day. To the Commandos went the credit for seizing Port-en-Bessin—the first French port to fall into Allied hands.

Each carrying a 90lb load, these troops struggle through the water.

The troops try to get away from the ramps, on which the enemy concentrate their fire.

Ramps ready, the infantry keep low as their craft comes in.

Ready for action, the British head off the beaches into the scrub.

19

The Harbours set sail

PORT-EN-BESSIN would be useful, of course, but the overriding need now was for one, or preferably two, full-scale supply harbours.

These were already on their way across the Channel—the Magnificent Mulberries!

The urgent need of some reliable port was being underlined, meanwhile, on D + 1, when the build-up of supplies to sustain the bridgehead began. Eight ship convoys were due to arrive on D + 1. One of these, consisting of nine large personnel ships, came from the Thames, and this convoy, ETP.1, was in fact the first group of large ships to pass the Strait of Dover for four years.

While M.L.'s ("motorlaunches") and aircraft of the Fleet Air Arm laid smokescreens ready for ETP.1 to slip between Dover and Calais, a motor transport convoy of smaller ships preceded ETP.1. Enemy batteries on the French coast picked these up, however, and scored a direct hit on one ship, which sank. Admiral Ramsay had to decide whether or not to risk a daylight passage for the big ships. ETP.1 was then ahead of time, so a signal flashed across to it to turn back round the East Kent coast, while the M.L.'s could put in and replenish their supplies of smoke. By mid-afternoon a most effectively dense screen hung in the Strait, and at 1700 on D-Day ETP.1 put on full speed and passed through without any enemy interference. The next morning the other convoys from the Thames were at their proper places off the Normandy coast, and all eight began unloading. At midday, however, the wind force from the north reached well over 15 m.p.h., and unloading became extremely difficult. Small craft plied to and fro through choppy water in this unpleasantly exposed spot.

Everything cried out for the sheltered water of a harbour. We must now turn back forty-eight hours to when the sixty Gooseberry blockships were steaming slowly up Channel past *Warspite, Ramillies, Dragon, Frobisher, Danae, Aurora, Mauritius.*

"Serial 1 in force."

So the blockships knew now. That meant D-Day was June 6, and H-Hour 0720. But exact timing was not yet vital.

All that day they literally ploughed E.N.E. up Channel, past the comforting sleekness of destroyers. Portland Bill broke the southwesterly seas. Already dozens of small craft were leaving Poole Harbour, bound for Piccadilly Circus and Normandy. "Change at Piccadilly," as some wag had inevitably said.

The blockships saw them go, and saw too the majestic minesweepers which would soon be clearing those ten vital channels south. The rising wind blew over the dusty beaches of Sandbanks, and a little beyond lay Bournemouth, "occupied" by the Royal Air Force, but still very much a holiday resort, even though the piers had been halved in the days when a German invasion had been feared. The wheel had turned full circle indeed.

In Poole Bay the Gooseberries learned that Serial 1 was still in force and that D-Day would be the next morning. They learned, too, for the first time the official orders for their scuttling. There was scarcely any need to stress the importance of their mission, or of the dangers from mines in waters outside their specified channels.

A Wren at Rosyth had spent three days working continuously on duplicating the detailed orders. Sixty ships, and each to be sunk in an exact spot. Here had existed one more possible source of security leakage, yet the invasion was launched with complete surprise.

Now they only had to wait. The silent stream of craft from the east end of the Solent faded into the distance and the dark, as the bombers began their early raids. But soon the blockships stirred at anchor almost alone, accompanied only by an unreal peace to end the day. Could this be the beginning of an armada unparalleled in history? Yet the signs were there. And the last log of the day reported that the British ex-battleship *Centurion* plodded up to join the Gooseberries all the way from the Mediterranean—and she almost looked as if she were out of breath from the effort.

Lieutenant-Commander Taylor on *Durban* (whose captain was in charge of the operation) dozed off to the drone of more bombers, to be awakened by his steward the next morning. It was only 0700, but the steward knew that this was D-Day. Soon the world would rejoice. But now the old ships had their duty to do. A strange, sad job, and their last. The French battleship *Courbet*, and near-by merchant ships launched as long ago as 1903—these were typical of the ships ordered to commit suicide. Forty-one years, and this was to be their end. Yet how much more

honourable than the breaker's yard was this, the greatest combined operation of all?

The white horses galloped around the smaller ships in the convoy
as they sped at a full six knots towards the Far Shore! They had time to
spare, luckily, and during the afternoon reached Area Z: Piccadilly
Circus. These were safe, swept waters, so orders were to stay in them
till the whole convoy was ready to proceed, some time after midnight.
A strange way to spend D-Day, some of them on board thought,
but their turn was still to come, their part in the pattern. Meanwhile, in
the intense dark, some support landing ships pushed part of the
Gooseberry convoy to the east as they steered an urgent, if inaccurate,
course south.

So the convoy, too, steamed south, through the small hours. All the
channels had been swept the previous night, but now this night became
punctuated by the staccato and then deep eruptions of mines. As each
mine fired it threw night into day, and then returned it to its obscurity
again. Another mine, and another. So the way was not necessarily plain
sailing. There might yet be some excitement. For many sailors in this
convoy, and other D-Day escorts, things had been "bloody boring," to
quote one expression.

D + 1. *Durban* drifted with the strong on-shore seas and might well
have been in any of the swept channels—or inbetween any two! Others
in their particular group of the convoy seemed to be sailing sedately
enough.

Suddenly out of the half-light came a craft reeling towards *Durban*.
Apparently out of control, she loomed from the grey gloom of a
wild horizon, only just missed *Durban*, and then spun crazily away
again.

Full day now and round to the right the soon-to-be-familiar sight:
smoke signalling a ship afire. And sounds as well as sights filled the morning air. The naval barrage yesterday had been laid down by 640 big guns.
Now it seemed as if there were just as many today, as enemy emplacements inland received a pounding. The first convoy of forty-five blockships arrived in the assault area at 1230. No time to be lost. *Alynbank*
would be the first to go, effecting her transformation from ship to outer
breakwater.

The official "Planter" would try to place each ship in the precise position needed to create an unbroken line. This was beginning to the
accompaniment of more gunfire from four of the warships whom
the Gooseberries had seen so lately off the Dorset coast. Also part of
the D + 1 scene were the repeated return journeys of every kind of craft,

returning home to come a second and third time with reinforcements of materials or men.

But before the blockships began to be sunk the enemy launched air and sea attacks in the area. During the previous night, June 6–7, German *R*-boats ventured out of Le Havre, and *E*-boats sailed from the western port of Cherbourg. The strong Allied coastal forces at once intercepted them, and inflicted damage on several boats before the enemy veered round back home again.

The next night this was repeated, and the Luftwaffe also mustered itself to try and attack the beaches and shipping. This raid of June 7–8 was not serious, but unluckily one of the early attacks soon after midnight co-incided with the arrival of some Allied aircraft carrying airborne reinforcements. The Dakotas carrying these troops were fired on by ships of the Eastern Task Force, and at least one Dakota was shot down, with the loss of crew and paratroops.

This marked the start of the battle of the Seine Bay, fought by the whole Navy with every kind of craft. By day, during these early days, the German coastal guns blazed at the battleships, but received more than they gave. By night the Luftwaffe began to drop parachute mines. And, also at night, the *R*-boats and *E*-boats were augmented by desperate devices like human torpedoes, midget submarines, and explosive motor-boats—all striving somehow to break up the line of warships and light craft which protected the beaches.

Part of this strong line was composed of L.C.G.'s ("landing-craft gun") and L.C.F.'s ("landing-craft flak"), and both of these helped to hold the vital seaway. This row of craft, 6 miles or so north of the invasion shores, was called the Trout Line, and its screen extended out to sea from the very mouth of the river Orne.

By the accuracy of their fire, the L.C.G.'s and L.C.F.'s particularly were responsible for foiling most of the enemy lunges at the line. During these first days they had their first taste of the German explo-sive motor-boats, which were unmanned, and, after they had been directed on to the course, moved at high speed towards the Allied ships. The gun crews needed cool wits to tackle these motor-boats, for if they engaged them at too long range they sometimes found that the motor-boats were still heading straight in when all the magazines were empty. The defending craft often waited till these unnerving boats reached a range of 50 yards before firing. Several were sunk from even closer quarters.

Inside the screen of the famous Trout Line *Durban* survived the night of June 7, and the next morning the total time that the captain had been rooted to his bridge, as the senior naval officer, came to 56 hours. Two days, two nights, and eight hours, without a break.

Alynbank was the first vital vessel in the plan to be scuttled. She was first right enough, but swung round so that she ended bow-and-stern to the coast instead of parallel to it—not surprisingly, perhaps, since some doubt did exist about whether the old ships would go down on an even keel. To try to ensure that they did, they had all been ballasted, but in *Alynbank's* case this did not do the trick.

One down, fifty-nine to go.

Then there started the long line of scuttled ships: 5½ miles of break-waters for the two Mulberry harbours. Over in the other area S.S. *Alymare* settled low, her number in the convoy, 504, only a few feet above the water. Off Omaha and Gold beaches they went down not like ninepins, but with their funnels or masts projecting like pins after they had been sunk.

The tugs' tasks were almost insuperable, yet somehow they grad-ually got each vessel roughly into place. Nor was the firing itself an enviable job. A man set the charge on the poop of *Saltersgate* and then retired rapidly, but silence continued. He had to return to the poop, check that the charge was not going to fire, so that the reserve charge could be set off, and evacuate for a second time. This time all went well, and the ship went down with a slow shudder, before settling on the bottom.

The five lines of ships being formed were called Gooseberry One, Two, Three, and so on. A last meal was being prepared in the galley of a ship in Gooseberry Four. Soon only ghosts or fish would swim around the messdecks and cabins, while the water lapped its wet way up to the superstructure. Four ships had gone down in Gooseberry Five, enough to bear the first fruits of the plan—breaking the will of the angry Channel before it reached and damaged the small craft.

D + 3, and *Durban* soon to be scuttled. Meanwhile there was never a dull moment as she found herself in the midst of a slogging match between giant guns of the Navy and the Germans. The other blockships were too close to shore for them to find it fun. Taylor slept through much of the gun duel, having earlier met the captain of the *Courbet* by launch and promised to pass on a request that he should be allowed to get some French soil before leaving the invasion area.

Courbet's time drew near. Four years before, just after Dunkirk, she had steamed at top speed across to Portsmouth. Now she returned to her native shore for the final act. The Free French flag and the tricolour flut-tered in the morning wind as tugs drew her high form forward. They towed as quickly as they could, because the shells from enemy batteries spumed into the sea quite close to the dignified, if dated, old warship. At last she was in position.

Then the explosion. She dropped the short three feet from the surface to the bottom, and in a few minutes it was all over.

The endless succession. Mixed feelings were experienced by the various crews. Some of the men were comparative strangers to their ships. Others, not. The Dutchmen of *Sumatra* all went for'ard as the fatal charges sent her the few feet to rest.

Next one. So to the *Durban* herself, due to lie by *Sumatra*. Spasmodic enemy shelling actually threatened to sink her before she could be scuttled in the proper place. Shells still burst on both sides of her as the last rites were administered. Then, vicious and violent, the blast roared out its message. *Durban* was down. The captain could at last leave, and he even relaxed enough to allow the captain of the *Courbet* to get his handful of native earth.

Sixty ships lay off Normandy, only their funnels, masts, and superstructure showing: like some strange, stunted fleet, half marine, half submarine. Which, of course, they were. An ill assortment of shapes and sizes, but one which at once smoothed the sea on their landward side. Planes passing overhead saw with amazement how the water was suddenly changed from rough to calm as its force was broken by the long line of vessels.

Now started the task of creating the inner installations to make Mulberry A and Mulberry B—two harbours, each the size of the one at Gibraltar.

The harbours would consist of outer floating breakwaters, inner fixed breakwaters made of concrete caissons, and floating piers running from the pier-heads to the shore. The vast towing task started on D-Day as innumerable tugs emerged with the results of the work of 15,000 men. Just as the whole invasion was by far the biggest ever, and the minesweeping and other constituent operations also all the largest of their kind, so was Mulberry the greatest tow in history. From the Sussex coast and the Solent emerged masses of floating ironmongery and the fabulous Phoenix creations. These concrete giants varied in weight from 1500 to 6000 tons, according to their sinking positions; in all, 146 were constructed in eight months.

The concrete caissons were looming on to the invasion scene while the last blockships were being sunk. The first of the Phoenix and Whale units and the inner Bombardon breakwaters arrived off the Far Shore on the morning of D + 2. Placing the Phoenix caissons was extremely tricky. A slack tide and a light wind were necessary, which was like asking for the moon that week. Also, after the sea-cocks were opened the tugs had to hold the concrete caissons with absolute accuracy as they sank to the sea floor. Any mistakes could be catastrophic. Luckily the tugs were handled skilfully by their American masters, and the first consignment of 1½ million tons of gear for the two Mulberries went into place.

The Whale floating-roadway units were less lucky, even before they reached the end of their sea trip. The strong wind was, of course, quite unfavourable for cross-Channel towing, and a number of dramas were played out between the unwieldy Whales and the struggling crews of tugs. The result of this match was: 40 per cent. of Whale roadways lost, including those damaged near the beaches upon arrival, and 60 per cent. safely towed. Several of the voyages with these units began in reasonable conditions, but then the tugs would be overtaken by bad weather when they were half-way across and it was too late to turn back. So Whale roadways careered off on their own down the Channel, to be battered by the sea on to some strange shore.

The Bombardons arrived more or less intact; they were placed in position by a fleet which was composed of carriers, net-layers, and boom-defence vessels. The first batch was laid on D + 1, before the blockships were sunk, and by D + 5 the complete floating breakwater at Mulberry A—Omaha beach—was ready and operating. Within another twenty-four hours the Arromanches Mulberry too had all its Bombardons safely placed, although much deeper than originally intended.

The build-up gathered ground as the Mulberries came into use. Already coasters with flat bottoms could come right to the beaches, sheltered by the framework of the harbours which were rapidly taking form. Once there, little D.U.K.W.'s took off vital supplies and sped ashore with them, while the coasters could make good time back to Britain.

Then, with the awe-inspiring sight of long necklaces of pontoons carrying floating roadways, the bigger ships steamed in. Through the line of sunken Gooseberry vessels they came, and tied up at the Spud pier-heads, where they were unloaded and their cargoes rushed into vehicles to be driven down the roadways to the shore. At intervals of each one or two hundred feet there rose from the sea itself the amazing Spuds, like torpedoes turned on end.

So there it all was. The lines of blockships, bow to stern—or sometimes bow to bow—lying steady out there in the tide. And within, the floating causeways, connecting pier-heads with shore, scarcely rising or falling on their mesh of metal and the pontoons underneath.

The Mulberries were made. An amazing achievement in prefabrication. The troops carried forty-eight hours' emergency rations to cover D-Day and D + 1. Food, ammunition, and all their other supplies had to be brought in after that—if not sooner. So the Mulberries were invaluable. Then a week later came the storm.

20

The Great Storm

D URING that first fortnight the Gooseberry blockships and the floating breakwaters formed more or less the only shelter for the innumerable supply ships, and, although the Mulberry projects were even now not yet completed, already vast numbers of men and their stores had gone through these two partially constructed ports.

But the weather continued to be bad, and from D + 8, June 14, deteriorated steadily until June 18. Even by this time the prefabricated harbours were not finished, for 1½ million tons of equipment had still to be conveyed across the Channel by 150 tugs. Most of the massive Phoenix caissons reached their resting-places, but the long pier roadways needed calmer weather and seas to be towed. Some of the sections had been taken across in the adverse conditions of the first fortnight, and it took all the efforts and skill of the tug crews to keep the roadways afloat for the 90-mile trip.

Then a temporary improvement in the weather during the night of June 17–18 raised false hopes of getting the rest across. Many lengths of pier roadway remained in English ports just waiting for this break in the weather. So the problem seemed to be solved for Rear-Admiral Tennant, who was in charge of the operation, as the next evening (June 18) was so wonderfully calm that he could follow a ripple right the way to the horizon. Back in Britain, Tennant's staff took immediate advantage of the weather to send twenty-two tows of roadway on their way to the French coast from the Solent. The meteorological report could not have been better, with a high barometer. The wind was westerly, at Force Three, indicating a gentle June breeze, and after only a few hours the tows reached the Piccadilly zone without incident. All seemed set fair for a quiet crossing.

Then it happened. That same night there was a sudden, sweeping change. The warm front from the Golfe du Lion stopped.

D + 13, at 0800. The barometer fell, the wind rose—from Force Three, to Five, to Eight. Gale force without a warning. And not only a gale, but the worst north-easter for forty years, and a couple of days short of midsummer. Half-way across the Channel the twenty-two tows of pier road-ways and some Phoenix units met the maelstrom utterly unprepared. The gale gusted down from the North Sea and diagonally across the Channel, blowing into the invasion beaches. It lashed the water into large rollers that hammered the tows heavily, over and over, until they had no chance of survival. The men on the tugs fought for their charges every inch and min-ute, but one by one they broke up, snapped their tows, and sank. There were wild scenes as loose roadways rose and fell in the grip of the gale, to be dashed finally against some part of the French coast, if not driven to the bottom. Freshening each hour, the storm reached full gale force, till by the end of the day only one of the twenty-two tows still survived to reach France.

At the beachheads the storm struck just as devastatingly. All unloading stopped in the stunning, mountainous storm. Larger vessels in the invasion area struggled to sea to escape the effects of being driven into the lee shore. Inside the two harbours the high spring tides made matters worse, for the water was deeper than usual. But despite this, some 500 smaller craft crawled for shelter under the lee of the blockships to try and ride out the storm. Here they hung on desperately without food or rest, as the waters swirled round the half-hidden blockships. Somehow they survived. Hundreds of others did not. They were picked up and hurled ashore, capsized or upright. Many lay smashed on the shore. Even one of the larger landing-craft got out of control, unable to punch back against the power of this gale which made the D-Day water look like a millpond by comparison.

The tide rose higher still, coming right over the main deck of *Durban* and the low quarterdeck of *Sumatra*. *Courbet* gave welcome complete pro-tection to a crowd of craft cowering behind her, and not even this gale could touch her Cross of Lorraine, still streaming straight out in the wind.

Sixteen blockships and twenty-four Phoenix caissons were planted at Arromanches, the Mulberry B harbour. As the water and wind lashed hour after hour at these the sea finally rushed through the Phoenix caissons to the craft sheltering inside. Yet only four of the caissons actually disin-tegrated. Beyond the breakwater it was the same story. Some ships survived, others did not. Throughout the night a window-shutter smashed against a deserted house. Day again, and the gale was still gusting. A littered tangle of steel marked high water. Piece by piece, some of the caissons started to crack. And the Bombardon breakwaters finally gave way, too, torn free by the force of waves 15 feet high and 300 feet long. These outer bulwarks had resisted the sea for thirty hours: a day and a quarter. But the strain was too much; they broke and drifted ashore. Under a cliff a destroyer lay listing towards the sea. She had been damaged by enemy action; now the storm took its turn. At 0400 on the second morning the barometer rose fractionally, but the wind went on—and on. The Calvados Reef did much to arrest the fury of the storm outside Mulberry B.

Not so at Mulberry A, where disaster was almost complete.

This harbour at St Laurent had been built speedily, and in deeper and more exposed water than that at Arromanches. The Americans had planted their blockships hurriedly to try and finish the harbour quickly, and there were still great gaps in the middle. This certainly made communication with the shore easier for their assault craft, but it also let in the full force of the gale. Even sooner than this, though, the ships themselves were suffering from the gale. Several blockships, including the *Centurion*, broke their backs. And as the wash of the sea scoured away the shifting sand in the harbour others settled deeper on the bottom and let in more of the storm.

Head on to the north-easter, the Mulberry A Phoenix caisson breakwater cracked, crumbled, and finally disintegrated. Far out, too, the 200-foot semi-submerged floating steel Bombardon bastions were ripped loose, to be flung and flailed against the crumbling Phoenix caissons.

Through the breaches the sea struck at the roadways and piers and everything in range, so that they were soon starting to submerge. The harbour was crammed with craft as the storm struck. Now they broke free, drifted down to the half-submerged Whale piers, and battered at the floating supports till they sank. And all the while craft, equipment, piers, and lengths of steel roadway were driven relentlessly inshore, till along the edge of the sea lay grotesque piles of wreckage, trailing into the distance. The wind went on howling as the destruction became complete.

So Mulberry A had to be abandoned. As much of its equipment as possible was salvaged and transferred to Arromanches, where a remarkable harbour was developed later.

The gale eased slowly on June 22, and the sea had subsided by the next day, when Admirals Ramsay and Tennant could survey the sad scenes at Arromanches, and, especially, at St Laurent. Apart from the total loss of Mulberry A, the most serious result was that some 800 craft of all types stood stranded, causing a shortage of ferry-vessels. As these stood high and dry, there seemed to be only a remote chance of their being refloated before the next spring tides; but, quite remarkably, 600 soon went back into service repaired and refloated, with a further 100 a fortnight later. So seven-eighths of the casualties to craft were saved.

Yet to all this there is a really remarkable postscript. If General Eisenhower had postponed D-Day from June 5–7 the next possible dates would have been about June 17 or 18. And remember, it was on June 19 that the great gale and storm swept down on those bare beaches. What would have happened? The armies might have been stranded in France without sufficient supplies to fight their way inland—or have been unable to hold on to the beachhead. No one knows. But it could have changed the course of history.

Meanwhile history was being made as the storm smashed the American harbour at St Laurent.

Cherbourg had to be held at any price. So spoke Hitler as the Americans raced across to seal off the Cotentin peninsula and then swung north towards the port. The American infantry pierced line after line of German defences during that week until at last they reached a point only 3 miles from Cherbourg. At the height of the sea storm the Americans started their last assault on the ditches, wire, and mines which were the port's last lines of defence. The enemy refused to surrender on June 21, and three more days of fanatical fighting followed before the Americans could enter the port. Even then the harbour forts held out for yet another three days until the capture was completed on June 27. Now the Americans had at their disposal a real port with which to replace the artificial one which they had only recently lost.

While the mopping up still went on in Cherbourg special naval frogmen were embarked from Falmouth. Their destination was to be the French port, as soon as it had been taken. On June 27, the day of the surrender of Cherbourg, they were anchored off Utah beach, where they received orders to hurry overland to the port.

The United States port authority had not been idle, for the frogmen received confirmation from them of a new German mine about which they had heard in London. A "K" type, it was known to the sweeping service as "Katy," and consisted of an explosive charge set in a concrete block surmounted by a tripod of steel tubing. The mines were lowered to the bottom of the harbour, and from them floated long greenish snag-lines almost impossible to detect. The Germans' intention was that a vessel should foul these snag-lines with its propellers, haul them taut, and fire the charge.

The frogmen went to work at once; but at first they had no luck, finding only an old Lee-Enfield rifle!

But soon came success. Able-Seaman M. H. Woods dived to look for mines in a large dry dock which could not be pumped dry because the machinery had been destroyed. Woods had a buoyant rubber float attached to him to indicate his position. The two maintenance men in the dinghy saw this float travelling along and then suddenly stop. They rowed over at once and gave one pull on the line to ask Woods if he was all right—but received no reply signal. After two more attempts they assumed that he had blacked out and started to haul him up. But even with their officer's help the two sailors could not move him. Then, to their amazement, Woods suddenly surfaced quite a long way off. He had found a K mine and, to be sure of being able to discover it again, had cast off his float line and secured it to the mine. So the men had been trying to haul up a live mine weighing almost a ton. Lieutenant-Commander Harries[1] dived down to the mine, and satisfied himself that it was a K which was wired up for electrical control from the shore. Harries rendered it safe on the bottom of the dock, and then the mine was recovered.

Soon afterwards Harries had a narrow escape when he went out with Commander De Spon in a motor-boat to investigate the reported presence of "Katy" snag-lines. While they were searching the area, the screw of their own boat fouled a mine's snag-lines. Harries spotted the danger quickly and ordered that the boat go astern. Fully clothed, he dived overboard and swam round to the stern to disentangle the line before it could take the strain, go taut, and blow them to bits.

So Cherbourg's channels, docks, and harbour were all cleared for Allied traffic—and for one of the most invaluable and imaginative projects of all the amazing achievements associated with D-Day: PLUTO—Pipe Line Under The Ocean.

Now that the Allied divisions were driving the enemy back, they had to have fuel for the attack. And that meant petrol. Tanks, trucks, jeeps, motor-cycles, and all other military vehicles would be powerless without it. So the brainwave was born—pipe it under the Channel.

Back in 1942 a 1000-mile network of pipelines was being built in Britain to take petrol landed at the safer western ports to London, and the south and east coasts. From Avonmouth on the Bristol Channel and Stanlow on the Mersey it flowed south and east to Thames Haven and the Isle of Grain.

But if it could be carried across England why was it not possible to continue the pipeline to France? So the back-room boys set about it and eventually evolved a three-inch-diameter pipe. The next step was to build the pumping stations on the Isle of Wight and at Dungeness. The station at Dungeness was intended to take fuel across to Calais at a later stage of the War; the first pipeline would be laid from the Isle of Wight to Cherbourg.

Royal Engineers and Royal Army Service Corps troops were trained to

[1] Afterwards Rear-Admiral D. H. Harries, C.B.E.

work the pumps, and the stations were carefully camouflaged to keep the plan secret. Next were needed special ships big enough to carry two-mile coils of this piping. After months of preparation, the first 70-mile span to Cherbourg was started, soon after D-Day. At a steady five knots the vessel advanced, and as she did so the pipeline unwound and rattled over a roller at the stem of the ship. Then, after two miles, another vessel moved forward with another length of heavy coils—and so on. Seventy miles were laid, and at last the final stage was reached when a barge came out to join the pipeline to the beaches. Then three more of these cross-Channel links were formed, making a total of four pipelines under the ocean. Just one more miracle to add to the story of D-Day.

A track has been laid to enable armoured vehicles to drive over the beach
without becoming bogged down.

Tanks and other vehicles advance inland against heavy fire.

Infantry advance through a shattered village, in the wake of tanks.

War comes to the peaceful French village of La Délivrande.

21

Hitler's Final Fling

HITLER'S final fling came secretly, silently. It was his last throw against the invasion coast, and he knew that if it failed the War would eventually be lost. So it was now or never.

His first secret weapon had been the magnetic mine. His last one was the oyster mine. And to trace the course of this strange story, we have to go right back to the days of Dunkirk. By 1940, thanks to the courage of Commander John Ouvry and others, the British had found the answer to the magnetic mine. Soon they were taking counter-measures against the acoustic mine. And throughout the first four years of the War they were busily developing an oyster mine—and trying to discover a satisfactory way of sweeping it. For it was all very well to be able to lay a mine; if the enemy retrieved one and copied it, and if an antidote were not known, the idea would boomerang.

In fact, both the Germans and ourselves produced this top-secret weapon. It took advantage of the principle that the wave-trough of a ship causes a drop in water-pressure on the sea-bed. A unit was evolved which would react to just such a change—and fire a mine as the ship passed overhead. But despite every conceivable effort, no antidote could be found. The oyster could not be swept, and if one side used it the other could retrieve it and copy it. Yet only in desperate circumstances would it ever be considered for service while anyone resorting to it was without a counter-resource.

While our own oyster progressed to this stage, without once being put into operation, the Germans were also working on one too, *completely unknown to us*. Neither John Ouvry nor any of the civilian scientists of H.M.S. *Vernon* had an inkling of what the enemy were doing.

The Germans' efforts all stemmed from an idea of one of their naval officers, Lieutenant-Commander Fett, who got hold of a constructional survey of the English canal system—ironically enough—in which he noticed that as a ship pushed an extended wave ahead of her, this trough caused a variation of water-pressure beneath her. The fact soon suggested an application to triggering a sea mine, but Fett's brain-child met with little enthusiasm until the War was well advanced. Then the Germans, thinking that it might be wise to explore every possible secret weapon, took the idea a step further and decided to combine it with some additional firing "trigger"— just to make the mine even more difficult to sweep. Two oysters were then developed along independent lines—one by the Luftwaffe, the other by the Navy. The Luftwaffe were producing "acoustic oysters," relying on water-pressure plus the trigger of the sound of a ship, while the Navy gave birth to "magnetic oysters," combining the change in water-pressure with the ship's magnetic field to fire the mine. These developments were completely unknown to the Allies, and not seriously suspected by them.

By the end of 1943 both these branches of the German forces had workable versions of the oyster—with nothing to counteract them. The mines were put into production and actually assembled, but it was ordered that they were not to be laid unless a national emergency occurred.

Realizing that an Allied invasion was likely soon, Hitler ordered 2000 oysters to be sent to France, ready for rapid laying the moment an assault was reported. A further 2000 were held in readiness first in Germany and Norway, and then later in Holland. So great was the secrecy surrounding them that no one—not even those senior officers of the Luftwaffe who would be called on to supervise the laying of them—was instructed in their nature or preparation until April 1944.

They were to be laid only on receipt of an explicit personal command from the Führer.

April turned into May, and at the beginning of that month an amazing stroke of luck happened—the first of two, but for which the invasion might well not have succeeded.

Goering suddenly ordered that all oysters were to be returned to Germany. This took time, and the whole operation was not completed until the first few days of June, when the last batch reached Magdeburg— only a day or two before the invasion!

This unfortunate decision was taken by Goering for two or three reasons. He knew that the rubber bag, which was the vital pressure part of the mine, would have a fairly short life and was due to be superseded by another one made of a better ersatz material. In fact, the original rubber bag would have lasted long enough in the water for the short-term shock purpose intended.

The decision was also influenced by German intelligence, which informed Goering that it expected that any Allied landings in the immediate future would be made on the west coast of France, opposite the Atlantic. Oysters were considered of less use in these deep, exposed waters of the Biscay seaboard; the swell was liable to fire them, and the depth was too great for their full effect to be made. In addition, the order was intended to prevent the mines stored at Le Mans from being captured before they could be used. So long as the Germans remained ignorant of where the assault would come, they could not lay their oysters with the devastating effect they hoped for. They just had to wait and see.

So it happened that the unsweepable oysters were far away in the shrinking Fatherland, more or less unavailable as the thousands of vulnerable Allied warships and landing craft prepared for the great assault. If the enemy could lay the oysters very soon after the invasion, and the seas kept calm, then ships could not survive, and the supply lines would be broken.

Meanwhile the British were wondering what sort of enemy mines were likely to be laid in order to foil the armada. The recent mine-laying raids in the extreme western Solent—in which two mines had been recovered from the shallows near Milford-on-Sea and rendered safe—had revealed only that the enemy was still relying on advanced forms of acoustic circuits. The specimens told the British nothing new about the mines which were likely to be met off Normandy. But to be ready to meet an emergency, H.M.S. *Vernon* trained several R.N.V.R. officers to accompany the invasion and try to find fresh mines—wherever they could. The orders were to look for any interesting variations of the types they had been taught about.

Then came D-Day. And at once an order came through from the German High Command: "Lay your oysters."

But during the first week of June the British and American air forces had been blasting all lines of communication between Germany and France—and that meant Magdeburg and the advanced enemy airfields from which the oysters would be flown to the French coast. Precious days passed, turning into a week and more before the order could be implemented.

While the oysters were being hurried by road and rail—wherever any lines remained—the Germans intensified mining and other naval activities, as soon as they had recovered from the initial shock of D-Day itself. They reinforced their E-boats in Le Havre and Cherbourg, and the first signs of their mine-laying in the actual assault area came on June 9, when E-boats tried to restrict the build-up of vital supplies by laying a mine barrier on the northern flank of the Western Task Force, the Royal Navy's route to the British invasion coasts. Most of these surface attempts were beaten off, but soon afterwards the Luftwaffe began mine-laying, too, which proved very hard to prevent. It was, moreover, difficult to mark accurately mines which had been laid by either naval or air forces, as both the E-boats and the aircraft operated only at night. But the heavy R.A.F. Bomber Command attacks on Le Havre on June 14 and 15 put an end to *E-* and *R*-boat attacks at least.

Admiral Ramsay soon saw that the most serious threat to the Allied shipping in the assault area would be from mines. Low-flying aircraft were coming in too quickly to be picked up by our Radar, and so they could avoid Allied night fighters.

It was at about this time that the Germans managed to get the first of their oysters back from Magdeburg, and they were rushed into service at once.

This was a vital period for both sides. The Allies were well established in Normandy, but not for a moment dare they risk an interruption to their supplies. And these came completely by sea, through waters liable to be mined. The build-up would take a long time, and it was essential that the Seine Bay be kept free for the ships which were constantly coming and going: the lifeblood of the assaulting armies.

For the Germans, this was the moment—the now or never, make or break.

Suddenly Allied ships started to be sunk. Steaming through swept channels, one broke its back on top of the deadly, devastating eruption of an enemy ground mine. Men struggled in the sea as the bows vanished from view. Soon another ship went down, the bows this time pointing high to heaven before she plunged into the grave of the Seine Bay. The problems of sweeping non-contact ground mines became more and more worrying, since the complicated minesweeping paraphernalia was inevitably liable to foul other ships and craft. If the minesweepers were heckling an acoustic mine there was the added uncertainty about the distance from the sweeper at which the mine might fire—a constant menace to neighbouring ships moored in the Bay. Sweeping an open sea was plain sailing, but finding and firing magnetic or acoustic mines which were lying on the seabed right among the Allied ships proved dramatically difficult.

Day by day ships were sunk and men died—by drowning or by blast. D + 10 ... D + 11 ... D + 12.

The sinkings went on.

The naval officers detailed to search for new enemy mines were beginning their task as the beachhead became more firmly established, but they could not be expected to retrieve mines dropped from the air into several fathoms off the coast.

Then, on D + 14 at Luc-sur-Mer, came a stroke of luck!

Long before, in November, 1939, the Luftwaffe had deposited a magnetic mine in the mud at Shoeburyness. History was now repeated.

On the night of June 19-20 enemy aircraft flew through the rising gale to lay their latest batch of mines in the Seine Bay.

The sound of the planes sent our ack-ack guns into action, and other personnel sought shelter. What with the dark night, the gale beginning to blow, and the heavy fire from the ground, one pilot lost his sense of direction and jettisoned his mines too soon. Sub-Lieutenant Young, R.N.V.R., was one of the men sheltering below at Luc-sur-Mer. He heard a deafening explosion as one mine came down, not in the sea, but on the town. Then, a moment later, a second, more muffled explosion.

The next morning Young went to investigate. He found a house flattened by the first mine, which was designed to explode on contact with the ground if dropped on land by mistake. Another weapon lay with only the end blown off. He recognized it as a mine at once and examined the outside of its rear end, which concealed all the mechanism. Yes, it seemed to be one of the sort he knew. There was the bulge which indicated the presence of the photo-electric cells. These devilish devices had been included in many enemy mines in an attempt to prevent our stripping the mines to see what was inside. The arrangement was that as soon as some one unscrewed the rear door of the mine and let in a scrap of light, the photo-electric cells made a contact and fired the whole mine, killing anyone within range. Yes, he knew all about these.

Then suddenly he spotted something he did *not* understand: an extra fitting on this rear end. It was only a slight variation, but this little addition seemed significant.

Young spoke to his senior officer. "I think we ought to get it back to *Vernon* at once, sir, don't you?"

His superior agreed, and they had it transferred to a temporary advance airstrip, where a Spitfire flew it across to Thorney Island, the nearest airfield to Portsmouth, where men of H.M.S. *Vernon* were waiting to have a look at it.

Meanwhile, as the gale blew itself out on the Far Shore, Ramsay was really worried by the mine menace. It was the hopelessness of not being able to do anything. Was it just that sweeping could not be done efficiently in the cramped conditions over there? Or was there something else they did not know?

"Casualties to our ships due to enemy mines were becoming serious," he said in his official report.

This was due partly to the "ripening" of mines which had been laid earlier but had not been exploded by our minesweepers, since at the time of sweeping the mines were passive, and so proof against sweeping. Then, after a time-delay clock had operated, they became active again and fired the first ship which actuated them. So there had to be frequent sweeps to overcome these mines.

The new lays were also worrying Ramsay, but there was still not much which could be done until a definite diagnosis of their character could be given. It was useless trying to cure something you were not sure about. That was why any new specimens which were recovered intact might be important.

Over at Thorney Island the mine which Young had found was unloaded carefully from the plane: a shorn-off relic of the dark, cylindrical shape it had been before it was blown in half.

"Look at that." Some one pointed to the external rubber fitting.

"My God, it looks like an oyster!"

But they could still not be sure till they had stripped the rear end and analysed the complicated contents. So at once the scientists started the procedure which even fifteen years later was still secret. They had to try and find out what made the mine work without losing their lives in the process.

Every one who had started to strip a mine in the past two or three years would remember only too well how six men had been killed in H.M.S. *Vernon* by a booby trap set inside a mine to prevent it from being examined. Nowadays the techniques were safer, but an element of risk still remained—even when the mine had apparently already exploded.

The strange shape on the rear end made the scientists wary of this one as they put into practice the drill for tackling any mine equipped with photo-electric cells, as this one obviously was. They trepanned holes in the rear end by a remote-control trepanning machine, lying concealed at a respectable distance, and only when it was dark did they risk completing the openings and disconnecting any remaining leads. Now it was safe. But what would it tell them? Interest in the specimen was mounting now.

They started examining the complicated mechanism and found a microphone indicating an acoustic circuit. Then quite quickly they were able to handle the rubber pressure unit.

"It's an oyster, all right. No doubt about it."

Working fast, they checked the circuits to make sure, and then, as soon as they were sure, a telephone call to the Admiralty reported: "An acoustic oyster."

To detonate it, this type of mine needed both the sound of a ship's engines plus the altered water-pressure caused by the vessel as it passed overhead.

An electrifying air encompassed the *Vernon* team as they went on with their examination. But they had revealed the vital news.

Still no solution was known, but at least counter-measures could be tried. That would be better than sitting waiting for something to happen. The Navy knew what it was up against now.

Within hours of the report reaching the Admiralty, all ships in invasion waters were ordered to reduce speed to a minimum when within the actual assault area. This rule was strictly enforced, and although only a makeshift expedient, it cut down the casualties to a fraction of their former level, since it reduced the volume of sound from the engines and also the change in water-pressure.

Then the minesweepers went into action again. Less ships were being sunk, but the mines had to be swept somehow. Acoustic and magnetic oysters were both being laid now, but neither had much more success.

A third stroke of luck contributed to this. The first two strokes of luck had been the fact that the oysters had not been ready for D-Day, and the discovery of the mine at Luc-sur-Mer. Now the weather, which had so seriously struck at the Allies, came to their help instead. The Luftwaffe had counted on the period after the invasion being fairly calm, with no rough seas. But the periodic high sea swell triggered the pressure, or oyster, side of the firing circuits of the acoustic oysters, without any ship passing overhead. This left the sweepers only the other half of the circuit to actuate, which they could do acoustically, so that the mines fired safely out of range. Plain acoustic sweepers, with their vibrating hammers, thus defeated the acoustic oysters.

The magnetic oysters too were often spoiled by the swell, which made the pressure side actuate prematurely. And the reduced speed of the ships also caused a drop in the magnetic field they created, so that they failed to fire the magnetic side of the circuit.

By July 3 it was estimated that, including spontaneous explosions caused by the elements, nearly 500 mines had been accounted for by the sweepers, and although the threat lingered on, the worst danger was over. By the end of July more than 2000 oysters had been laid in the Seine Bay, but, like so many others of Hitler's secret weapons, this one had misfired.

But if the oysters had been laid on D + 1 day, and the weather had kept calm afterwards, the whole invasion would have been endangered, with the Allied soldiers stranded on the Far Shore.

Now the moment of danger had passed. The seas were clear, the way was open to victory. And as the armies advanced only sunken hulks and battered buildings remained as reminders of the splendour and the pain, the grimness and the glory, of D-Day, 1944.

Index